MEASUREMENT
AND EVALUATION
OF READING

MEASUREMENT AND EVALUATION OF READING

ROGER FARR
Indiana University

HARCOURT, BRACE & WORLD, INC.
New York   Chicago   San Francisco   Atlanta

Preface

This book describes procedures that should be useful to classroom teachers, reading specialists, and school administrators as they go about the important task of evaluating their students' reading performance and their school or class reading programs. The articles contain practical advice, based on sound theory, about evaluation. The effective utilization of these practical procedures must, of course, be based on a careful consideration of the total reading program and school environment in which they are to be used.

To be effective, reading instruction needs to be based on a valid and reliable evaluation of the student's reading ability. Teachers need to know the present reading level and the strengths and weaknesses of each student's reading skill development. Teachers and administrators also require information about the effectiveness of materials and organizational patterns.

A reading evaluation program is frequently viewed as the administration of standardized reading tests to a group of students. While group test scores are useful, they are only one aspect of a total evaluation program; other types of information about students' reading behavior must be gathered. In addition, continuous evaluation of teaching procedures, instructional materials, curriculum organization, and the objectives of the program must be planned as an integral part of the total evaluation program.

Assessing the reading ability of students involves major problems. Foremost among them is estimating reading growth. Several articles describe aspects of this problem and suggest evaluation methods that should provide for more reliable and valid estimation of reading improvement. Another serious problem classroom teachers continually face is the diagnosis of students' reading skills. Standardized reading tests, although they include separate subtests of reading ability, are usually lacking in diagnostic validity. Teachers should be aware of these shortcomings and should be able to utilize other means for diagnosing students' reading skills.

Each of the five sections of this book considers one of the areas or problems mentioned above. Articles in the first section present a discussion of the broad scope of evaluation in reading education and attempt to answer the question, "What can and should be evaluated in reading education?" The second section includes articles describing procedures that can be utilized in evaluating reading programs and students' reading abilities. The third section continues the discussion of assessing students' reading abilities; however, the major focus is on informal reading diagnosis within the classroom. The fourth section addresses the problems of measuring specific reading skills. The final section considers problems and procedures in estimating improvement of reading ability.

Each section of the book is preceded by a brief description of the articles in that section and also by questions to direct the reader's study of the articles. Following each section is a list of suggested readings for further study.

This book should be of value to anyone directly concerned with the teaching of reading. Instructors and students in graduate and undergraduate teacher-training courses in reading will find that this book is a useful guide to the discussion and study of the essential aspects of reading ability and reading programs. Classroom teachers, reading specialists, and curriculum supervisors will find that this book provides practical answers to present evaluation problems.

It is the hope of the present author that this book will help to improve the teaching of reading through more complete and more reliable evaluation.

R. F.

Contents

MEASUREMENT
AND EVALUATION
OF READING

Section One

WHAT CAN BE EVALUATED IN READING EDUCATION

Most evaluation programs in reading education are too limited. In assessing the abilities of students, teachers tend to place too much emphasis on the results of standardized reading tests and fail to consider such pupil behaviors as what students read, attitudes toward reading, and use of reading to search for answers to personal problems. The effectiveness of reading programs is also assessed almost exclusively in terms of standardized reading test scores. Certainly student reading ability as measured by such tests is a most important consideration in assessing the value of a reading program, but teachers and administrators need to consider other criteria and methods for evaluating teaching procedures, instructional materials, and curriculum designs.

In the first two articles, Bamman and Kingston describe the need for a variety of procedures in assessing students' reading abilities. They hold that evaluation must be systematic and continuous and recommend that it take the form of a search for answers to specific instructional questions. This procedure demands that evaluation be preceded by a careful delineation of what is to be measured.

In the third article, Lennon reviews recent research meant to help determine the skills of reading that can be measured. The contrast between the intentions of the subtests of existing standardized reading tests and Lennon's conclusions about what can in fact be measured should cause deep thought and perhaps a sense of alarm. If Lennon's conclusions are accurate, most standardized reading tests are not even attempting to measure the reading skills that research studies indicate can be measured.

In the final article in this section, Strang describes the number of variables that can be evaluated in reading education and gives general guidelines for their evaluation.

The reader may wish to keep in mind the following questions as he proceeds through the section:

1. What is the ultimate outcome of an evaluation program? What long-range goals should be considered?
2. Do reading tests validly describe reading behavior?
3. What testing conditions limit the validity of evaluating reading behavior? How can these limitations be overcome?
4. What are the goals for evaluating students' reading abilities? Are these the same or different from the evaluation of reading programs?
5. What general guidelines should be followed in evaluating reading programs and materials?

1

Assessing Progress in Reading

HENRY A. BAMMAN

Perhaps the prime purpose of considering assessment of progress in reading should be a determination of how assessment practices or techniques may be used to effect changes and improvements in the general curriculum, which would necessarily include reading for all purposes in all subjects. Still another purpose would be the determination of the methods of instruction, the types of materials, and the nature of the relationship to be established for and with the individual child.

Another approach to a consideration of assessing progress in reading might be a discussion of the relative weaknesses and strengths of formal and informal instruments now being used in our schools. Certain critical questions immediately arise. What components of the reading act are now measured adequately? Are we measuring children, teachers, administrators, or the instructional program? Are we differentiating between what reading ultimately becomes in the life of the individual and what it is now during a particular stage of development? What measuring instruments do we need to determine more accurately how well the individual child is progressing and to predict his future progress?

REPRINTED with permission of Henry A. Bamman and the International Reading Association. "Assessing Reading Progress in the United States," in *Reading Instruction: An International Forum*, Marion D. Jenkinson, ed., Proceedings of the First World Congress (Newark, Delaware: International Reading Association, 1966), pp. 312–17.

To attempt to discuss all phases of assessment of reading progress in a paper such as this is impossible. I propose to discuss briefly four statements about assessing progress in reading. These statements are (1) that assessment of reading progress should be continuous; (2) that assessment should be directed toward specific information to be gained; (3) that through informal measures one may observe systematically and carefully how a child reads; and (4) that assessment of reading progress must include some knowledge of how the individual uses what he reads.

For all of us, the word *assessment* should mean more than obtaining test scores or diagnostic data from a child or from numbers of children. The term itself includes the act of *valuing* what is measured—values to be determined for and by the child, in terms of the curriculum and in terms of definite goals that are educationally reasonable and practical. We should ask ourselves concerning data we have gathered: What is the relative value of these data in terms of the total reading program? What is the worth of this information in terms of the child's total development in language skills? Too frequently, we accumulate masses of statistical data on children, commit those data to statistical analyses, and publish our assessments of methods, materials, and programs. While this type of assessment may serve as an integral part of a good program of evaluation, it may detract from the core of our concern: the individual child who is frequently lost in descriptions of and prescriptions for the masses.

All agree, probably, that a balanced assessment of reading should include certain basic ingredients: standardized tests of the various reading skills, informal inventories to determine strengths and weaknesses, measures of linguistic abilities, measures of thinking abilities, and measures of psychological and physiological status. Surely the experienced teacher would agree that the data from these measures cannot be obtained before we begin to teach the child to read; in fact, most of the data will be gathered as we teach the child, from day to day and from year to year.

Assessment of reading progress should be continuous. It is possible to assemble data on all aspects of the child's functioning at a given time and to determine the type of instruction that the child should be given. But, once instruction has begun, critical changes may occur. A child apprised of his weaknesses may quickly correct many of them through concentrated effort. When we measure a child's reading, we are assessing the child's current functioning level of performance. We may not know, at that time, that the child has given his maximum performance—a performance which he can infrequently duplicate. We may not know, on the other hand, that the child's current performance is one that is much less distinguished than his usual functioning. Many factors of threat in the testing situation may prevent the child's functioning as he does in the less threatening atmosphere of his classroom. The point to be made, then, is that an assessment of reading progress at any given time may be only an indicator of what should be followed up through observation in order to substantiate what we feel and conclude about the child's current functioning.

The goal, then, of continuous assessment is a composite picture of reading progress over a period of time. Standardized tests which may give us information relative to the child's silent reading abilities; formal and informal oral tests which yield specific information regarding the child's ability to recognize and call words, to respond to questions which are asked by the examiner, and to summarize what has been read; and day-by-day observations of the child's development of interests and tastes and his application of his reading skills to all types of reading should be included in a longitudinal assessment of an individual or of a group of children.

Assessment should be directed toward specific information to be gained. Too frequently we hear a child's progress summarized by such statements as "He doesn't read well," "He does poorly on comprehension exercises," or "He has difficulty with word recognition skills." Each of these statements lacks the specificity that is essential for planning a good program of instruction. Yet, each may provide a beginning point for further assessment. The next step, obviously, is to discover which skills, among the multiple skills of comprehension and word recognition, represent the child's specific weaknesses.

The survey test may give an indication of the child's independent reading level, as his performance is compared to the performance of others of similar age or educational level. However, survey tests are limited in what they can tell us. They represent a limited sampling of the wide variety of reading skills and of types of reading materials. They may indicate broad areas of weakness and strength in the reader. But, the standardized test does not currently exist that will give sufficient information regarding a child's background of experiences, his independent and instructional levels of reading, his recognition vocabulary, his thinking abilities, his word analysis skills, his oral language abilities, or his interests in and attitudes toward reading.

General information regarding a child's performance on a standardized test is necessary as a beginning point of assessment. But, immediately we must follow through with clearly defined measures of individual skills. Many of the measures we use will be informal or semi-structured observations and tests.

Through informal testing, we may observe carefully and systematically how a child reads. The informal, quasi-structured nature of an informal test or inventory may give the teacher an opportunity to evaluate far more than a child's reading performance. Before the child reads, and as he reads, there are opportunities to explore his oral language background. How well does he express himself, in terms of fluency and depth of statement about familiar ideas and events? Does he respond accurately to directions? Does he speak spontaneously or with labored effort? What does he reveal about his experiences, his interests, his attitudes toward reading?

Faced with the responsibility of reading aloud for the examiner, the child may reveal vital information regarding his language development. For instance, let us consider the child whose dialect is divergent from the "standard" written and spoken language. He may habitually mispronounce many words; he may omit parts of words; he may fail to recognize and grasp the meaning of idiomatic language; and he may hesitate frequently in his reading because he does not follow standard patterns of syntax. I think immediately of the boy who reported to me, during an oral reading test, that he had broken his "feets." I responded, "Did you break both of your feet?" "No, sir," he replied. "I breaks jus' one my feets." He could not recognize the word *foot* in a reading selection; the word simply did not exist in his language. The problem of such a child is one of basic language development. This child frequently cannot read and think about language which is unfamiliar in his own patterns of listening and speaking.

Using an informal test, the examiner has an opportunity to probe how well the child comprehends what he reads. Questions can be structured to fit any need. They may be designed to measure the child's recognition of the meaning of a word in a particular context, his ability to recognize and to relate essential details to a main idea, his skill in inferring meaning by using the minimum clues supplied by the writer and applying his own experiences, or his ability to relate ideas in proper sequence. The examiner may determine how well the child can paraphrase what an author has stated by giving in his own words the ideas that he has read. The examiner should follow the clues and on each succeeding selection shift the nature of the questions in order to obtain a more discrete picture of the child's functioning both in reading and speaking.

In the specific area of word recognition skills, the informal techniques of assessment may provide important information. If the teacher or examiner suspects that the child is weak in word recognition skills, a test may be designed to confront the child with specific tasks. Does he lack an immediate recognition vocabulary? Fluent reading is not a matter of analyzing words as they are met, but rather the immediate recognition of virtually all of the words in the selection. We cannot expect the individual to develop skills of analyzing words unless he has a broad recognition vocabulary. True, we can teach him to analyze laboriously each word as he meets it; but, is this really reading? Does it not lack the spontaneity and the flow of natural language? The child who goes through the mechanical exercise of making responses to a series of visual stimuli becomes so preoccupied with the act of responding that he fails to think. If reading is thinking that is stimulated by the printed word, then printed words must flow as spontaneously and as naturally as spoken language, if thinking is to occur.

If we suspect that the child has difficulty with word analysis, then we should confront him with tasks that will give evidence of specific strengths and weaknesses. It is not sufficient to conclude merely that a child has a difficulty with phonetic and structural analysis. Specifically, what areas of word analysis call for attention and training? Is the child too dependent upon initial letter clues? Does he fail to generalize from familiar words to unfamiliar words in terms of phonetic principles of our language? Does he fail to recognize a familiar word in an inflected form? There are available several standardized tests which aid in gaining a more specific assessment of word analysis skills; these should be supplemented by informal tests, designed not only to yield more exact information, but also to measure the child's progress over a period of time.

Assessment of reading progress must include some knowledge of how the individual uses what he reads. All of us are engaged in our classrooms in testing orally the child's immediate recall of what he has read. We may become acutely aware of those children who never seem to grasp a general impression of a selection and fail to recognize main ideas. We know which children are capable of establishing relationships among main ideas and details. We observe those children who have difficulties in recalling a sequence, following directions, and reacting critically to what they have read. But how well do we assess the child's ability and inclination to *use* what he reads?

Do our students develop habits of applying information gained through reading to the solution of problems in all areas of study? Do they share information enthusiastically and effectively using one another as sounding boards for refining their thinking about ideas? Do they apply their reading skills to ever increasing levels of materials? Have they developed, through reading, both deeper and broader interests? Have they learned to think, speak, write, and listen more critically as a result of reading about the ideas, the dreams, and the deliberations of wiser and more experienced men and women?

The questions posed cannot be answered sufficiently through the use of standardized measures. The answers can be found only through critical observation by the parent, the teacher, or the friend, who through the long years of a child's development watches, records, corrects, admonishes, and encourages that child as he moves through pain and pleasure from the initial stages of recognizing the simple symbols for his familiar language to the mind-stretching, self-fulfilling period when reading in reality is an integral part of his daily life.

A distinguished American reading specialist, Marjorie Seddon Johnson of the Reading Clinic at Temple University, has written these words concerning assessment of reading achievement of children:

> No instructional program can be any better than the teacher's knowledge of the children for whom it is planned. If they are known only superficially, the instructional program will be superficial at best, totally inappropriate at the worst. In order to plan effectively, the teacher must first determine achievement levels, then specific strengths and weaknesses of each child. Evaluation must not stop at any point in the program but rather be carried on through all instruction. This evaluation must be broad in scope, tapping all the factors that are related to reading achievement. It must have adequate depth to provide a strong foundation of information on which instruction can be built. In a word, a teacher must teach someone. Unless he knows, in the broadest sense, who each someone is, he cannot teach.[1]

[1] Marjorie Seddon Johnson, "Identifying Individual Needs in the Classroom," *Proceedings of the Annual Reading Institute at Temple University.*

2

Measuring Reading Performance

ARTHUR S. McDONALD

The program of this year's Conference amply demonstrates recognition of the necessity of developing and utilizing sound theories of reading. Measurement is useless without a clear theoretical sub-structure. Unless we know what we are trying to find, the utility of our measures will only be a function of our uncertainty.

Measurement of human performance must be multi-faceted because of the complexities of human behavior. The meaning of information gathered by measurement techniques must ultimately depend on human judgment. The foregoing statements seem elementary platitudes. Unfortunately, reference to thirty years of reading research will show that little more than lip service has been paid them. Measurement is commonly equated with administration of one or two standardized instruments whose scores are accepted as real units. ("Sam grew 9 months in reading achievement in only six weeks of instruction.") Kingston[1] has pointed out the need

---

[1] Kingston, Albert J., "Is Reading What the Reading Tests Test?" In Eric L. Thurston and Lawrence E. Hafner (eds.), *The Philosophical*

REPRINTED with permission of Arthur S. McDonald and the National Reading Conference, Inc. "Measuring Reading Performance," in *New Frontiers in College Adult Reading*: The Fifteenth Yearbook of the National Reading Conference, George B. Schick and Merrill M. May, eds., 1966, pp. 216–21.

for a concomitant advance in measurement techniques and has shown the lack of such improvements.

Perhaps, therefore, it will not be amiss to state how measurement will be used in this discussion. Measurement is considered as the collection, selection and interpretation of data about a student or students relevant to reading performance. Such assessment and appraisal of performance is highly dependent for its adequacy on the appropriateness of the educator's theoretical frame of reference. Innumerable experiences suggest that skillful human judgment, based on adequate theory, can compensate for malfunctioning equipment or poorly conceived measures. For example, on several occasions in World War II, submarine commanders rejected the problem solutions of their electronic computers because such solutions were not consonant with their interpretation of the total situation. Using relatively primitive techniques these commanders achieved their objectives of torpedoing enemy shipping.

Data cannot be collected, selected and interpreted without reference to objectives. What is being measured? Why is measurement being carried on? The effectiveness of any kind of measurement depends on appropriate division of the field of activity into operationally differentiated categories. The establishing of criteria as measures of achievement is also necessary. The *reason* for measurement will be a material factor in determining the *methods* of measurement.

For example, if the purpose is to identify groups of slow, average, rapid and "super" readers, some kinds of rate measures must be chosen. (The defensibility or desirability of this purpose is not the object of this illustration.) On the other hand, should the purpose be that of ascertaining the student's ability to understand a given type of reading, more complex and sophisticated measuring techniques will be necessary.

What type of reading performance does the teacher want to measure? Procedures of assessment will vary as the type is changed. The reading performance of a group of students in relation to a regional or national norm is relatively easy to

and Sociological Bases of Reading, Fourteenth Yearbook of the National Reading Conference. Milwaukee: National Reading Conference, Inc. 1965, 106–109.

determine (although perhaps not very useful). Finding out the special instructional and counseling approaches necessary to assist a student overcome specific reading deficiencies presents a measurement problem of quite a different magnitude.

All data secured from people—by whatever means—are samples of performance. Accounts of behavior observed by others, scores on standardized tests, self-reports, etc., are all only samples. Obviously, the greater the number of reports, the more varied the situations in which behavior is observed, the larger the number of observers and the longer the period of time covered, the more useful the samples are to the trained interpreter in evaluating behavior.

As the foregoing suggests, there are numerous ways of securing information about performance in a given skill or type of situation. For a number of reasons—not the least of which is conservation of time—the greatest reliance has been placed on standardized tests for measuring reading performance. From a review of the reading research, it would appear that users of these tests frequently forget that they are also only observations of a limited sample of behavior. True, the behavior sample is observed under standard and controlled conditions in such a fashion that one or more quantitative scores are obtained. Nevertheless, the standardized tests are still measures of performance at a particular place and time under certain conditions. Their scores represent a relationship which is believed to exist between standing on the test and performance in real life.

Commonly, in assessing reading performance—for whatever purpose—the standardized tests measuring the familiar triad: rate, vocabulary and comprehension, are used. Despite the accumulation of studies showing the stark inadequacy of such tests, they continue to be used. Although compressed into 40 to 50 minutes, considerable reliance is placed on their subscores. Confounding errors are sometimes introduced, e.g., treating *percentiles* as *per cent* of comprehension correct. Simplifying constructs are used such as "speed of comprehension." The fallacy of this latter has been demonstrated many times. Are two students with identical speed-of-comprehension scores of 200 performing equally well? Of course the answer depends on the elements making up the score: student A reads 200 wpm and gets all the questions right; student B reads 800 wpm and misses three-fourths of the questions. Are they likely to perform equally well in reading situations? Let us suggest that no one knows. But, speed-of-comprehension scores serve to obscure even the limited data provided by this kind of reading test.

Spache[2] has asserted that general improvement of reading rate does not exist as an entity and has warned that speed is not independent of numerous other aspects of the reading process.

May we suggest rate measures are used because they are easy to administer and score, because rate *appears* to be related to reading achievement, and because group gains after almost any form of training appear with comforting regularity? Many research reports conclude that X method resulted in significant gains in rate with the same or better comprehension.

Commercial speed reading programs have only carried this emphasis on rate to its logical conclusion. Thus, advertisements appear guaranteeing that customers completing Z method of training will be able to read 11.3 times faster with equal or better comprehension to that initially tested. It would not be outside the guarantee, therefore, if a trainee began the program reading 100 wpm with 20 per cent comprehension and ended with scores of 1200 wpm and 20 per cent comprehension. Without suggesting what action any given program would take, it can be observed that the conditions of the guarantee have been met. (Need it be observed, in passing, that guarantees of performance are contrary to the Codes of Ethics of many professional associations, including the International Reading Association, National Reading Conference, American Psychological Association and American Personnel and Guidance Association?)

It is time to abandon the enticing constructs of rate, vocabulary, and comprehension as exemplified by most standardized reading tests. What is needed, instead, is an indication

[2] Spache, George D., "Reading Rate Improvement—Fad, Fantasy, or Fact." In J. Allen Figurel (ed.), *Improvement of Reading Through Classroom Practice, International Reading Ass'n Conference Proceedings.* Newark, Delaware: International Reading Association, 1964, 28–30.

of how well the student can achieve his purpose for reading.

In measuring reading performance, then, techniques should be used which enable the reading specialist to determine:

1. Under what conditions and with what kinds of reading material is the student effective (i.e., able to achieve his purposes for reading)?
2. Can the student vary his reading approaches to suit the nature of different reading selections and purposes for reading?
3. When is the student an efficient reader (i.e., achieves his reading purpose with expenditure of time and energy appropriate to the magnitude of the task)?
4. What deficiencies hinder the student from reading effectively or efficiently?

Measurement of performance usually includes comparing an individual with his class; comparing a group with other groups in school; matching scores against a norm group. Measurement may extend to comparing a student's reading performance with that of an idealized individual who embodies the teacher's standards. (Thus, we get the aspiration to end the program of instruction with all students "reading above average.")

Of crucial importance, although often overlooked, is a thorough assessment of a student's initial reading status, including interacting non-academic factors in a number of reading situations.

Appraisal of reading performance cannot be satisfactorily carried out unless the educational objectives of the school have been defined in operational terms. Account also must be taken of the "institutional press." Does the student *need* to read? Perhaps his instructors *tell* him what he needs to know to pass his courses. Perhaps his curriculum is one in which reading plays a subordinate role—for him, at least. The above statements, displeasing as they may be to persons dedicated to reading, do reflect real life conditions. While this paper does *not* contend that a person is better for *not* being able to read efficiently, nevertheless, for many students reading plays a small role in their lives. Thus, the demands for reading performance of the school must be identified and defined in testable terms.

Competent appraisal demands adequate operational answers to the following questions:

1. What is the student's current reading performance?
2. What learning experiences does he need in his school and curriculum to perform at his highest probable level of achievement?
3. What combination of instructional materials, techniques, independent work and counseling is best for him?

It should be constantly borne in mind that *no* reading test is in and of itself diagnostic. Appropriate appraisal of a student's needs and abilities which is diagnostic can come only from the preparation of a tentative hypothesis based on the analysis of carefully selected data covering significant aspects of the student's life-space. Especially should the appraiser insure that measuring techniques test all facets and aspects of the reading process required to achieve school and student objectives.

Discussions during past meetings of this Conference have shown how complicated and difficult is assessment of improvement in reading for either a group or an individual. Articles by Davis[3,4] and the review of research by McDonald [5] may be found useful references in this tricky area.

All appraisal must provide protection against invalid judgments because of oversimplification, Hawthorne, placebo and Rogers-Dymond effects or appraisor-student bias.

Measurement is only impeded by setting up facile objectives (e.g., "Why can't we read as rapidly as we think?"). Useful for research as this may be at the present stage of the

[3] Davis, Frederick B., "The Assessment of Change." In Emery P. Bliesmer and Albert J. Kingston (eds.), *Phases of College and Other Adult Reading Programs, Tenth Yearbook of the National Reading Conference.* Milwaukee: National Reading Conference, Inc., 1961, 86–95.
[4] Davis, Frederick B., "Measurement of Improvement in Reading Skill Courses." In Emery P. Bliesmer and Ralph C. Staiger (eds.), *Problems, Programs and Projects in College-Adult Reading, Eleventh Yearbook of the National Reading Conference.* Milwaukee: National Reading Conference, Inc., 1962, 30–40.
[5] McDonald, Arthur S., "Assessing the Effects of Reading Programs." *Journal of Reading,* 8:417–421, May, 1965.

art, the previous question is not testable. How fast do we think? What is meant by thinking? Perhaps we can read faster than we can think—if by thinking is meant constructing an entirely new conceptual framework. The author may have presented the new conceptual structure so clearly that the reader grasps it much more rapidly than the writer was able to build it.

On the other hand, we may read a statement relatively quickly and then be slowed up by our thinking about its implications. For example, consider the statement "a ship which floats displaces the amount of water which is equal in weight to its own." The reader who is familiar with the sea might hesitate to sail on a ship designed by a person making such a statement. A ship which displaces water equal in weight to its own weight will be submerged in a state of neutral buoyancy. This means that a ship will neither rise nor sink. Such a condition will hardly win customers for a shipping line. Did the reader read faster than he thought? Or, was he slowed up by reflecting on the meaning of what was said? Or, did he accept the statement at face value?

Measurement of reading performance, then, requires the selection of data-gathering devices suitable to the amount and type of appraisal wanted. It demands the assessment by a trained teacher of the data collected. Such measurement will be used to draw only those inferences clearly supportable by the evidence at hand. The assessment will take into account the sad truths that deductions from *a priori* reasoning are not always borne out in human performance and that *statistically significant* differences are not always of *educational importance*.

A logical *a priori* assumption is that a reader can voluntarily change his reading rate to suit his purpose. We conducted a modest "experiment" on the entering classes of 1964 and 1965 to determine to what extent such a change can take place. 3,500 students were asked to read material differing markedly in readability and conceptual difficulty as well as in purpose. The mean and median scores for difficult material on which the instructions were to read thoroughly with care to understand the author's major premises, supporting ideas and important details were 230 wpm while the mean and median scores for fictional material to be read for what happened to whom and who did it were 270 wpm. Statistically significant, these scores can hardly be considered educationally important.

Three hundred students were asked to read non-fiction history selections "as fast as you can. You will not be asked questions about what you have read." The mean score was 400 wpm. When the instructions were varied to say, "Read this passage as fast as you can. When you have finished, you will be asked questions about its meaning"; mean score was 240 wpm. Purpose had been changed from "eyeballing the print" to some form of reading.

This study—congruent with more defensible research—is cited merely to verify the complexity of reading behavior and to illustrate the difference between statistically significant and educationally important behavior. It also exemplifies the need to assess student perception of the measurement task.

Above all, then, the meaning for the student of the situation in which the data were collected must form part of the final judgment about performance.

3
What Can Be Measured?

ROGER T. LENNON

We can look back today upon virtually a half-century of experience in the development of objective, standardized tests of a wide variety of reading skills and abilities. Such tests, numbering well into the hundreds, have been making their appearance year after year since about 1910; some have enjoyed decades of apparently satisfactory use, others have lapsed into disuse after relatively brief careers. The period since 1910 has witnessed prodigious research activity in the reading field; for the past several decades, an average of a hundred or more publications per year have swelled the literature devoted to this endlessly fascinating topic. Much of this research literature has been concerned with analysis of reading skills, speculation and experimentation concerning the nature and organization of reading abilities, and development and utilization of appropriate instruments. To undertake even the most cursory review of the reading tests that have appeared, or of the implications of the voluminous research with respect to reading measures, is far too ambitious a task, and yet an answer to the proposed question requires at least passing cognizance of some of the history and research.

REPRINTED with permission of Roger T. Lennon and the International Reading Association. "What Can Be Measured?" in *The Reading Teacher*, vol. 15, no. 5 (March 1962), pp. 326–37.

THE PROBLEM

What can be measured? An unsuspecting student who sought to answer this question from an examination of test catalogs, or of the instruments which they describe, might say, "We can measure paragraph comprehension, word meaning, word discrimination, word recognition, word analysis skills, ability to draw inferences from what is read, retention of details, ability to locate specific information, rate of reading, speed of comprehension, visual perception of words and letters, ability to determine the intent of a writer, ability to grasp the general idea, ability to deduce the meaning of words from context, ability to read with understanding in the natural sciences, in the social sciences, in the humanities, ability to perceive relationships in written material, ability to sense an author's mood, or intent, ability to appreciate poetry, ability to grasp the organization of ideas, ability to read maps, charts, and tables"—The list may be extended, if not *ad infinitum,* at least *ad* some seventy or eighty alleged reading skills and abilities. And this, mind you, from an inspection only of tests that are labeled as reading tests, without any consideration of other tests which look very much indeed like blood brothers to the reading tests, but which mask their familial ties under such beguiling aliases as tests of "critical thinking," of "educational developments," or even—most artful deceivers of all —as tests of "mental ability," "intelligence," or "scholastic aptitude."

Surely, no reader is so naive as to suppose that there really corresponds a separate, identifiable skill or ability to each of the test names. What then may we assume we are actually measuring with the scores and scores of differently named tests?

It is one thing—and a necessary thing—to make a careful analysis of reading ability, to spell out its various supposed components in detail, and to prepare extensive lists or charts of the specific skills or abilities to serve as statements of desired goals or outcomes of the reading program. It is quite another thing to demonstrate that these manifold skills or abilities do, in fact, exist as differentiable characteristics of students; and still a third thing to build tests which are in truth measures of one or another of these skills, and not of some more general, pervasive reading ability.

But if the number of abilities or dimensions of reading is not the seventy or eighty indicated, what is it? And how can we tell? Can we reduce this vast complexity to a single, global measure of reading ability, as some have concluded— or three, or five, or ten? Twenty years ago Dr. Arthur Traxler[1] addressing a conference on problems in measurement of reading, adverted to this same issue, and remarked that "What is apparently needed is a mathematical resolution of the difficulty by means of a thorough-going factor analysis of the abilities which enter into silent reading." Even as Dr. Traxler made his plea, such empirical attacks on the problem were under way, and during the decade or so following, there appeared a series of excellent studies of this kind that shed much light on our topic.

REVIEW OF RESEARCH

Traxler himself in 1941[2] reported an analysis of the Van Wagenen–Dvorak Diagnostic Examination of Silent Reading Abilities, one of the most impressive tests of this kind that had appeared up to that time. He sought to ascertain whether the several parts of the test yielded "measures which are independent enough to warrant their separate measurement and use as a basis for diagnostic and remedial work." Studying the results on these tests for a group of 116 tenth-grade students, Traxler concluded that the "measures of Central Thought, Clearly Stated Details, Interpretation, Integration of Dispersed Ideas, and Ability to Draw Inferences appear to be measuring closely related reading abilities. There is at least

[1] Traxler, Arthur E. "Problems of Measurement in Reading." *Proceedings of the 1941 Invitational Conference on Testing Problems* (mimeo.). American Council on Education, pp. 65–73.
[2] Traxler, Arthur E. "A Study of the Van Wagenen–Dvorak Diagnostic Examination of Silent Reading Abilities." *Educational Records Bulletin* No. 31. New York: Educational Records Bureau, January, 1941. Pp. 33–41.

reasonable doubt concerning whether or not the separate scores contribute anything greatly different from the reading level score." He found most of the parts so highly correlated that diagnosis based on the scores had little real meaning. In fact, when the intercorrelations were corrected for attenuation, most approached unity.

Even before Traxler's call for research, Gans in a 1940 study[3] had analyzed the relation between a specially built measure of "the critical types of reading required in the selection-rejection of content for use in solving a problem," and a reading composite based upon two standardized reading tests, Thorndike-McCall and Gates Silent Reading, and four sections of the California Test of Mental Maturity. (Worthy of note is the fact that Gans justified the composite as a general measure of reading comprehension on the basis that the intercorrelations among the components approached their respective reliabilities—even though the components were as superficially varied as the Thorndike-McCall score, Gates' scores on Appreciating General Significance, Predicting Outcome, and Noting Details, and California Delayed Recall, Numerical Quantity, Inference, and Vocabulary.) Analysis of the results of a group of 417 intermediate-grade pupils led Gans to conclude that "the abilities (i.e., the reference-reading abilities) are not closely enough related to those in the reading criterion to be measured by tests designed for discovering the criterion abilities," and "the composite which functions in reference reading is made up of a number of variables, with reading ability, as measured by the reading criterion one factor, and the selection-rejection pattern another." ". . . another factor operates which possibly includes some function of delayed recall."

A trail-blazing study, and probably still the best known of all the investigations of this type, was that reported by Davis, originally in 1941.[4] Davis sought to identify some of

[3] Gans, Roma A. *A Study of Critical Reading Comprehension in the Intermediate Grades.* New York: Teachers College, Columbia University. Contribution to Education No. 811 (1940).
[4] Davis, Frederick B. "Fundamental Factors of Comprehension in Reading." Unpublished doctoral dissertation, Graduate School of Education, Harvard University, 1941; and in *Psychometrika* 9 (1944), 185–197.

the fundamental factors in reading comprehension and to provide a means of measuring them. On the basis of a comprehensive survey of the literature, he listed nine supposed categories of basic skills of reading comprehension. He proceeded to develop test questions to measure each of these skills, administered the tests to a group of subjects, and computed the intercorrelations among the nine tests. He interpreted a factor analysis of the results as indicating the presence of nine factors, six of them clearly significant. These latter included word knowledge; ability to manipulate ideas and concepts in relation to one another—"reasoning in reading"; ability to grasp the author's expressed ideas; ability to identify the writer's intent or purpose; ability to follow the organization of a passage; and knowledge of literary devices and techniques. Of Davis' nine factors, word knowledge accounted for by far the greatest part of the variance, followed by the so-called "reasoning in reading" and the literal meaning factors.

Davis concluded that at least two factors, the word knowledge and the reasoning factor, were measured in his tests with sufficient reliability for practical use, and that adequately reliable measures of three other factors—literal meanings, inference, and ability to follow the organization of a selection—could be developed as a practical matter.

A re-analysis of Davis's data by Thurstone,[5] employing a somewhat different factor analysis technique, led Thurstone to conclude that a single factor was sufficient to account for the obtained correlations. The apparent conflict in interpretation reflects different purposes served by the respective types of factor analysis employed in the two investigations. Davis, reacting to Thurstone's re-analysis of his data, continued to maintain that his first six factors, at least, represented significant dimensions of reading comprehension, though admittedly, several of them accounted for very little variance in reading scores.[6]

---

[5] Thurstone, L. L. "Note on a Reanalysis of Davis' Reading Tests." *Psychometrika*, 11 (1946), 185–188.
[6] Davis, Frederick B. "A Brief Comment on Thurstone's Note on a Reanalysis of Davis' Reading Tests." *Psychometrika*, 11 (1946), 249–255.

Langsam in 1941 [7] reported a factor analysis of results of six reading tests, yielding fourteen scores, and one intelligence test yielding seven scores. She identified five factors, labeled respectively a *verbal* factor, concerned with word meaning, a *perceptual* factor, a *word* factor denoting fluency in dealing with words, a *seeing relationships* factor, perhaps concerned with logical organization, and a *numerical* factor. The factors were found to overlap to a considerable degree, beclouding their interpretation.

Conant in 1942 [8] undertook to answer the questions: "Is there a general reading comprehension, or does reading proficiency depend upon skills using a number of different reading techniques? If there are different reading abilities, how are they interrelated? She developed an outline of a test to measure the following skills: (1) Reading to get in detail the pattern of the author's thought, including comprehension of the main points, comprehension of specific facts which support main points, comprehension of cause-and-effect relations, and comprehension of words in context. (2) Ability to interpret and make a critical evaluation of material read, including selection and organization of facts relevant to a more general idea, and ability to draw inferences.

Conant developed tests designed to measure these skills and administered them, together with the Nelson-Denny Reading Test and American Council Psychological Examination. Intercorrelations among all the measures except five were above .50, leading Conant to state that there was no evidence "that students in general employed relatively independent abilities in this study-type reading." She concluded that the results were largely accountable for in terms of a single factor, tentatively defined as general comprehension. Three other factors appeared, but accounted for extremely small parts of the variance. Conant pointed out that her results by no means precluded the possibility that some individuals may show

[7] Langsam, Rosaline. "A Factorial Analysis of Reading Ability." Unpublished doctoral dissertation, New York University, 1942. Abstract in *Journal of Experimental Education*, 10 (1941), 57–63.
[8] Conant, Margaret M. *The Construction of a Diagnostic Reading Test.* New York: Teachers College, Columbia University. Contributions to Education No. 861 (1942).

marked differences in their relative abilities to use different
reading techniques.

A doctoral dissertation by Artley in 1942 [9] explored the
relationship between general comprehension ability, as measured by the Cooperative C-1 Level of Comprehension test, and
hypothesized special reading abilities in the social studies
area, measured by the Cooperative Tests of Social Studies
Ability, Proficiency in the Field of Social Studies, and Survey
Tests in the Social Studies, including ability to obtain facts,
to organize, to interpret, to generalize, to perceive logical relations and to evaluate arguments. For a group of two hundred eleventh-grade students, Artley found the correlation
between general comprehension measure and the composite
of the specific measures to be .79 (.86 corrected for attenuation). He found also that the correlations of the several
specific measures with total reading comprehension all fell
within a fairly narrow range, from .6 to .8, and he concluded
that one could not "dismiss the possibility that there are a
great number of pupils who might profit from a specific type
of instruction." Artley interpreted his findings as "evidence
that there exists a significant degree of specificity in the
measures relating to reading comprehension of the social
studies."

Hall and Robinson reported in 1945 [10] an attempt to
develop independent measures of various aspects of reading.
After analyzing the research and the available tests produced
up until the time of their study, and concluding that these
tests left very much to be desired from the standpoint of
diagnostic potentiality, they developed a battery that included
twenty-five measures, many of which were tests of reading of
non-prose material. Factor analysis of the results of administration of this battery of tests to one hundred college students
yielded six factors, which Hall and Robinson defined as "at-

[9] Artley, A. S. "A Study of Certain Relationships Existing between
General Comprehension and Reading Comprehension in a Specific Subject Matter Area." Unpublished doctoral dissertation, The Pennsylvania
State College, 1942; and in *Journal of Educational Research*, 37 (1944),
464–473.
[10] Hall, W. E., and Robinson, F. P. "An Analytical Approach to the Study
of Reading Skills." *Journal of Educational Psychology*, 36 (1945), 429–
442.

titude of comprehension accuracy"; an "inductive" factor; a verbal or word-meaning factor; a "rate for unrelated facts" factor; a chart-reading factor; and a sixth undefined factor. In other words, six factors, one of which was quite nebulous, were sufficient to account for the variance in the twenty-five separate reading measures.

Harris in a 1948 study[11] identified seven skills or behaviors called for in comprehension of various types of literature, as follows: recognition of synonyms for uncommon words and groups of words; recognition of words or groups of words that are used figuratively; recognition of antecedents of pronouns, or subjects and predicates in loosely organized statements; recognition of summary of ideas expressed or implied; recognition of summaries and characteristics of persons or characters; recognition of author's attitude toward his characters, of his mood or emotion and of his intent; recognition of relationship between technique and meaning.

After administering a battery of tests designed to yield measures on each of these seven skills to two groups of adults, and factor-analyzing the results, Harris concluded that "(1) one and only one ability is common to the comprehension of these literary passages of different types; and that one general factor is adequate to account for the intercorrelations of the seven variables."

Maney and Sochor in 1952 studies[12, 13] sought to develop tests to measure specific factors in comprehension of science and social studies material. Their tests yielded measures of "literal comprehension" and of "critical interpretation" in these two areas. Administering these tests together with the Gates Survey Test and the Pintner General Ability Tests (Verbal Type) to some five hundred fifth-grade pupils, they found correlations from .61 to .67 between the literal and the critical reading scores; from .60 to .76 between these scores and scores on the Gates test; and from .67 to .75 between

[11] Harris, C. W. "Measurement of Comprehension of Literature: II Studies of Measures of Comprehension." *School Review*, 56 (1948), 332–342.
[12] Maney, Ethel Swain. "Literal and Critical Reading in Science." Unpublished doctoral dissertation, Temple University, 1952.
[13] Sochor, E. Elona. "Literal and Critical Reading in Social Studies." Unpublished doctoral dissertation, Temple University, 1952.

these scores and scores on the Pintner tests. The "critical" scores correlated slightly lower with the general reading ability or the intelligence test scores than did the "literal" reading scores. Maney and Sochor interpreted the findings as showing considerable independence between literal and critical reading skills, and between the specific abilities required for critical reading and "general" reading comprehension. In other words, they saw a high degree of specificity in the types of processes involved in different reading situations.

Another 1952 study, the doctoral dissertation of Lyman Hunt[14] represents one of the most competent studies in this area. Hunt sought to determine whether the six factors identified by Davis would reappear in an independent investigation, or, more generally, whether reading comprehension is made up of aspects sufficiently specific to be measurable as independent variables. Hunt developed tests to measure each of the six factors, taking great pains to insure that every item included as part of the test for a given factor was judged with very high consistency by competent consultants to be measuring the ability in question. For a group of 585 college students he first compared item-discrimination values for every item with respect to each of the six postulated factors. Despite the fact that the items had been constructed specifically to measure a carefully defined aspect of reading ability, and had been judged qualified consultants to be measuring that particular ability, Hunt found that in general the items classified in any given area—as, for example, vocabulary items, or items intended to measure reasoning—correlated no higher with the total score on the ability they were supposed to measure than with the score on any of the other abilities. That is to say, there was no evidence in the item-discrimination statistics that the items possessed any differential validity as measures of one aspect of reading comprehension rather than another. Factor analysis of the scores led to the same general conclusion—that, except for the vocabulary test, the other measures "may be measuring much the same function of reading comprehension." Com-

[14] Hunt, Lyman C. "A Further Study of Certain Factors Associated with Reading Comprehension." Unpublished doctoral dissertation, School of Education, Syracuse University, 1952.

paring the factor structure revealed in his study with that reported by Davis, Hunt reports emergence of a first factor somewhat resembling Davis' reasoning factor, a second factor similar to Davis' word knowledge factor, though appearing much less important than it did in the Davis study. He found a third factor like Davis' organizing ability, but it accounted for only 8 per cent of the total variance. He also found three other factors, all probably not significant.

A later study by Stoker and Kropp[15] reported a factor analysis of results of Iowa Tests of Educational Development administered in 1959 to a sample of ninth-grade students. Three sub-tests of the Iowa are concerned respectively with ability to interpret reading materials in the social studies, in natural science, and literary materials. Stoker and Kropp found intercorrelations (uncorrected for attenuation) among these three parts from .67 to .76. A first factor, identified by them as "general mental ability," had extremely high loadings on these three sections and on the Verbal section of the Scholastic Aptitude Test; no other factor contributed significantly to the variance on these parts of ITED. They concluded, therefore, that there were no differentiable reading abilities in the three areas, at least as measured by ITED.

Most of the references cited above have to do with the state of affairs that exist at the secondary or college level. We may very well ask whether reading ability has not become so highly organized at this stage that an individual's performance on all kinds of reading tasks is pretty much of a piece, defying diagnosis or differentiation. It is certainly conceivable that at lower grade levels reading ability is much less highly organized than it is at the high school, college, and adult levels. We may readily suppose that in the beginning stages of reading, emphasis is on the perceptual and mechanical aspects of the task to a greater extent than on central thought processes; and that, since the requisite perceptual skills are being acquired at varying rates by children, there may exist among pupils more readily differentiable degrees of proficiency in

---

[15] Stoker, Howard W., and Kropp, Russell P. "The Predictive Validities and Factorial Content of the Florida State-Wide Ninth-Grade Testing Program Battery." *Florida Journal of Educational Research*, 1960, 105–114.

various components of reading ability. Such a conclusion
seems probable, but it should be said, too, that this belief is
buttressed by no such amount of experimental data as are
available concerning the nature and organization of reading
abilities at the higher levels—and, indeed, there is some contrary evidence, as in the intercorrelations among the subtests
of the Gates Primary Batteries, or the several reading tests
of the Metropolitan Achievement Tests. Virtually all of the
tests of lower-level reading abilities that purport to be diagnostic are based upon *a priori* identifications of the various
reading skills; and however expert one may consider the
analysis and the identification, it nevertheless remains true
that we still have little experimental evidence about the
reality of the distinctions that are made among the various
reading abilities and about the validity of supposed diagnostic
profiles of reading skills. In the realm of vocabulary, for example, we have measures that are labeled tests of "word
recognition," or of "word discrimination," or of "phonetic
analysis skill," all of which characteristically yield quite substantial intercorrelations relative to their reliabilities.

IMPLICATIONS

The studies cited above are not the only ones bearing upon
the organization of reading comprehension ability, but together they comprise a representative sample of the research
in this area. Even from brief recapitulations, one can sense
a lack of consistency in the findings with respect to the generality or specificity of comprehension abilities. What are we to
make of it all? Shall we conclude that the reading experts,
with their lengthy lists of objectives, of finely differentiated,
ever more specific skills, have simply been spinning a fanciful
web that bears no relation to the realities of the nature of
reading ability? Or shall we charge the test makers with a
lack of ingenuity in devising test exercises to provide reliably
differentiable measures of the several skills, with a failure to
provide instruments that will match in their comprehensiveness and sensitivity the goals elaborated by the reading experts? The truth, it seems to me, is to be found between the

two extremes. The following discussion is an attempt to make sense of the research findings, and to suggest their implications for the question, "What can be measured in reading?"

One generalization seems to emerge with very considerable support. With distressing sameness, or with gratifying consistency, depending upon one's point of view, the studies agree that most of the measurable variance in tests of reading competence, however varied the tests entering into the determination, can be accounted for in terms of a fairly small number of factors, certainly not more than six being required to account for better than 90 per cent of the variance. One investigator after another has launched his battery of tests, with all segments neatly labeled, carefully segregated and packaged in separate if not watertight compartments, only to have the vessels founder on the shoals of hard data, with the cargo jumbled together in a single heap, or in a few mixed-up collections. It seems entirely clear that numerous superficially discrete reading skills to which separate names or titles have been attached are, in fact, so closely related, as far as any test results reveal, that we must consider them virtually identical.

It would seem that we may recognize and hope to measure reliably the following components of reading ability: (1) a general verbal factor, (2) comprehension of explicitly stated material, (3) comprehension of implicit or latent meaning, and (4) an element that might be termed "appreciation."

The "verbal factor" in this context is intended to connote word knowledge: breadth, depth, and scope of vocabulary. Every investigation shows vocabulary to be substantially related to other measures of reading ability. Extensive word mastery, or fluency in handling words, is almost a prerequisite to attainment of high competence in any type of reading skill. We are well equipped for reliable measurement of this factor at virtually every level.

Under "comprehension of explicitly stated material" is included such skills as the location of specifically stated information, comprehension of the literal meaning of what is written, and ability to follow specific directions set forth in what is read. Many reading tests are available that measure these skills acceptably; probably the most widely used tests measure this type of reading ability to a greater extent than any other.

The third component, "comprehension of implicit meanings," embraces all of those outcomes that we tend to label as "reasoning in reading." Included here would be the ability to draw inferences from what is read; to predict outcomes; to derive the meaning of words from context; to perceive the structure of what is read—the main idea or central thought, and the hierarchical arrangement of ideas within a selection; to interpret what is read, as manifested either by applying the information to the solution of a problem or by deriving some generalizations or principles from it; in a word, all those abilities that demand active, productive, intellectual response and activity on the part of the reader. The research, in my opinion, does support the belief that this type of reading ability can be differentiated from the ability to comprehend what is explicitly stated though we should always expect to find the two correlated because the ability to get at the implicit meaning of what is read presupposes the ability to understand the explicit or literal meaning.

Test makers have been, and are, devoting more effort to the measurement of the inferential, interpretive abilities, and such abilities are well represented in the reading tests produced in recent years. It is perhaps not inappropriate to comment in passing on what seems to be a false issue that has sometimes been raised by those who object that reading tests which stress this factor are too much like intelligence tests. My view is that the intellectual operations or processes that it is common now to include in the notion of reading as a thinking process are indistinguishable from at least some of the operations and processes that we define as comprising "intelligence." In other words, it is inconceivable that a good test of reading as reasoning should not also be a valid measure of some aspects of the complex we term intelligence.

Finally, we have the factor termed "appreciation." By this is meant such things as sensing the intent or purpose of an author, judging the mood or tone of a selection, perceiving the literary devices by which the author accomplishes his purposes, etc. Existence of these types of outcome as distinct from the ones enumerated above seems less clearly established by the research findings, but here some of the blame may perhaps be laid at the feet of the test makers, who have, by and large, been less concerned with the development of suitable instruments in this area than in the three general areas suggested above. We may reasonably hope that more satisfactory measures of outcomes of this kind will be produced.

SPEED

Thus far the measurement of our old friend, rate or speed, has been neglected. That speed of reading is an important and desired outcome of reading instruction goes without saying. Evidence concerning the extent to which a pupil is improving in rate of reading is highly desirable in any evaluation of a reading program. Our assessment of rate, however, leaves much to be desired, though paradoxically enough, we are better off today because we have a keener appreciation of the limitations of our speed measures than we were twenty-five or thirty years ago, when it was not uncommon to encounter the belief that measurement of rate was a fairly simple, straightforward operation.

Our problems in the measurement of rate stem from the fact that we are never really concerned with pure speed— that is, with just the rapidity with which the subject can move over a given number of words or lines of written material. Rate is only meaningful as it defines the rapidity with which the reader covers material at a particular level of comprehension. We are all now well aware that an individual's rate is a function of the level of difficulty of the material being read; and some would say also of the type of material, though the experimental data on this question are inconsistent. Indeed, this ability to change rate of reading is accepted as one of the desired outcomes of reading instruction; we want the student to adapt his reading to the demands of the particular material, to move as rapidly or as slowly as the requirements of the material and his own purposes in reading dictate. The question of the relation of speed and comprehension is a perplexing one, to which the experimental data give no single clear-cut answer.

We are troubled also in the measurement of rate by the fact that the test situation poses quite a different motivation for the reader than does the normal, unsupervised reading situation. Unfortunately, from the standpoint of validity the difference between the test situation and the normal reading situation, as far as motivating property is concerned, varies from one subject to another, and our interpretation of rate of reading scores derived in test situations must, therefore, always be subject to some reservation—at least in the case of rate measures obtained when the subject is aware that his speed of reading is being appraised.

Nevertheless, our measures of rate are not without usefulness. For the estimation of change or development, rate measures derived from the same test are quite serviceable. Research, moreover, suggests that while rate measures are not perfectly correlated by any means, there is an appreciable community among the various measures. We thus may identify with a good deal of confidence those readers who are excessively slow; and this is perhaps the most important use of rate measures.

CONCLUSION

As important as what *can* be measured in reading, perhaps, is what *cannot*. There remains the uneasy feeling that no matter how excellent our measure of comprehension, whether of explicit or latent meaning, no matter how clever our techniques for assessing "critical" reading skills may become, our evaluation still leaves much to be desired. Whence this dissatisfaction? Is it sensible to anticipate that we can develop wholly adequate objective measures for "reading ability"? Consider what reading is, or should be. Not only do we read what we read; in the layman's peculiarly apt term, we read *into* what we read—that is, we read something of ourselves into the written word. We bring to bear on the material we are reading our total experience, background, interests, understandings, purposes, and so on. The response that each person makes to a given piece of reading matter, therefore, is necessarily and desirably a unique, personal kind of response. When we set before a student an exercise in arithmetic, or a word to be spelled, or a problem in algebra, there is only one response that is desired and that is to be considered correct. When we are concerned with appraisal of a person's ability to read insightfully and meaningfully, we almost assume that there will be many different but equally acceptable responses to the stimulus material. Under these circumstances it looms as a very difficult task to conceive a completely objective test that will permit us to assess the quality or richness or correctness of each person's interpretation of a given selection.

"Reading," in the words of Francis Bacon, "maketh the full man"—and this neatly epitomizes the goal of reading instruction. It is important for people to learn to read because reading can enrich their lives so enormously. We want people to be able to read the sign that says "Stop," so that they will not endanger themselves and others at crossings. We want people to be able to read the directions, simple or complicated, that enable them to comply and cooperate with the practices necessary for getting along with others. We want them to read because in no other manner can they so readily share in the experiences of the rest of mankind that will inform and ennoble them. For these purposes, surely *what* a person reads is as important as how well he reads it, but I am afraid that we have no measures of the wisdom with which persons make their choices of reading matter, nor have we any measures of the extent to which they profit from their reading in the manner suggested above, and I for one am dubious that we shall ever have such measures.

Like many other students who have considered reading tests, I have suggested that the labels on the tests are perhaps poor indicators of the jobs the tests actually perform. I am less dismayed by this fact than some critics have been, for I feel that it does not preclude the possibility of considerable usefulness and value in these measures. Insofar as uncritical acceptance of test names as representative of their contents leads to erroneous descriptions and improper diagnosis, such names are, of course, harmful. But, in a fortunate way, the very difficulty that surrounds our efforts to develop differentiating measures of various reading skills becomes our salvation in the instructional program. If these abilities are substantially related and overlap to the extent that the various studies make it appear, then it is entirely likely that efforts devoted to improving one or another of the types of skill will carry over to improvements in the other types of skill. There is nothing in the research reports which would lead us to believe that it is fruitless to attempt to set up varied types of goals or outcomes, to prepare exercises calculated to develop power in these several skills, and even to use these analyses as bases for developing tests. Indeed, in no other way can we sensibly plan or conduct the instructional program.

4

Evaluation of Development
In and Through Reading

RUTH STRANG

Evaluation is like Tennyson's "flower in the crannied wall"—
it reaches out in the whole universe of the reading field. It
is concerned with the individual's reading development and
the effect of reading on his personal development. Evaluation
recognizes that improvement in any reading skill may not
only affect the acquisition of subsequent skills but also the
individual's self-confidence and concept of himself. Growth in
reading ability may also lead to improved relationships with
parents and teachers. As the child grows older he uses reading increasingly as a tool to further intellectual growth. The
knowledge obtainable through reading helps him grow socially,
educationally, and vocationally. Evaluation, therefore, must be
comprehensive and continuous; it must change somewhat with
successive stages of development.[1]

The evaluation process begins when we state the goals
of teaching reading. Some of these are fairly specific, such as

[1] *Evaluation of Reading.* Compiled and edited by Helen M. Robinson.
Proceedings of the Annual Conference on Reading Held at the University
of Chicago, 1958. Supplementary Educational Monograph, No. 88.
Chicago: University of Chicago Press, 1958.

REPRINTED with permission of Ruth Strang and the National Society for
the Study of Education. "Evaluation of Development In and Through
Reading," in *Development In and Through Reading:* The Sixtieth Yearbook of the National Society for the Study of Education, Nelson B. Henry,
ed. (Chicago: University of Chicago Press, 1961), pp. 376–82 and 392–97.

learning to recognize words; others are more intangible, such as enjoyment and appreciation of literature. These goals should be stated as specific abilities, habits, attitudes, appreciations, activities, and interests that can be observed or measured in the teaching-learning situation.

To obtain evidence of these changes—which, if desirable, imply growth—we must select or devise methods and instruments. After we have obtained the evidence, the next step is to evaluate, in the light of our objectives, the adequacy, effectiveness, and worth of the teaching-learning experiences that have been offered. After this has been done, administrators, teachers, and students should apply the results of the evaluation to improve instruction in reading. Thus, evaluation helps produce growth as well as appraise it.

WHY EVALUATE?

Evaluation is essential to learning.[2] It is an incentive to students, an intrinsic part of teaching, and an aid to the administrator and the specialist in improving the program.

For students, evaluation facilitates learning and gives them a sense of direction. Psychological experiments have repeatedly shown that students learn more effectively when they know how well they are doing and what specifically they are doing wrong. Appraisal as a part of teaching helps them identify the reading processes or methods that they can use successfully.

Awareness of one's progress helps build self-confidence. Every student needs the stimulus of success. When the retarded reader sees objective evidence that he can learn to read, he begins to overcome his longstanding sense of failure. Encouraged by evidence of progress, students tend to take more initiative and responsibility for their improvement in reading. "Nothing succeeds like observed success."

Teachers, too, need a sense of progress and the stimulus of success. A comprehensive evaluation process, by broadening and sharpening objectives and highlighting the results

[2] Virgil E. Herrick, "Purposes and Needs for an Evaluation Program," in *Evaluation of Reading, ibid.,* pp. 153–58.

that have been achieved, gives teachers an increased sense of the value of their work. On the other hand, an evaluation based on narrow tests of skills is discouraging to the teacher who is broadly concerned with attitudes, new interests, and appreciations.

Evaluation also shows the teacher where to begin. By trying to estimate students' readiness and capacities as well as by measuring their present skills and interests, the teacher can provide the learning experiences that the students need. Evaluation serves as a guide to the choice of procedures and materials.

For the administrator, evaluation may show the strengths and successful features in the program as well as indicate needs for changes in curriculum, instruction, and administrative policy. As it reveals failure in the common effort to attain objectives that have been agreed upon, the administrator asks "why?" Do the students' inadequacies in reading stem from an unsuitable curriculum, from poorly prepared teachers, from failure to detect incompetency in the teaching of beginning reading, from lack of suitable reading materials for the wide range of reading ability that is found in most classes, or from homes or communities that are unfavorable to improvement in reading? Naturally, the administrator uses the results of evaluation in explaining the reading program to the community.

To the reading specialist, evaluation reveals strengths and weaknesses in the program. It may show that he has devoted too much time to individual cases and small groups and neglected work with and through the teachers. It may suggest strategic points in the program at which he should concentrate his efforts, such as a developmental reading course for all students or special classes for the gifted.

From the standpoint of research and contributions to the literature in the field of reading, we should have better evaluations of programs and procedures. Future writers should avoid two faults that often occur in the reports now available: (*a*) A program or procedure is merely described without evidence of its effectiveness; (*b*) results are presented statistically with no concrete description of the organization, methods and materials by which they were achieved. The evaluation process will be described in this chapter, and instruments and methods for obtaining evidence will be suggested.

WHAT IS EVALUATED?

The nature of the evaluative process varies with the accepted concept of reading. Evaluation is a relatively simple matter if reading is conceived as merely pronouncing printed words correctly with little or no regard to their meaning. If reading is broadly defined to include thinking and feeling, the exercise of imagination and character traits, such as determination to overcome difficulties, persistence in practice, and self-confidence in attacking new tasks,[3] then evaluation becomes complex, indeed. In this chapter, the description of evaluation accords with the broad view of reading that is presented in this yearbook.

Main Goals

The goals to be evaluated have been stated in previous chapters, both broadly and as specific behavior that can be observed. In evaluating them, we must remember that they are not separate steps; they are interwoven in the reading process from beginning reading to maturity.

How to State Objectives: With Reference to Students

The stated objectives for development of reading abilities and for personal development through reading should possess those characteristics that are indicated in the following paragraphs.

Be Specific General goals should be broken down into specific objectives and stated operationally as definite reading skills or behavior. For example, the objective, "acquire skill in word recognition," should be broken down into specific be-

---

[3] Calvin D. Cotterall and Phillip Weise, "A Perceptual Approach to Early Reading Difficulties," *California Journal of Educational Research,* X (November, 1959), 212–18.

havior which can be observed or tested, such as: (*a*) shows progress in associating the initial sounds of words with the appropriate letter symbols; (*b*) becomes proficient in identifying sounds in words; (*c*) improves in facility to give words that rhyme with the word presented; and (*d*) year by year becomes more skillful in using various methods to determine the meaning of unknown words—context clues, structural analysis, syllabication, phonic analysis, and use of the dictionary. The stated objectives should also include items relating to the students' personal development—for example, is encouraged by success and evidences of progress in word-recognition skills.

Be Realistic and Clearly Stated   Objectives should be realistic and precisely rather than vaguely stated. Similarly, we should avoid the use of words that may make the objectives ambiguous or obscure.

Accent Growth   We should try to appraise the student's growth as well as his reading status. Growth is especially difficult to measure. Progress is always relative to the capacity of the student and to his opportunities for learning. As measured by gains on standardized tests, progress should be checked to determine whether it is merely a chance difference or real evidence of growth.

Show Relative Importance   It is also necessary to determine the relative importance of each objective at different stages in the child's development. For example, in beginning reading, acquiring a sight vocabulary and word-recognition skills are basic, dominant learnings, although thinking and feeling are also part of the pattern of objectives in the primary grades. In the intermediate grades, learning through reading in new fields becomes increasingly important. During high-school years, still deeper levels of interpretation and critical thinking occupy a central position in the pattern of objectives. Evaluation must take into consideration these changing emphases at different stages in reading development.

Recognize Individual Differences   Some objectives are more important and appropriate for certain students than for others. To determine this relative importance, we must have a knowledge of students' interests, abilities, and backgrounds. For example, for a retarded reader in high school, growth in basic vocabulary and word-recognition skills may be the most important evidence of progress to evaluate. For an able student who reads little, an increase of interest in worthwhile reading is most important. Some individuals who are above the test norms for their ages and grades are still achieving below their potential reading ability. On the other hand, a score that is several years below the norm may represent real achievement for a less able learner.

Show Progress in Patterns   Ideally, patterns of objectives paralleling the development from beginning reading to mature reading should be described. For example, a pattern of objectives at the developmental level of junior high school, applied to reading a short story, might include: (*a*) show increasing interest in reading short stories; (*b*) comprehend most of the words; (*c*) apply word-meaning skills to unfamiliar words; (*d*) are keen to pick up clues of character and plot from the descriptions of physical appearance, speech, actions, and response of others to a certain character; (*e*) respond in an appropriate manner emotionally to examples of courage, cruelty, and other human qualities; (*f*) communicate more effectively to others their thoughts and feelings about the story; and (*g*) modify their point of view, attitude, and behavior in a desirable direction.

By setting up sequential patterns of reading development, it is possible to see more clearly how children's improvement in reading might progress simultaneously on all fronts through the school years or how a retarded reader, starting with his present pattern of reading development, might make progress.

Consider Causes   If evaluation is to lead to improved practice, it is important to ascertain conditions that may be responsible for the observed growth or lack of growth. Neither teacher nor student can do much to remedy a bad situation or to improve a good one unless he knows what is causing the success or failure. These causes or conditions are complex and can best be recorded and synthesized in a reading case study for each student.

Objectives: With Reference to Staff Responsibilities

The objectives described thus far have been stated as desirable changes in students. These are the ultimate focus of evaluation. However, an effective reading program may also be evaluated with reference to co-operation, communication, and other constructive attitudes and practices on the part of administrators, supervisors, and teachers.[4,5] An evaluation concerned with students' development should consider how well informed the administrator and supervisory personnel are about the reading program, how effectively they assist teachers in improving instruction in reading, and how adroitly they interpret the reading program to the public and use community resources. It would also be necessary to ascertain how well teachers were combining planning, teaching, and evaluating, and whether they were making appraisal of student progress an intrinsic part of instruction in reading.

GUIDES TO EVALUATION

General procedures for evaluating may be briefly summarized as follows:

1. Evaluation should be continuous rather than periodic.
2. It should be a part of the instructional program, not apart from it.
3. It should obtain evidence on the extent to which the stated objectives have been achieved.
4. In obtaining this evidence, it should use both formal and informal methods.
5. The data collected should be used for the improvement of program and procedures.

---

[4] Elizabeth Zimmermann Howard, "Appraising Strengths and Weaknesses of the Total Reading Program," in *Evaluation of Reading*, Helen M. Robinson, pp. 169–73.
[5] Mildred C. Letton, "Evaluating the Effectiveness of Teaching Reading," in *Evaluation of Reading*, Helen M. Robinson, pp. 76–82.

6. Increasing emphasis should be placed on self-appraisal as the student grows older.
7. Evaluation of a reading program should be carried on by a team that includes administrators, reading consultants, other specialists, teachers, students, and parents.

EVALUATION OF GROWTH IN INDIVIDUAL STUDENTS

The evidence on each of the several aspects of reading development should be evaluated against a background knowledge of the situation and the students. The real test of an individual's potential reading ability is the progress that he, through the best possible instruction, is able to make. The "best possible instruction" would, of course, vary with the individual's age, interest, and reasons for his reading difficulties.

Appraising a student's progress with reference to his capacity presents many difficulties. In estimating potential reading ability, it is important to study all the available evidence about a student: his scores on standardized intelligence tests and listening comprehension tests, observations of his mental alertness in everyday situations, family background, and early school experiences. A discrepancy between the student's potential ability and his present achievement may be caused by poor teaching, lack of purpose or persistence, negative parental attitudes toward education, too much pressure or indifference on the part of parents, and a great variety of emotional disturbances.

The case study should bring together information about the interrelated aspects of home background, health, school and social conditions; results of individual tests of mental ability, listening comprehension, and reading achievement; and observations of interests and personality. It relates changes in reading development and personal development through reading to causative conditions. The case-study approach emphasizes simultaneous growth in all aspects of reading important for an individual. At every point, it takes into account his ability and learning opportunities.

A well-designed reading program stands or falls on the

basis of desirable changes in student development, both with respect to personality traits and advancement in reading skills. In working with an emotionally disturbed girl changes were noted, not only in test results but also in subjective impressions of her improvement in reading and personal development. Her reactions were described as a more relaxed attitude, less anxiety, less self-depreciation, more pleasure in reading, extended areas in which she could concentrate, increased awareness of reading methods she could use most successfully, and day-by-day improvement in comprehension of different kinds of material.

Evaluation of these more subtle aspects of development may be made by noting evidences of changes in a pupil's attitude toward reading, toward school, toward himself, and toward his family, as in the case of Donald. The quotations are from tape-recorded interviews and are given in the order of their occurrence from the beginning of the first to the end of the twenty-seventh interview:

Donald's chronological age, on November 10, was 13 years 3 months; mental age on the *Stanford-Binet Test,* 14.2; I.Q., 108; 68 percentile; reading expectation, seventh grade. *Gray's Oral Reading Paragraphs,* given at about the same time, indicated that he was reading on about the 1.8 level. Also significant was his mastery of the Dolch basic vocabulary, his ability to read many signs and directions, and his efforts to get some ideas out of his eighth-grade social-studies books.

Although there was definite improvement in Donald's reading during the time he was coming to the Reading Center, the most important change was his attitude toward himself and to reading. He came to the Center with a negative attitude toward reading and anything pertaining to it. But even in the first interview he showed a ray of hope. In response to the question, "Did you want to come to the Reading Center?" he said, "Nothing to lose. Everything to gain." He expected to fail but hoped there was some magic that would make it possible for him to read better.

Even during these first interviews he made some positive comments: "I could do the tests if I could read them." When told he was reading much better one week, he said, "I know."

Although he resisted word study on certain days, he showed interest in reading the names on the subway map and names of airplanes and engines. In the sixth interview, when given words in an envelope to make into sentences, Donald said, "This is like TV. 'Beat the Clock.' It's fun. . . . It's easy to do when you know the words."

After the seventh interview, comments like the following became more frequent: "Don't you have a little harder vocabulary cards?" "Could I have some homework to take home?" "I came by myself today. My father wrote down the directions." "I want to read. I want to read a book. I want to read some hard books—hard-cover books."

At home the father, too, noted progress. At the end of the series of interviews, the father wrote, "I realize there has been an improvement. . . . You're the first teacher he really respected."

The study of movement in a series of verbatim interviews can be made more scientific by making a content analysis, charting changes in the number of comments the client volunteers, the attitudes which he states or which can be inferred, and the kind of responses he makes to certain teaching techniques.

Similarly, changes in parents' perception of and attitude toward the child with reading difficulties can be traced over a period of five group-discussion sessions which have been tape-recorded. Changes in the expressed attitudes of one mother were as follows:

> Session I. My son is just plain lazy. The guidance director told us he was below average in intelligence and this seemed to fit in with what we thought of him.
>
> Session II. I still think it is a form of laziness or maybe impatience. Possibly my child has as much intelligence as an average child, but he is not using it.
>
> Session III. I'm letting up on the pressure now and have stopped criticizing him constantly.
>
> Session IV. I am taking it easier with him; maybe it's working. He doesn't seem to be any worse anyway.

Session V. Well, I am relaxed for the first time, sitting back and letting things go by for a little while and, believe it or not, the child seems to be much better.[6]

APPRAISAL OF THE READING PROGRAM AS A WHOLE

Instead of attempting to evaluate a given method of teaching reading by making inconclusive experimental control-group studies, it would appear to be more rewarding to recognize the complexity of the problem and to describe the combination of methods and materials that result in reading growth of many individuals and groups of different ages, abilities, and backgrounds. It might then be possible to vary one method with the same group of individuals and measure subsequent improvement or note lack of improvement.

To appraise reading material, well-known formulas such as the Gray-Leary, the Dale-Chall, and the Lorge may be used to estimate the structural difficulty of a given piece of material. But other aspects of readability should also be taken into account—organization and the interrelation of ideas, interest, difficulty of concepts, unnecessary technical words, vividness of expression, originality, imagination, and personal references. In appraising reading material we should also consider its contribution to solving personal problems, lightening one's burdens through laughter, furthering ethical development, understanding one's self and associates, and studying the nature of the world.

Numerous descriptions of school and college reading programs have been published, most of which have been presented with practically no evaluation. The only evaluation in the majority of the other reports is based on differences between initial and final scores on standardized reading tests. Very few of these reports consider the standard error of measurement with respect to the test scores and the standard error of the difference between the initial and final scores. Still fewer

---

[6] Janice MacDonald Studholme, "Changes in Attitudes of Mothers of Retarded Readers during Group Guidance Sessions." Unpublished Doctor's project, Teachers College, Columbia University, 1960.

observers have attempted to measure the persistence of gains made after the experimental period. Rarely does any investigator report the frequent use of short, informal tests charted to show students' progress. Evaluations of reading programs are still seriously lacking in reliability and in valid appraisal of reading, broadly conceived.

Only brief references may be made to several different patterns of the evaluation procedures reported. Durrell and others obtained evidence of the effectiveness of their beginning reading program from group and individual tests, including standardized and informal types, tests of word-recognition abilities, and others pertaining to oral reading and paragraph reading.[7] Quite a different approach to evaluation is directed toward administrative provision and teacher behavior, e.g., "Is a definite time set aside in the school program for the teaching of reading skills in each grade?" Tormey and Patterson[8] depended largely on student statements and suggestions for evidence of the effectiveness of a developmental reading program. Baron and Bernard[9] emphasized the use of informal evaluation techniques in the classroom. Applying the analysis of co-variance technique, McDonald and Paul[10] evaluated the Cornell University reading program with respect to increase in vocabulary, speed of comprehension, and three measures of academic achievement. In the evaluation of the reading and study program at the University of Missouri, Ranson[11] obtained evidence on the progress and the superiority of those enrolled in the reading course from grade-point averages, results of reading rate and comprehension tests converted to t scores, and subjective appraisal by students.

[7] Donald D. Durrell, Alice Nicholson, Arthur V. Olson, Sylvia R. Gavel, and Eleanor B. Linehan, "Success in First Grade Reading," *Journal of Education*, CXL (February, 1958), 1–48.

[8] Mary K. Tormey and Walter G. Patterson, "Developmental Reading and Student Evaluation," *Journal of Developmental Reading*, II (Winter, 1959), 30–43.

[9] Denis Baron and Harold W. Bernard, *Evaluation Techniques for Classroom Teachers*. New York: McGraw-Hill Book Co., 1958.

[10] Arthur S. McDonald and Walter Paul, "Teaching College Freshmen To Read," *Phi Delta Kappan*, XXXVIII (December, 1956), 104–09.

[11] Kathleen M. Ranson, "An Evaluation of Certain Aspects of the Reading and Study Program at the University of Missouri," *Journal of Educational Research*, XLVIII (February, 1955), 443–54.

The effect of one group-therapy session per week in a college reading program was evaluated by means of an elaborate battery which included the *Wechsler Adult Intelligence Scale,* the *Diagnostic Reading Test Battery, McDonald-Byrne Reading Versatility Inventory, Michigan Vocabulary Test,* several personality tests, and a semi-structured diagnostic interview.[12]

CONCLUDING STATEMENT

Evaluation of reading programs is not an end in itself, it is a means to better reading. Consequently, it should be closely associated with instruction. Moreover, evaluative techniques are more likely to be used immediately if evaluation is an intrinsic part of the teaching-learning process. Data should include evidence not only of acquired knowledge and skills but also of the conditions favorable or unfavorable for learning. Probably few teachers view instruction and evaluation as inseparable.

In-service education is needed to help teachers learn convenient ways of evaluating student growth in reading. As the student progresses through school he becomes an active participant in the evaluation process. He should have a clear and concrete conception of his reading goals or purposes and assist in gathering evidence of his progress toward these goals. With the help of the teacher and the stimulus of his fellow students he should overcome difficulties that are hindering his improvement.

We have a long way to go in reaching a scientific experimental type of evaluation. Progress will be made as standardized tests measure the attainment of broader objectives; informal methods become more precise; and evidence from various sources is analyzed, interpreted, and synthesized more expertly.

The present emphasis of evaluation of reading seems to

[12] Arthur S. McDonald, Edwin S. Zolik, and James A. Byrne, "Reading Deficiencies and Personality Factors: A Comprehensive Treatment," in *Starting and Improving Reading Programs,* pp. 89–98. Edited by Oscar S. Causey and William Eller. Eighth Yearbook of the National Reading Conference. Fort Worth: Texas Christian University Press, April, 1959.

be on continuity of appraisal and instruction, cooperation or the team approach, and complexity, which recognizes the broad view of reading instruction presented in this yearbook.

For Further Reading

Austin, Mary C., Bush, Clifford L., and Huebner, Mildred H. *Reading Evaluation: Appraisal Techniques for School and Classroom.* New York: Ronald Press, 1961.

Austin, Mary C., and Morrison, Coleman. *The First R.* New York: Macmillan, 1963.

Chandler, Theodore A. "Reading Disability and Socio-Economic Status," *Journal of Reading* 10 (October, 1966): 5–21.

Goodman, Kenneth S., and others. *Choosing Materials to Teach Reading.* Detroit: Wayne State Univ. Press, 1967.

Horrocks, John E., and Schoonover, Thelma I. *Measurement for Teachers.* Columbus, Ohio: Merrill, 1968.

National Education Association. *The Three R's Hold Their Own at the Midcentury.* Washington, D.C.: National Education Association, 1951.

Penty, Ruth C. *Reading Ability and High School Drop-Outs.* New York: Bureau of Publications, Columbia University, 1956.

Robinson, Helen M., ed. *Evaluation of Reading: Supplementary Educational Monograph No. 88.* Chicago: Univ. of Chicago Press, 1958.

Section Two

PRACTICES IN EVALUATING PROGRAMS AND STUDENTS

The purpose of this section is to propose models and methods for evaluating programs and students. The teaching of reading can be improved if teachers and administrators will encourage the systematic and continuous evaluation of reading programs and students' reading abilities. These evaluation procedures must be based on instructional objectives. The models described should be modified to meet the specific conditions of the instructional setting where they are to be used.

The first essay in this section, Article 5 by Chall, includes a discussion of the use of standardized tests in evaluating students' reading behaviors. Chall demonstrates the use of these tests in planning effective instruction.

Article 6, by Smith, outlines the procedures he and his co-workers utilized in conducting a national evaluation of federally funded reading programs. Their evaluation was based on specific program objectives—the objectives set forth in the federal act that authorized the funding of the programs. The evaluation of an entire school district, an individual school, or a single class-room could easily adopt the general evaluation model suggested in this article.

The last five articles in this section are detailed exam-inations of reading program evaluation at various levels—from pre-primary to adult. In Articles 7 and 8, Barrett and Mattick point out that evaluation at the readiness level should be concerned chiefly with measurement which determines instructional needs. Ironically, once readiness tests are diag-nostically valid, it will be feasible to define the purpose of reading programs as being to *invalidate* the predictions of reading readiness tests.

In Article 9, Harris describes the total evaluation of an elementary reading program. Included in the Harris model are procedures for assessing students, teachers, teaching proce-dures, and instructional materials. Both this article and Article 10 by Hill on evaluating the secondary school reading program are complete evaluation models. They include many specific suggestions and examples that are of practical use to reading supervisors as well as to reading teachers.

The last essay in the section, Article 11 by Brown, raises some serious questions concerning the measurement procedures used with adult illiterates. The pertinence of the discussion is not limited to work with the special population of adult illit-erates; the essay also illuminates measurement problems that arise in connection with many other groups that differ from the socioeconomic middle class, for whom most standardized tests are developed.

The reader will identify many important ideas in this section if he searches it for answers to these questions:

1. How are the objectives of the reading program determined?
2. Are the objectives for reading programs different from those for improving student's reading abilities?
3. Can teaching procedures be validly and reliably evaluated?
4. How can the information from an evaluation program be utilized so it will have an impact on the instructional program?
5. Is the evaluation program different from the instructional pro-gram?
6. What special characteristics of the school environment should be considered in planning a reading evaluation program?

5

Interpretation of the Results of Standardized Reading Tests

JEANNE S. CHALL

Essentially, tests are only samples of behavior and measure only what a person does at a particular time and place. Some people do their best reading on tests; others do their poorest.[1] In interpreting the test results of a *class* or *school,* the "best" and "worst" performances may balance out, and the average scores may represent the group's actual performance. For the individual pupil, however, it is well to remember that his test performance is only a sample of his daily functioning, and the sample may be biased. Furthermore, tests are samples of the particular skill or ability tested. Reading is a complex of skills encompassing many general and specific abilities, understandings, and attitudes. Although standardized reading tests purport to measure the most important aspects of reading, they lag behind our recognition of these factors at all levels.

The reading readiness tests correlate positively, but not perfectly, with success in beginning reading. It is therefore not surprising to find that Mary, who scored below average

---

[1] Alex C. Sherriffs and Donald S. Boomer, "Who Is Penalized by the Penalty for Guessing?" *Journal of Educational Psychology,* XLV (February, 1954), 81–90.

REPRINTED from *Evaluation of Reading,* Supplementary Educational Monograph No. 88, "Interpretation of the Results of Standardized Reading Tests" by Jeanne S. Chall by permission of the University of Chicago Press and the author. Copyright, 1958, The University of Chicago Press.

on the readiness test, is more advanced at the end of the first grade than John, who scored above average. The high school or college student who scores below the mean on a standardized reading test may in fact be a better reader, from the viewpoint of integrating and using what he has read, than the student who scores above the mean.

The assumptions that standardized test results may not always be unbiased samples of a student's reading ability and that the standardized reading tests do not measure all the important objectives of reading instruction, especially for a particular school,[2] often lead to rejection of standardized tests in favor of informal teacher observations. However, standardized reading tests, even with their limitations, can make an important contribution to reading instruction. The remainder of this paper will suggest how the results of standardized reading tests can be interpreted to evaluate, first, achievement and, second, instructional needs.

TEST RESULTS AS MEASURES OF ACHIEVEMENT

The most common use of standardized reading tests is to determine over-all reading achievement of individuals and groups in comparison to that of the general population. The grade levels or percentile ranks afford both a measure of achievement and a comparison with the population on which the test is standardized. The results reveal the level in reading achievement of a school system, a class, or an individual. But what we do not know is how "good" or "bad" the results are. For this, we must take into account the capacities of the students. Test scores alone tell us "how much" but not "how good."

For example if one third-grade class in a school averages at grade 3.9 on a reading test, and another at only 2.8, we cannot, from this information alone, determine which can be more proud of its achievement. By merely scoring at the

---

[2] Walter W. Cook, "Tests Achievement," in Walter S. Monroe (ed.), *Encyclopedia of Educational Research*, pp. 1461–78. New York: Macmillan Co., 1950.

national norm, the first class may not be doing well enough, since the children may be superior in intelligence and should be achieving even higher. The class that scored below the national norm may be below normal in intelligence and may, in fact, be achieving even better than the first in terms of the capacities of the children.[3,4]

Since the capacities of poor readers are often underestimated, their low reading achievement may appear justified. According to expectancy formulas, pupils may appear to be achieving up to their capacities. Also, since children are selected for remedial and corrective programs on the basis of discrepancies between their intelligence quotients and reading, the children who have "low" intelligence quotients because of poor reading will be penalized further. We often reason erroneously that children achieve below grade level in reading because their intelligence quotients are low. The truer picture is that in many instances their intelligence quotients, as revealed by group tests, are low because their reading is so poor.

LIMITED RANGE OF READING TESTS

Standardized reading tests designed for a few grades frequently give a distorted picture of reading achievement, particularly at the extremes among the poorest and the best readers. The selections and vocabulary are suitable for typical students in those grades. Hence, if students are significantly retarded or advanced for their grade, they will be unable to reveal their true achievement levels.

It may well be that the usual finding that bright children do not work up to potential is sometimes due to the restrictions at the upper levels of achievement tests. The best achievers cannot show how well they can really read because they can complete all items.

It would be well to select tests for those who achieve at

[3] George Spache, "Intellectual and Personality Characteristics of Retarded Readers," *Psychological Newsletter*, IX (September, 1957), 9–12.
[4] H. F. Burks and P. Bruce, "The Characteristics of Poor and Good Readers as Disclosed by the Wechsler Intelligence Scale for Children," *Journal of Educational Psychology*, XLVI (December, 1955), 488–93.

the extremes on the basis of their estimated reading level rather than their grade placement. Two or three levels of standard tests may have to be given to one grade if the range of reading is wide. Where this cannot be done, the lowest achievers should be retested on lower level tests and the higher achievers on tests designed for higher grades.

THE INFLUENCE OF RATE

Slow readers, especially above the primary grades, often find it impossible to complete the test before time is called. For this reason, some tests now give longer time limits. Some even have separate sections that are designed to measure the rate of reading. However, unless the time limits on vocabulary and comprehension are long, the scores of slow readers will be affected adversely.

To illustrate, the following were culled from test batteries of three children who were given additional time to complete their tests:

		Grade scores	
Reading comprehension tests with	*Level of test*	*Standard time*	*Untimed*
1. Ample time limits	For Grades V–VI	5.0	6.2
2. Ample time limits	For Grades V–VI	4.9	6.2
3. Very short time limits	For Grades IV–VIII	7.3	11.2 +

Which of the foregoing are the truer scores? If our purpose is to measure power of comprehension, then the higher ones are probably more accurate. When a school uses tests with short time limits, perhaps some adjustment can be made to permit those students to finish who think they can continue. A test may be scored both with and without time limits by drawing a line under the last item completed within the specified time. Such dual scoring gives additional information about instructional needs.

TEST RESULTS AS INDICATORS OF INSTRUCTIONAL NEEDS

The grade equivalents from standardized reading tests can give clues to selecting appropriate reading materials, to suggesting the level and type of reading instruction, and to grouping of students.

The grade scores from the reading comprehension subtests of survey and analytic tests indicate the general level of difficulty of material that can be read. In most instances a score of 4.5 indicates that a pupil can read with a reasonable degree of facility and understanding material on a fourth-grade level of difficulty. If a junior college freshman averages only ninth-grade reading level, it means that his textbooks should be easier than those published for average college freshmen. Therefore, the grade level scores from standardized tests can help the teacher set the level of basic reading instruction. If groups are formed, the grade scores can be used as the first approximation of the level of the basal reader most suitable for that group.

Some teachers assume that the standardized test scores indicate a pupil's frustration level or top level of performance and have therefore selected readers on a grade lower than the standardized test scores. This may not always be wise, since for many children, especially those who lack confidence or have an unusually slow rate of reading, the standardized scores may give a minimal estimate of performance. Such children can actually benefit more from a higher level of materials. Informal tests on the basal readers should supplement the standardized scores in order that children be given instruction neither too difficult nor too easy for them. This is especially important for retarded readers, who may be discouraged further by basal readers several grades below their maturity levels.

DIAGNOSTIC INTERPRETATION FOR GROUPS AND INDIVIDUALS

The most penetrating kind of interpretation of standardized test results is concerned with the pupil's strengths and weaknesses in reading. To answer questions about specific aspects of reading achievement, the analytic or diagnostic type tests, with separate subtests, are especially useful. However, even the survey tests (the usual reading tests on achievements batteries), if studied and interpreted carefully and supplemented with oral reading tests or just "listening" to the pupil read, can be used to diagnose specific needs.

Limitations of space prevent my going further into this particular aspect of interpretation. However, some basic issues which should be considered suggestive will be discussed.

DIAGNOSTIC INTERPRETATION AT THE ELEMENTARY SCHOOL LEVEL

Most reading readiness tests afford a separate evaluation of knowledge of concepts, understanding of directions, visual discrimination, auditory discrimination, and visual-motor coordination (copying). These subtests are usually too short to give a reliable index of each aspect of readiness, but they can give the teacher a clue to weaknesses that can be observed more thoroughly by informal tests. For example, if a child scores low on the visual discrimination subtest, his teacher can look for this deficiency in class activities in matching of pictures, forms, words, and letters.

Recent findings on the importance of visual [5] and auditory discrimination[6] for success in beginning reading suggest that the results from these particular subtests should be studied carefully to locate those children who may be weak in these areas.

In general, the readiness subtests can be divided into two areas—language background and specific auditory-visual skills. These two areas are not highly intercorrelated, and if a child is high on one and low on the other, the kind of instruction needed to get him "ready" would differ. If a child is high in language background and low on auditory and visual skills, he

[5] Jean Turner Goins, *Visual Perceptual Abilities and Early Reading Progress*. Supplementary Educational Monographs, No. 87. Chicago: University of Chicago Press, 1958.
[6] Donald D. Durrell *et al.*, "Success in First Grade Reading," *Journal of Education*, CXL (February, 1958), 1–48.

may not need the enriched experiential background usually considered a must for "low readiness" children. He may, instead, need more concentrated help in matching words and letters and in listening for rhymes and beginning sounds.

On the primary, intermediate, and upper elementary levels, most of the standardized silent reading tests contain only two subtests—word meaning and paragraph reading. Separate grade scores are derived for each subtest. Usually the two scores are fairly close to one another. However, it is not uncommon to find significant discrepancies between the subtests. Some children may score considerably lower on the word meaning subtest than on the paragraph reading part. What does this mean? If we consider only the names of the subtests, we may infer that the pupil needs help in word meanings and that general comprehension will also improve if the child's meaning vocabulary is expanded. However, in some instances his meaning vocabulary is quite extensive for his age, but he cannot recognize the words. Thus faulty word recognition may lie behind the low word meaning score. On the paragraph comprehension subtest, context may be used to arrive at general meaning. Thus paragraph comprehension scores may not be affected as much by poor word recognition, especially for brighter pupils. A standardized or informal oral reading test, together with a diagnostic test of word analysis skills, can determine whether the problem is primarily word recognition, word meaning, or comprehension. If the oral reading score is low and word analysis skills limited in a child with normal or above normal intelligence, we can usually infer that the major problem is not comprehension but probably still word recognition.[7]

On the other hand, higher scores on oral reading tests together with significantly lower scores on silent reading tests may indicate a need for help in comprehension and rate. However, here too, especially if the pupil has normal intelligence, the lower silent reading test scores may reflect a difficulty in working independently or in concentration—abilities needed for completing a standardized silent reading test.

[7] Jeanne S. Chall, "The Roswell-Chall Diagnostic Reading Test of Word Analysis Skills: Evidence of Reliability and Validity," *Reading Teacher*, XI (February, 1958), 179–83.

As mentioned earlier, beginning with intermediate grade levels, rate becomes an important factor to consider. Power of comprehension may be considerably underestimated if the time limits are short. Since reading instruction would differ depending upon whether the major problem is rate or comprehension, it is well to analyze the scores and the test booklets to see whether rate is a problem.

What about the diagnostic and analytic tests that give separate grade scores for word meaning, different kinds of comprehension, rate, and study skills? The profiles of scores on such tests can help pinpoint strengths and weaknesses. Thus it may be found that a group of eighth-grade pupils score high on comprehension of details and low on comprehension of main ideas and critical reading. Appropriate steps can then be taken to remedy their weaknesses. However, for very poor readers, the discrepancies in scores may reflect not so much the specific weaknesses in different kinds of comprehension and study skills but a more fundamental deficit in reading skills. Each of the analytic tests requires a minimal reading ability to make the subtest scores meaningful. If the pupil still has difficulty in reading the words, the weaknesses indicated by the tests may not be too helpful for remedial purposes.

DIAGNOSTIC INTERPRETATION AT HIGH SCHOOL AND COLLEGE LEVELS

Most standardized reading tests at this level are of the analytic type with many subtests. The same points about analytic tests made above for the upper elementary tests are relevant here as well. At the high school and college levels the content of the tests and methods of testing rate and comprehension vary so much that careful interpretation is needed.

Some tests contain passages of a general nature; others contain only social science and natural science materials. It is therefore more essential than for the elementary levels to study carefully the test manuals and the critical reviews in order to interpret what the results mean for instructional goals.

Some of the tests for high school and college students

have unusually short time limits on all subtests. For example, one student in Grade XII scored at the fourth-grade level on rate, fifth grade on comprehension, and sixth grade on word meaning.

To show how rate can influence comprehension scores on a test, I administered to him two subtests of a silent reading test widely used in high schools and junior colleges. This test has short time limits. He was given as much time as he needed, however. The subtests were then scored two ways—according to the standard time allotted and by the additional time he needed. The following were his percentile ranks on the word meaning and paragraph reading subtests:

	Percentile rank—twelfth-grade norms	
	Timed—standard testing procedures	*Untimed—given time to complete the subtest*
Word Meaning	5	58
Paragraph Comprehension	1	74

When given as much time as he needed, he was able to achieve average scores for his grade.

Since a deficiency in comprehension is usually associated with lack of intelligence, it is essential that we measure power of comprehension which is not influenced by rate.

CONCLUDING STATEMENT

There is more to interpreting the results of standardized tests than drawing profiles of grade scores or percentile ranks arrived at miraculously by modern scoring machines. As in medical diagnosis, the final decision about what the scores mean rests with human interpretation. The data secured from our more elaborate tests must ultimately gain their meaning and wise use from the teacher, the psychologist, and the administrator.

6

Evaluating Title I and Innovative Reading Programs: Problems and Procedures

CARL B. SMITH

PURPOSE OF INNOVATIVE READING PROGRAMS

Thousands of fresh new reading programs are shifting into high gear these days, especially under the impetus of the Elementary and Secondary Education Act, Title I. The spirit of experimentation has taken hold. Educators now generally agree that one method of teaching reading will not solve all reading difficulties, and they are searching for new methods and combinations. Recently, the specific problems of poverty children have received the greatest attention; several ESEA Title I programs will be used as examples in this discussion.

Because American education is spending over a billion dollars a year on innovative programs and because the lives of millions of children are at stake, judgments about the value of new programs must be made. What exactly must be judged and how to proceed are the concern of this discussion.

An evaluation proceeds from criteria. In the case of many innovative reading programs, the goals stated for the program constitute the major criteria for judgment. For Title I reading programs, the law indicates in broad terms that the objectives are to be (1) innovative curriculum approaches and

PRINTED here for the first time with the permission of the author.

(2) proposals to meet the needs of disadvantaged children. Innovative approaches have been taken to mean procedures or materials or services that were not previously offered. The language needs of disadvantaged children naturally vary from city to city, from one population to another, but there are some general needs that research has identified and that serve as guides for locating the specific needs in a given school district. Gordon and Wilkerson (1966) and the Bulletins from the ERIC Information Retrieval Center on the Disadvantaged (IRCD) have identified language problems, lack of school-type experiences, and environmental interference with attitudes as major and generalized problems in teaching disadvantaged children to read.

Assuming that a school system decides that one or all three of these general problems are needs that it must cope with, it still has to determine what the specific needs and deficits of its children are. A school system may find, for example, that the children's vocabulary is very different from the vocabulary of their basal readers or teachers. The school may also find that the children are unfamiliar with the syntactic patterns used by teachers and books or that their pronunciation is so different from that of their teachers that they have difficulty understanding the sounds (phonemes), syllables, and words that they hear in class. As these specific needs are identified, they have to be translated into behavioral goals— types of new behavior that can be measured after some educational treatment has been applied to produce them.

Once specific objectives have been established, procedures can be set up to accomplish them. If one objective is to teach the children to recognize and understand the meaning of the ninety most frequently used nouns, the school may decide to develop a series of slides and tape recordings to teach the children. (The development and use of the slides constitute an *innovative* approach to meet the need—an approach that hasn't been used in that school before.)

Types of Title I Programs

What are the innovative programs being developed? A national study of Title I reading programs by Austin and Smith (1967) identified six major types of programs according to their dominant purpose or goal.

1. Developmental programs in which children in regular classrooms in target areas received intensified help in reading;
2. Remedial reading projects that included reading clinics, remedial classes, and corrective classes for pupils whose retardation varied from severe to mild;
3. Enrichment programs that provided cultural experiences to supplement reading projects;
4. Special programs planned to overcome specific learning handicaps related to reading;
5. In-service education for teachers and administrators; and
6. Combination projects that usually involved two or more separate thrusts in reading and often were administered independently.

Table 1 shows that of the 632 Title I reading programs studied, 53.48 per cent were remedial programs. Furthermore, among the programs classified as "combination" (29.59 per

Table 1   Types of Reading Programs

Program type	Number of participating school systems	Per cent of total
Remedial	338	53.48
Developmental	81	12.82
Enrichment	10	1.58
In-service	8	1.27
Special	8	1.27
Combination	187	29.59

cent), most contained a remedial reading factor in the combination. It would be safe to say, then, that approximately 75 per cent of Title I reading programs were designed totally or in part as remedial reading approaches.

These remedial reading programs were usually trying to overcome the discrepancy between the potential and the actual reading performance of certain children. In many cases the discrepancy was defined as a two-year difference between potential and actual performance. Often the program was innovative only in the sense that no such program had been offered previously or that it tried to treat some of the language or environmental handicaps associated with disadvantaged children. The concept of the two-year deficit was not always central, however; developmental programs, enrichment programs, and programs of other types often assumed a generalized deficit in a factor related to reading, such as experience, language, a sense of identity with book characters, and motivation. New materials and approaches were then applied in the hope that they would raise the reading scores of the children and remove some of these deficits.

Other innovative methods, such as Words in Color, i/t/a, and the use of linguistics and audio-visual materials, are being tried in an attempt to improve children's reading performance. The problems of evaluating the effectiveness of the Title I programs are thus myriad. Evaluation is necessary, however; without it, there is no way of determining which were the most effective expenditures of time, resources, and effort.

Problems That Interfere with Evaluation

Multiplicity   Quite often innovation means more than the use of a new book or approach to instructing children. It may mean a long series of new things, any one of which may contribute to improved learning, each of which should be included in the assessment of the program's value, and each of which complicates the evaluation. A program may use different facilities, new material, a variety of personnel and more personnel per pupil, new time arrangements, and more specialized teachers. If the program shows improved learning, to what do you ascribe this improvement? Answering that question is a tall order, particularly since multiplicity of new elements is only one of the problems of evaluating innovative programs.

Title I program directors reported that their greatest problem was locating qualified personnel. Seventy-five per cent of the school systems reporting problems gave this as the major one. Sufficient numbers of trained reading teachers and reading specialists do not exist to fill all the positions open. A proper assessment of most Title I programs, therefore, has to include a statement that it operated without the specialists described in the program plan. Even the programs that some-

times had "specialists" didn't have good ones, but only classroom teachers who were put in "quickie" training programs in
order to prepare for their new jobs as remedial reading teachers and who taught as if they were still in a class of thirty-
five where everyone did the same thing at the same time.

Other operating problems that affected the outcome of
these Title I programs were: lack of consultants to train personnel for specialized roles, shortage of administrators to
plan and supervise, overabundance of children who met the
selection criteria, lack of school facilities, late delivery of materials, equipment, and supplies, scheduling the children into
special programs—especially troublesome at the secondary
level (Austin and Smith, 1967).

When such problems interfere with the planned instruction or experience, an evaluator must report the interference
and qualify his judgment about the program. With all these
problems, it is not surprising that the original program may
veer off course. The end product may not reflect clearly the
potential of the program. It may indicate the adjustments
made to circumvent obstacles, or it may indicate the void left
by the omission of a crucial ingredient, such as competent in-
service training.

Teacher Personality   The problems mentioned so far are
perhaps unavoidable. What about the personality of the
teacher? Is he enthusiastic? Does he communicate well with
children? Is his bias toward or away from the direction of the
new program? Is he well prepared for the subject or ill
prepared? Answers to questions about the teacher(s) may be
as significant in evaluating an innovative program as any
other set of questions. Bond and Dykstra (1967) found that
the teacher accounted for more of the variance in the 1965
first-grade studies than any other single factor.[1] Related to the
teacher's personality is his adherence to the instructional procedures that make up the innovative program. When a remedial reading program is initiated as a means of giving
individualized treatment to problem readers, for example, it
is a violation of procedures for the teacher to consistently

[1] In 1965, the U.S. Office of Education granted $1 million for an extensive
study of first-grade reading methods in thirty-one separate projects.

move all six students through the same activities at the same time. If he does so, he is using regular classroom procedures, and the only innovation is that he has six pupils to teach instead of twenty-five or thirty. Adherence to program procedures should be enforced through careful supervision and in-service training.

Mobility A particular problem in evaluating reading programs in inner-city schools is the mobility of the population. Some schools report as high as 140 per cent turnover within a nine-month school year. In reading, where the sequencing of skills is considered quite important, student turnover plays havoc with a simple evaluation scheme that says, "Here's what went into the class and here's what came out." Are the results due to what the innovative program gave the children or to what they had when they came in mid-year or in May?

Reading Tests Some Title I directors complained about the inadequacy of existing tests to evaluate their programs. In many cases they felt that the popular standardized reading tests did not suit the language and experience of their population. Another possibility, not often mentioned, is the fact that the standardized reading test was not a valid measure of the reading skills objectives of the program. What, for example, does a test with a vocabulary list and a few paragraphs measure? Probably, overlapping skills that might be labeled vocabulary and paragraph comprehension. Yet these may not be the main skills developed in the instructional program. A project that lays heavy emphasis on word analysis should test the children's ability to use word analysis skills. A silent reading test of paragraph comprehension does not reveal the effectiveness of the instruction in word analysis. An even more obviously invalid measure is a silent reading comprehension test used to determine the effectiveness of motivational activities.

All these problems should put the evaluator of innovative reading programs on his guard. Observation of any deviation between what was planned and what occurred, insistence on supervision and training, care in the selection of evaluation procedures and instruments, alertness to trends or indications as well as to hard data: all these will produce a better evaluation.

EVALUATION PROCEDURES FOR
INNOVATIVE READING PROGRAMS

The more one observes new programs such as Title I reading programs, the more one sees that they do not fit into an easy mold for evaluation purposes. These programs are not research studies in the strict sense. They have been created to meet one or more needs that a previous program did not meet. At their best, the new programs are a unique combination of elements that have arisen from someone's hypothesis about the best way to make up for past deficiencies. But the resulting combination of hardware, software, and personnel is usually stirred together in so big a pot that pinpointing the cause of success or failure defies the evaluation specialist.

Because of the large number of uncontrolled variables (remedial teachers, psychologists, books, reading pacers, tape recorders), evaluators of innovative programs must seek procedures and instruments that will answer some preestablished questions about each of the new elements. A gain score based on a pre-test and post-test simply will not suffice for an evaluation. Questions like the following have to be answered: What is the role of the new personnel? Are they enthusiastic about the procedures and materials they use? How do the students respond to the materials and the procedures? Do other members of the staff see results from the new program? Do they provide any evidence to support parts of it or all of it? Is the program easy to administer? Do the administrators know what each element in the program is supposed to contribute to the entire picture? And especially, is each part of the new program accomplishing the precise objective that was given to it?

With those questions in mind, a procedure for evaluation can be developed. It should be evident, first of all, that the evaluator forms an integral part of the project team. He must work with them from the start of the project: when the specific objectives for the new program are being formulated, the evaluator must provide guidance in setting objectives that can be measured.

Performance Objectives

To measure student behavior, teacher behavior, or the principal's behavior, an evaluator must have the objective spelled out in terms of observable performance. An objective aimed at increasing student interest in reading has to be put in terms of the number of books he reads or the number of times he uses reading to answer specific problems. An objective involving improved teacher competence has to be stated in terms of the tests he will be able to administer or the diagnostic profile he will be able to outline. Performance objectives not only give the evaluator something specific he can count but also indicate fairly precise steps for proceeding with the new program. Teachers and administrators thus have a better idea of where they are going and what instructional procedures they have to take to get there.

In a sense, then, evaluation of a new program begins with an evaluation of the objectives. Are they aimed at specific needs? Are they stated so everyone in the program knows what may be measured as success? In Title I, programs are designed to improve the reading of poverty children, and the programs must be innovative. Because some of the overriding needs of poverty children are known, it is safe to say that the objectives often will seek to alleviate one of these problems: poor attitude toward reading and learning, inadequate school language, lack of experiences that will help in reading books, background of school failure, vision and hearing problems. And these needs may be attacked through programs that are developmental, remedial, enrichment, or in-service for teachers. Specific innovative elements are woven into the general program format. Are these new elements being used as intended? Is there an indication that it is worth retaining them in future instruction? An innovative element may be materials like programed books or pacing machines, a scheme for individualizing reading instruction, or a teacher whose only job is to work with disabled readers. Tables 2 and 3 summarize

Table 2   Prescribed Program Goals for Title I Reading Programs

General goal and program structure	Poverty children					Innovation				
	Lan- guage	Experi- ence	Atti- tude	Failure	Health	Ma- terial	Per- sonnel	Organ- ization	Facili- ties	Remedi- ation
Developmental										
Remedial										
Enrichment										
In-service										
Special										

Note: This schema identifies major areas that a Title I reading evaluator may want to evaluate. These general goals must be transformed into specific performance goals.

some typical long-range goals for reading programs. The specific means for reaching a goal constitute intermediate steps that must be evaluated as the program operates week by week.

Table 3   Typical Goals for Reading Instruction;
Goal Area: Students

Name of goal	Guiding question: Can the child . . .
Word Attack	sound out and understand words not in his sight vocabulary
Vocabulary	understand the meaning of words appropriate to his reading level
Comprehension	understand and relate ideas to one another
Oral Reading	read aloud well enough to give and receive enjoyment and/or information
Listening	retain, organize, and evaluate the speaker's ideas
Work-Study	use appropriately a wide variety of reference resources and study skills
Speed	vary reading rate according to the material and purpose
Literary Interpretation	understand and recognize various purposes and styles
Critical	arrive at logical conclusions, see relationships, and pull together isolated facts
Interests and Appreciation	find personal value in reading and become aware of broader horizons
Personal Development	relate reading to enhance his own life

Source: Farr, Laffey, Smith, 1968.

One step to improving attitude toward reading may be setting up a classroom library with many books of high interest. In regard to this objective, the following evaluation questions might be posed: Are the books there? Are the children using them? Is the teacher encouraging use of the books by providing browsing time, giving informal talks, and showing enthusiasm for the shelf's contents? In other words, are the short-term procedural objectives being carried out? This question can be answered only if regular observations are made on the operation of the program.

In the Austin and Smith study (1967), interviews with directors, principals, teachers, and children called for evidence that their reading program was worthy of their enthusiasm. They responded with things like: children want to come back after school, more books are being taken from the library, vastly improved class attendance, fewer discipline problems, willing to discuss stories and books with their peers, knows all of the 220 Dolch sight words, can reread and find answers to specific questions. The teachers and principals knew that there was evident progress. Unfortunately, most projects did not provide for systematically collecting that kind of evidence. Most projects did not include specific measurable behavior in the statement of objectives. As a result, most Title I projects were evaluated on the basis of gain scores on pre-tests and post-tests. Some included teacher "enthusiasm."

Guiding Questions

Some questions that the Austin and Smith study asked of Title I directors might serve as guides to the kinds of questions evaluators would ask.

Does the program meet the needs of the school system? Which ones?

What evidence is there that the reading program is helping your school?

What interests or excites you most about this program?

Are the teachers interested in the new program? Do they follow the designated procedures?

Were the teachers trained in the new procedures? How do you know the training made a difference?

Do you have material to fit the new program?

Is there a sufficient quantity of material? Is there a wide enough variety?

Were the teachers trained to use the new material?

What criteria are used to select the children and to determine when they have finished the program?

In what ways are individual differences provided for?

In areas outside the reading class do other teachers report a difference in the behavior of the children?

Are the parents and the community involved? In what way?

AN EVALUATION MODEL

How does one proceed with evaluation? Constructing a model helps the evaluator to see and remember the process. Several models could be discussed, some simple, some complex. There is, for example, evaluation that uses a kind of computer format —*input* and *output*. The child is the computer into which teachers, books, facilities, and instructional activities are fed. The child's score on a reading test may be called the output. If the only question the evaluator wants to ask is: "Does he score better on a test now than he did nine months ago?" then all input is considered as a conglomerate contribution to the one act of reading on a test.

In some cases, that answer may suffice. But, in the case of Title I reading programs and many other innovative programs, a narrative model may suit the situation better than a computer model will. The evaluator has to tell a story. There are characters (students and teachers) in a setting (neighborhood and school) with a problem to solve (poor reading and use of language). Their steps toward a solution will involve some trials (innovative arrangements and instructional activities). If their first plans do not succeed, they will adjust and try something else. As time progresses, the characters change (comprehend better and are enthusiastic about school). They charge confidently into the climax (the annual standardized achievement test) and leave school saying they are going to college, while the weary librarian restacks cartloads of books they have just returned. The parents write letters of commendation to the newspaper, and the principal takes off for Florida because there are no failures for summer school. At least that is what the proposal suggests will happen.

Because of the lack of scientific controls in most innovative teaching programs and because there is evidently more to reading than a score on a paragraph meaning test, the narrative serves as a better model than a more rigorous research evaluation model. Hard data must still be collected, of course; many observations must be made throughout the program. But the data are placed in the perspective of a drama in which the learner, armed and advised, does battle with the dragon of reading disability. The weapons, the battleground, the plans of attack can all be described and assessed.

INSTRUMENTS AND TECHNIQUES
FOR EVALUATION

Since formal tests often do not give pertinent information about the success of an innovative program, other techniques and instruments must be employed. Naturally, the techniques will be governed by the objectives set up for the program. If a Title I program is concerned with establishing some new arrangements, facilities, materials, or personnel, an evaluation must be made as to how well these features contribute to a change in student or teacher performance.

General techniques found useful by some Title I evaluators include a teacher log, periodic observation, interest and attitude inventories, parental and community questionnaires, checklists, and personal interviews. The teacher log (a sample is shown in Figure 1) provides the primary means of determining whether the instructional procedures are being carried out as designated. It enables an evaluator to count the number of days a teacher spent on any one of the established objectives and whether he found the materials and procedures workable. Deviations or adjustments can be noted, and the evaluator can decide whether the reported adjustments are substantial enough to merit mention in the evaluation report.

Figure 1   Teacher Log on New Program

Date (of instruction)

Objective

  1. State the specific program objective as it appears in the program proposal.
  2. State the performance objective for today's lesson.

Procedures and Materials

  1. Indicate how today's performance obqective will be accomplished.
  2. List or describe the materials to be used in today's lesson.

Evaluation

  1. Did the children accomplish the performance objective?
  2. Were the procedures and materials appropriate and effective?

Adjustments

  1. What changes in the plan, procedures, or materials should take place in order to achieve the objectives?

Periodic observation by a supervisor can be a means of providing continuous direction to classroom teachers in carrying out the program; a record of those observations can serve the evaluator in noting the strengths and weaknesses reported by the supervisor and at what points clarification or adjustments were made or were desirable. Figure 2 represents a structured observation form that enables the observer to relate what is anticipated in the program plan to what the teacher actually does. Comments under "action to be taken" let the evaluator know what kind of interference there is and what recommendations can be made as part of his report.

Interest and attitude inventories can be given to students early and late in the reading program. Such instruments can be quickly constructed along the lines of the one shown in Figure 3. Teachers, too, should fill out attitude inventories, such as the Minnesota Teacher Attitude Inventory, to see what effect in-service training has or what effect working with the new program has on their approach to students. Some

Figure 2   Observation Form

Directions: Compare the recommendations from the proposal with what you see in the classroom.

Date

Program Area

Program Objective   Evidence of Program Goal

Recommended Procedure   Observed Procedure

Recommended Material   Observed Material

Student Behavior   Action to Be Taken
                                              discuss with teacher
                                              change new program
                                              reject unacceptable material,
                                                procedure
                                              accept change as improvement
                                                or as necessary adjustment

Teacher Behavior

school systems have engaged in sensitivity training as part of their in-service approach to teaching reading to disadvantaged youngsters. Since the objective of this training is the changing of attitudes, the results of an attitude inventory seem quite appropriate.

School people are deluged with questionnaires and may have some aversion to them, but parents and other interested community people will usually respond to short questionnaires that can provide additional data and valuable observations about the child's behavior outside school. Does the child read

Figure 3   Inventory of Reading Attitude

Yes   *No*

		1. Do you like to read before you go to bed?
		2. Do you think that you are a poor reader?
		3. Are you interested in what other people read?
		4. Do you like to read when your mother and dad are reading?
		5. Is reading your favorite subject at school?
		6. If you could do anything you wanted to do, would reading be one of the things you would choose to do?
		7. Do you think that you are a good reader for your age?
		8. Do you like to read catalogs?
		9. Do you think that most things are more fun than reading?
		10. Do you like to read aloud for other children at school?
		11. Do you like to tell stories?
		12. Do you like to read the newspaper?
		13. Do you like to read all kinds of books at school?
		14. Do you like to answer questions about things you have read?
		15. Do you think it is a waste of time to make rhymes with words?
		16. Do you like to talk about books you have read?
		17. Do you feel that reading time is the best part of the school day?
		18. Do you find it hard to write about what you have read?
		19. Would you like to have more books to read?
		20. Do you like to read hard books?
		21. Do you like to act out stories that you have read in books?
		22. Do you like to take reading tests?

Key: Questions 2, 9, 15, and 18 should be answered no; the remaining questions usually should be answered yes.

at home? Has his attitude toward reading and school changed? Does he go to the library? Do magazines and newspapers now seem to mean more to him? Answers to these questions offer positive feedback to the school personnel, and the questionnaire serves as an inexpensive public relations instrument. A questionnaire can inform the public about the school's work and involve the community in an evaluation of program effectiveness.

Checklists are easily constructed instruments for identifying the existence or lack of material, facilities, a good atmosphere, certain procedures, and particular interests. Figure 4 shows a simple checklist to determine the variety of materials that can be seen in the classroom. A quick tally can tell the evaluator much about the availability of reading materials that should be evaluated.

Personal interviews are not often used as evaluation

Figure 4   Materials for Teaching Reading

Check the categories that are treated by the books and instructional materials seen in the classroom.

Skill area	Related subskills	Difficulty level
_____ Word Attack	_____ consonants _____ blends and digraphs _____ vowels: short and long _____ sight vocabulary _____ context clues _____ structure clues: syllables and affixes	_____ easy (beginning) _____ average (middle grades) _____ difficult (mature reader) _____ all grades
_____ Comprehension	_____ specific details _____ main ideas _____ sequences _____ conditions— relations _____ follow directions _____ sentence clues _____ paragraph clues	_____ easy (beginning) _____ average (middle grades) _____ difficult (mature reader) _____ all grades
_____ Study skills	_____ table of contents _____ dictionary _____ maps and charts _____ references— encyclopedias	_____ easy _____ average _____ difficult _____ all grades
_____ Selecting books	_____ interests _____ information _____ enjoyment	_____ easy _____ average _____ difficult _____ all grades

techniques; according to Gage (1961), they consume much time and their reliability is not very high. The personality of the interviewer naturally plays a role in value of the data he collects. The same questions should be asked in exactly the same way in each interview. The questions should also ask for specific evidence whenever that is possible. Principals interviewed in the Austin and Smith study were asked these questions:

1. What specific things has the Title I reading program done for your school?
2. What positive results (evidence) have you noticed? Cite specific cases and individuals.
3. What negative results (evidence) have you noticed? Cite specific cases.
4. In connection with the program, what comments do the teachers make most often?
5. What do the teachers ask for most often?
6. In rank order give the elements of the program that seem to be its greatest strength.

Only samples of evaluation techniques and instruments have been mentioned here. There are numerous other devices, some of which have been collected in a U.S. Office of Education monograph "Taxonomy of Evaluation Techniques for Reading Programs" (Farr, Laffey, and Smith, 1968).

CONCLUSIONS AND RECOMMENDATIONS

Experience in evaluating Title I programs on a nationwide basis shows the relative impossibility of evaluating innovative reading programs on the basis of hard data as would be done in most controlled research. Contrary to tightly controlled research studies, most innovative programs are a conglomerate of loosely controlled elements being fed to the same learners without precise means of determining what, if anything, each of the elements is contributing to the status of the reader at the end of the instructional period. One of the messages of this article, then, is to encourage meaningful evaluation of new reading programs through the use of supplementary informal measures to report progress toward goals. One kind of evaluation is to describe each element from its introduction to the learner throughout its development, always relating it to the purpose for its being in the program. That kind of narrative evaluation gives a much clearer picture of individual elements and the success of the whole than does a gain score based on pre-tests and post-tests. It also enables readers of the evaluation report to make decisions when they face similar problems and circumstances.

To be adequate, evaluation must be a part of the program from start to finish—from the writing of measurable performance objectives through observing program operation to assessing the final product. To put the matter metaphorically and a little ironically, one might say that the gods of education decide that learners shall have a certain group of experiences to help them reach the nirvana of successful learning. The learners struggle with the elements as the gods watch. Occasionally the gods change the experiences because they see that the learners are only mortals and have not responded as anticipated. At long last, however, the learners attain nirvana, and the gods retell the struggles and the happy ending on Mount Olympus—an evaluation report to the Board of Education.

Recommendations

In addition to the obvious and usual checkpoints that evaluators have for reading programs, the following notations may stand as recommendations of possible elements for evaluation:

1. General Planning. It should provide for
   surveying the needs of children, staff, and facilities;
   designing a program guided by needs and in terms of measurable
      objectives;
   orienting the staff, parents, and community to the rationale of
      the program;
   training the staff and providing adequate supervision and direction;
   evaluating periodically, not just at the end.

2. Development programs. They should
   consider readiness for learning;
   observe the child's sensory-motor development, physical health,
   language proficiency, and experiential background.
3. Remedial programs. The evaluator should
   examine the corrective efforts of the classroom teacher before the
   child was admitted to the remedial program;
   note the number of different services (psychological, social,
   physical) that the poor reader has received.
4. Enrichment programs. The evaluator should
   consider enrichment as a different use of time instead of an
   exposure to art or music or city government;
   look for explanatory leaflets on enrichment activities for children;
   look for lesson guides for the teachers on the significant features
   of the enrichment activities.
5. In-service programs. The evaluator should
   consider in-service training as a means of changing attitudes as
   well as a means of increasing skill competency;
   note whether the in-service training is defined specifically enough
   to help the teacher accomplish specific tasks.

A new or different arrangement of reading methods,
materials, facilities, teachers, and pupils constitutes an innovative reading program. A great many have been inaugurated
in the past few years. Feedback from the kind of meaningful
evaluation suggested in this article would make decisions about
reading programs much easier and would likewise help to
improve reading instruction.

References

Austin, Mary, and Smith, Carl. "Survey of Title I Reading
    Programs Conducted in the Fiscal Year of 1966." Case
    Western Reserve University, U.S. Office of Education
    Contract 3-7-000168. Final Report. August, 1967.
Bond, Guy L., and Dykstra, Robert. "The Cooperative Re-
    search Program in First-Grade Reading Instruction,"
    Reading Research Quarterly 2 (Summer, 1967) : 5–142.
ERIC/IRCD Bulletins. Information Retrieval Center for the
    Disadvantaged. New York: Yeshiva University, 1967.
Farr, Roger, Laffey, James, and Smith, Carl. "Taxonomy of

Evaluation Techniques for Reading Programs," Indiana University, U.S. Office of Education Contract 0-8-980812. November, 1968.

Gage, N. L., ed. *Handbook on Research in Teaching.* Chicago: Rand-McNally, 1963.

Gordon, Edmund, and Wilkerson, Doxey. *Compensatory Education for the Disadvantaged.* New York: College Entrance Examination Board, 1966.

7

Predicting Reading Achievement Through Readiness Tests

THOMAS C. BARRETT

Interest in predicting first-grade reading achievement was the result of two occurrences in the middle 1920's. First, it was observed that children were being retained in first grade because of their inability to learn to read. The reason for many such failures was attributed to the general practice of introducing all children to formal reading instruction at the outset of school. Second, educators took the position that a reading readiness period at the beginning of first grade for certain youngsters would enable them to learn to read without undue difficulty. These events brought into focus the importance of one instructional decision: the point at which a child is ready for formal reading instruction. Also indicated was the need for predictive accuracy upon which to base this crucial instructional decision. As a result, the search has been under way since 1930 for measures of pre-reading skills, abilities, and understandings (factors) which best predict first-grade reading success.

REPRINTED with permission of Thomas C. Barrett and the International Reading Association. "Predicting Reading Achievement through Readiness Tests," in *Reading and Inquiry:* Proceedings of the International Reading Association, J. A. Figurel, ed., vol. 10, 1965, pp. 26–28.

THE CONTENT OF READINESS TESTS

One might expect that thirty-five years of research into the predictive validity of readiness factors would have produced a high degree of agreement in the content of commonly used standardized readiness tests. An analysis of five such tests,[1] however, did not fulfill this expectation, since the results, presented in Table I, indicated with two exceptions that there

Table 1   The Content of Five Standardized Readiness Tests

Readiness factor measured	*Number of tests measuring the factor*
Visual discrimination	5
Visual discrimination of words	4
Visual discrimination of letters	2
Visual discrimination and knowledge of letters	2
Visual discrimination of pictures	1
Miscellaneous visual discrimination	1
Auditory discrimination	3
Discrimination of beginning sounds	1
Discrimination of ending sounds	1
Discrimination of both beginning and ending sounds	1
Word meanings and concepts	2
Listening comprehension and use of oral context	2
Visual-motor coordination—copying	1
Learning rate of words	1
Number concepts	1
Word-picture relationships	1

was little agreement among the tests in terms of content. The exceptions in this instance were the general factor of visual discrimination, which was measured by at least one subtest in all of the tests, and the visual discrimination of words, a specific visual discrimination skill, which was evaluated by four tests.

[1] The tests analyzed were: Gates Reading Readiness Tests; The Harrison-Stroud Reading Readiness Profiles; Lee-Clark Reading Readiness Test; Metropolitan Readiness Tests; Murphy-Durrell Diagnostic Reading Readiness Tests.

From this point on, the table shows that there was an ever lessening agreement among the tests in the general and specific factors measured. Even with respect to the seemingly important general factor of auditory discrimination, the tests were not in unanimity, since two of them failed to include a single subtest that could be classified in this area.

If this disparity in the content of the five tests surveyed can be generalized to all tests, it suggests that test makers and test users might consider recent reading studies dealing with prediction to determine whether there are two or three specific readiness factors which should be a part of most readiness tests.

At this time, three specific factors appear to deserve careful attention. The first such factor is visual discrimination and knowledge of letters, which appears to be both an index of visual discrimination and experiences with printed materials. The value of this specific ability as a predictor of reading achievement is underscored in investigations by Gavel,[2] McHugh,[3] and Barrett.[4] Auditory discrimination of beginning sounds in words is a second specific factor which appears to possess useful diagnostic and predictive qualities. An investigation by Dykstra[5] comparing the predictive precision of a number of auditory discrimination tasks indicated its importance. A study by Clymer and Barrett[6] gave further support to the predictive significance of this factor.

Finally, Jean Turner Goins[7] found that the ability to keep a figure in mind against distraction, as demonstrated

[2] Sylvia R. Gavel, "June Reading Achievements of First Grade Children." *Journal of Education*, 140 (February 1958), pp. 37–43.

[3] Walter J. McHugh, "Indices of Success in First Grade Reading": a paper presented at the AERA-IRA Meeting, February 15, 1962.

[4] Thomas C. Barrett, "Visual Discrimination Tasks as Predictors of First Grade Reading Achievement." *The Reading Teacher*, 18 (January 1965), pp. 276–282.

[5] Robert Dykstra, *The Relationship Between Selected Reading Readiness Measures of Auditory Discrimination and Reading Achievement at the End of First Grade.* Unpublished doctoral dissertation, University of Minnesota, 1962.

[6] Theodore Clymer and Thomas Barrett, an unpublished investigation, 1964.

[7] Jean Turner Goins, *Visual Perception Abilities and Early Reading Progress, Supplementary Educational Monographs, No. 87.* Chicago: University of Chicago Press, 1958, pp. 41–87, 96–108.

by a student's ability to complete a mutilated design when a completed design was in view, was a relatively good predictor of first-grade reading achievement. Goins concluded that tests which measure this perceptual ability might prove to be valuable additions to reading readiness tests. Barrett [8] provided cross validation for both her finding and conclusion in a later study.

The point here is not that all readiness tests should be alike. On the contrary, it is that enough information is available in this general area of study to provide worthwhile suggestions about some specific factors that might prove valuable, both predictively and diagnostically, as a core for almost all readiness tests.

READINESS TESTS AS PREDICTORS OF READING ACHIEVEMENT

It would be good to be able to say that readiness tests, in their present state of refinement, are perfect predictors of first-grade reading achievement. Unfortunately this is not the case, since correlation coefficients between various readiness tests and standardized measures of reading have been reported to range from .40 to .70. This state of affairs should not be viewed as hopeless, however. In the first place, the predictive validity of present readiness tests is comparable to other instruments used for the purpose of prognosis in education. For example, intelligence tests are far from perfect predictors of school achievement, although some people use them as if they were. The fact is that tests and test scores are not infallible and that tests should be regarded in this light whether they are readiness tests, intelligence tests, or achievement tests. A second hopeful sign is that readiness tests appear to measure factors which do have a relationship with first-grade reading achievement. Moreover, it appears that the more closely these factors resemble the actual reading act, the higher the relationship between the readiness test and reading

---

[8] Thomas C. Barrett, "Visual Discrimination Tasks as Predictors of First Grade Reading Achievement." *The Reading Teacher*, 18 (January 1965) pp. 276–282.

achievement will be. Although not perfect predictors, readiness test results can help teachers predict future achievement and can, as a result, help them with instructional decisions.

Since the position taken in this portion of the paper implies that readiness tests have some value to teachers, it seems appropriate to close with three observations concerning the possible uses of readiness tests as predictors of reading achievement and indices for instructional decisions.

First, readiness tests should be selected with specific instructional situations in mind, since it is possible that tests may predict more accurately in certain school systems or groups of schools within a system than they do in others. Other variables, such as the reading program itself and measures used to evaluate the outcomes of the program, may affect the predictive validity of a given readiness test. Various readiness tests should be tried out in specific situations before a final decision on adoption is made.

Second, not all the important readiness factors are measurable with paper and pencil tests. Therefore, teachers can enhance their predictions by combining readiness tests results with systematic observations and evaluations in such areas as oral language facility, informational background, story sense, interest in reading, and attitude toward reading.

Finally, teachers should analyze their reading programs to determine whether certain skills and abilities appear to be vitally important to success in beginning reading. For example, one might hypothesize that visual discrimination of letters and words would be a critical skill in a room where the teacher employed a predominantly visual approach to teaching reading. Contrarily, if a teacher gives a strong emphasis to phonics from the beginning, auditory discrimination might be a crucial factor for success. With these and other possibilities in mind, teachers may find readiness tests helpful as diagnostic instruments which provide clues to specific instructional emphases needed by certain pupils.

8

Predicting Success in the First Grade

WILLIAM E. MATTICK

One of the most important tasks facing the kindergarten teacher at the close of the school year is the assessment of each pupil's readiness for the first grade. This responsibility is particularly crucial in a school which segregates pupils in the first grade according to ability, in programs such as the non-graded primary. In programs involving ability grouping, appropriate initial placement of the majority of children is essential to avoid later mass realignment of classes. Even in traditional graded programs, the first-grade teacher may devise within-class groupings more effectively at the beginning of the school year if she has reliable evaluations of children's abilities. In any type of school organization, valid evidence on pupils' potentialities is necessary to make well-founded decisions to promote or to retain in kindergarten.

The purpose of the present study was to compare judgments of kindergarten teachers with results of four standardized tests for effectiveness in predicting the success kindergarteners would have in early first grade.

REPRINTED from *Elementary School Journal*, Vol. 63 (February, 1963), pp. 273–76, "Predicting Success in the First Grade" by William E. Mattick by permission of the University of Chicago Press and the author. Copyright, 1963, The University of Chicago Press.

85

Subjects of the study were 972 kindergarten children in a suburban school district that had a total enrollment of fourteen thousand. All children were eligible to attend free public kindergarten. About half of the district's fourteen elementary schools operated non-graded primaries that encompassed Grades 1, 2, and 3. The other schools in the district had traditional graded primaries. In all schools the kindergarten was a separate grade level, not included in any other grouping arrangement in the schools.

In April, all kindergarten teachers in the district were asked to rate each pupil in their classes as having high, average, or low potential for success in the first grade. This rating was completed before the administration of any standardized testing.

During late April and May, each kindergarten pupil in the district took two of four standardized tests: Metropolitan Readiness Tests, Form R, Lee-Clark Reading Readiness Test, California Short-Form Test of Mental Maturity, and the Lorge-Thorndike Intelligence Tests, Form A. Combinations of two of the four tests were assigned randomly for administration at the various schools. Testing was limited to two tests for each pupil because it was believed that the administration of four tests to children aged five and six would be entirely unfeasible. The Lorge-Thorndike Intelligence Tests and the California Short-Form Test of Mental Maturity were administered to pupils at two schools, the Metropolitan Readiness Tests and the California Short-Form Test of Mental Maturity at three schools, the Lorge-Thorndike Intelligence Tests and the Lee-Clark Reading Readiness Test at two schools, the Lorge-Thorndike Intelligence Tests and the Metropolitan Readiness Tests at three schools, the California Short-Form Test of Mental Maturity and the Lee-Clark Reading Readiness Test at two schools, and the Lee-Clark Reading Readiness Test and the Metropolitan Readiness Tests at two schools.

During late October of the following school year, all first-grade teachers of the district were asked to rate the subjects (who were then in the first grade) as high, average, or low achievers in their classes. The lapse of two months of the school year before obtaining the ratings of the first-grade teachers was deemed long enough to allow the teachers to make a preliminary assessment of their pupils' achievement, but brief enough to avoid significant influence of first-grade instruction on this achievement.

Two sets of Pearson product-moment coefficients of correlation were calculated from the data: first, between the kindergarten teachers' ratings and the subjects' scores on each of the tests; second, between the first-grade teachers' ratings and the subjects' scores on each of the tests.

Table 1 presents the correlation data between the four tests and the kindergarten teachers' judgments. The highest

Table 1 Coefficients of Correlation Between Four Test Scores and Kindergarten Teachers' Predictions of Success in First Grade*

Variable	Number of pupils	Mean score	Standard deviation	r
Metropolitan total letter grades	829	3.55	.92	.546
Lee-Clark total	578	3.54	.70	.449
Lorge-Thorndike intelligence quotients	679	105.0	12.4	.378
California total intelligence quotients	634	114.9	14.9	.368

* Kindergarten teachers' judgment mean = 2.18. Kindergarten teachers' judgment standard deviation = .67.

coefficient of correlation of the four was between the Metropolitan Readiness Tests and kindergarten teachers' judgments. This coefficient of correlation was .546. The coefficients of correlation between the other three tests and the teachers' judgments were, in order of size, Lee-Clark Reading Readiness Test, .449; Lorge-Thorndike Intelligence Tests, .378; and California Short-Form Test of Mental Maturity, .368. All four coefficients of correlation were significant beyond the .01 level of confidence.

Coefficients of correlation obtained between the five kindergarten predictive variables and the criterion variable of first-grade teachers' judgments are shown in Table 2. The coefficient of correlation between the Metropolitan Readiness

Tests and the first-grade teachers' judgments was the highest of the five coefficients of correlation, .559. Kindergarten-teacher judgment was the second most effective predictor of early first-grade success, yielding a coefficient of correlation of

Table 2   Coefficients of Correlation Between Five Predictive Variables and Teachers' Assessments of Early Success in the First Grade

Variable	Number of pupils	Mean score	Standard deviation	r
Metropolitan total letter grades	563	3.55	.92	.559
Kindergarten teachers' predictions	972	2.19*	.67†	.429
California total intelligence quotients	471	114.9	14.9	.371
Lee-Clark total	392	3.54	.70	.370
Lorge-Thorndike intelligence quotients	518	105.0	12.4	.310

* First-grade teachers' judgment mean = 2.12.
† First-grade teachers' judgment standard deviation = .73.

.429. Coefficients of correlation obtained from the other three tests were, in order of size, California Short-Form Test of Mental Maturity, .371; Lee-Clark Reading Readiness Test, .370; Lorge-Thorndike Intelligence Tests, .310. All five coefficients of correlation were significant beyond the .01 level of confidence.

The means and standard deviations of the various measuring instruments are presented in Tables 1 and 2 in the following terms: Metropolitan Readiness Tests, score range from 5 to 1, 5 indicating an "A" letter score on the test, 1 an "E" score; kindergarten and first-grade teachers' judgments, 3 as "high" ranking, 2 as "average," and 1 as "low"; California Short-Form Test of Mental Maturity, total intelligence quotient; Lee-Clark Reading Readiness Test, score range from 4 to 1, 4 being "high" and 1 being "low," according to the designations suggested by the publishers; Lorge-Thorndike Intelligence Tests, total intelligence quotient.

Of the five predictors of early first-grade success evaluated in the study, the Metropolitan Readiness Tests were clearly the most effective. The coefficients of correlation of .56 and .55 between scores of these tests and the judgments of the two sets of teachers compared favorably with similar coefficients of correlation yielded by ability and prognostic tests used with older children.

It was especially notable that the Metropolitan Readiness Tests were superior to the kindergarten teachers' judgments in predicting early first-grade success. Similar studies conducted in higher grades have found that teachers' judgments are usually superior to any single standardized test in forecasting the future achievement of pupils.[1] While the high coefficient of correlation between the Metropolitan Readiness Tests and kindergarten teachers' ratings would indicate that the tests and the ratings measured many of the same characteristics, the Metropolitan Readiness Tests apparently assessed additional aspects of pupil ability closely related to first-grade expectancies of pupils.

On the basis of the findings of this study, the Metropolitan Readiness Tests may be considered to be highly useful in predicting early success in the first grade. Supplemented by the kindergarten teachers' judgments of their pupils, the tests should prove valuable in assisting in the placement of pupils in classes separated according to ability, in the formation of within-class groupings early in the first grade, and in making decisions concerning the promotion or retention of pupils in kindergarten. The data of the study offer no evidence, however, concerning the validity of the Metropolitan Readiness Tests or any of the other measuring instruments evaluated in predicting the school success of pupils at a time later than early first grade.

[1] James Robert Long. "Academic Forecasting in the Technical-Vocational High School Subjects at West Seattle High School," pp. 28–113. Unpublished Ed.D. dissertation. College of Education, University of Washington, 1957.

9

Evaluating a Reading Program at the Elementary Grade Level

LARRY A. HARRIS

Recently a young elementary school teacher who was returning to the classroom after an absence of only a year remarked at how "ignorant" she felt. "I graduated from college just five years ago," she observed, "and already I feel old-fashioned."

Educators appreciate the circumstances that create such a feeling on the part of this young teacher. Change and innovation are accepted aspects of education in our modern world. Indeed, one of the most encouraging trends in today's schools in their willingness to change—their increased acceptance of experimentation and variation in materials, the curriculum, and teaching method.

At first blush the flexibility and change that are evident in nearly every aspect of our schools may seem to be without a common purpose or cohesion. However, one factor is central to practically all contemporary educational change: individualization of instruction. Millions of dollars are invested annually in the development of stories that meet the special interests of individual learners and skill programs that overcome specific learning deficiencies. Countless other examples of the trend toward individualization could be cited to show

PRINTED here for the first time with the permission of the author.

that educational change is ultimately designed to provide for the unique needs of each learner.

The movement toward individualizing instruction is probably the most exciting and promising development in education today. Modern schools should be able to offer the child materials that meet his needs, concepts that enrich his understanding, and teaching methods that facilitate effective learning. One element still seems to be missing from this highly sophisticated and efficient operation, however: the diagnostician who determines the needs of the individual learner and prescribes the appropriate instruction.

It is the major premise of this paper that a classroom teacher must be skilled in determining the needs of pupils. A sound instructional program cannot be initiated without evaluative information, since learners, methods, and materials are effectively matched only on the basis of such data. The goals or objectives of the instructional program provide direction for the teacher's diagnosis as well as a standard against which progress can be measured. Therefore, this paper begins with a description of the objectives of the primary grades reading program. The means for collecting and analyzing evidence of progress toward these goals will then be discussed.

OBJECTIVES OF THE PRIMARY GRADES READING PROGRAM

The objectives of the primary reading program can be grouped into three categories:

1. Creating favorable attitudes toward reading
2. Developing fundamental reading skills
3. Building personal reading tastes and interests

It is not necessary to pursue in detail the significance of each of these categories; however, since evaluation should be conducted with reference to some stated goal, a brief description of the elements that comprise each objective is in order.

Attitudes Toward Reading

The foremost objective of the primary reading program is to build positive attitudes toward reading. The child should come to value reading as an important avenue to knowledge, recreation, and responsible citizenship. Some children enter first grade with a strong desire to read and a positive conception of reading as a useful and pleasant activity; others have never seen reading used by anyone to gain information or enjoyment.

It is imperative that children have successful experiences with reading. Failure at learning to read can build only negative associations and lead the child to avoid reading whenever possible. The primary reading program should build on whatever desire to read a child has and reinforce that desire with continuous success in reading.

Developing Skills

In its initial stages, reading is little more than decoding word symbols and associating literal meanings with those symbols (Chall, 1967). Therefore, the skills of greatest concern in the primary grades are those that lead to accurate decoding of word symbols. These skills are often grouped under the heading *word recognition* and can be divided into analytic techniques (sounding and structural analysis), contextual techniques, techniques of dictionary usage, and recognizing a growing stock of words at sight. A major objective of the primary reading program is to develop independence and flexibility in recognizing words through any or all of these four techniques.

Directly related to word recognition is vocabulary development. Considerable attention has been focused on the significance of language development to success in school and particularly success in learning to read. The special needs of disadvantaged children in this regard have been highlighted by numerous authorities (Witty, 1967; Riessman, 1964; Tiedt, 1967). Rich and accurate associations for word symbols are fundamental to success in reading. Therefore, another goal of the primary reading program is the development of vocabulary.

In addition to decoding a word symbol and associating a meaning with it, the primary grade child must be able to comprehend the message carried by the specific words that are gathered into phrases, sentences, and paragraphs. Termed literal comprehension, this is a skill of great importance since all subsequent higher levels of comprehension are built on this foundation. An example of literal comprehension is a youngster's placing incidents of a story in proper sequence. In the primary grades some time is spent developing higher levels of comprehension, those associated with interpretation and critical analysis. Even the beginning reader is asked to distinguish fact from fantasy. Therefore, some instructional time must be devoted in the primary grades to these skills and subsequent evaluation undertaken.

The skills required in locating and organizing information are also initiated in the primary grades. As in the case of comprehension, refinements of these basic study skills—such as using a table of contents or preparing an outline—are pursued in the intermediate reading program.

Tastes and Interests

While the school cannot dictate for the learner what he should and should not read, another major objective of the primary reading program is to begin the creation of personal tastes or standards by which reading material is judged. Furthermore, the range of topics that appeal to the learner should constantly be expanding. The reading tastes and interests of children should receive careful attention prior to formal reading instruction as well as throughout the primary grades.

TECHNIQUES AND INSTRUMENTS FOR COMPREHENSIVE EVALUATION

Evaluation of the primary reading program must be keyed to the progress that is being made toward the objectives previously described. In practice the tendency is strong to measure only the most obvious aspect of the program—the reading achievement of the pupils. Clearly, however, complete evaluation goes beyond the scores of children on standardized tests. Variables such as student attitude and home background should not be neglected in evaluation programs. Indeed, comprehensive evaluation goes beyond student-related variables to include the quality of the instructional program, the variety and amount of useful materials employed, and the effectiveness of the reading program on a districtwide basis.

In addition to being comprehensive in nature, evaluation of the primary program must be systematic and efficient. Therefore, the instruments to be employed in evaluating progress toward each of the program's objectives should fit into an overall plan or strategy. The following discussion will provide a plan for evaluating each aspect of the reading program. The use of evaluation techniques and instruments appropriate to each aspect of the program will then be discussed.

Evaluating the Learner

Bond and Tinker (1967) list eight general principles for reading diagnosis, which are helpful in planning an evaluation strategy at the primary grade level:

1. A diagnosis is always directed toward formulating methods of improvement.
2. A diagnosis involves far more than appraisal of reading skills and abilities.
3. A diagnosis must be efficient—going as far as and no farther than is necessary.
4. Only pertinent information should be collected and by the most efficient means.
5. Whenever possible, standardized test procedures should be used.
6. Informal procedures may be required when it is necessary to expand a diagnosis.
7. Decisions in formulating a diagnosis must be arrived at on the basis of patterns of scores.
8. A diagnosis should be continuous.[1]

[1] Guy L. Bond and Miles A. Tinker, *Reading Difficulties: Their Diagnosis and Correction*, 2d ed. (New York: Appleton-Century-Crofts, 1967), pp. 152–53.

Generally speaking, evaluation begins with gross measures being applied on a whole-class basis for the purpose of screening learners whose status and needs are rather apparent and easily identified. Subsequent measures become increasingly specific and precise for the purpose of further screening. Finally, intensive and detailed analysis is employed with the few cases that resist adequate assessment at each successive level. The successive levels of screening and the decrease in number of students at each level who require further analysis can be pictured as an inverted pyramid (see Figure 1):

Figure 1

Successive Levels of Screening

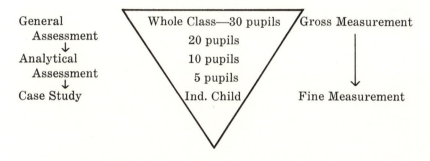

General	Whole Class—30 pupils	Gross Measurement
Assessment ↓	20 pupils	
Analytical	10 pupils	
Assessment ↓	5 pupils	
Case Study	Ind. Child	Fine Measurement

The successive-levels approach enables the classroom teacher to identify specific needs as well as classwide deficiencies. These needs must be identified to plan the instructional program; groups can be formed on the basis of mutual skills and interests as well as on reading level. The needs must also be identified so the school can later demonstrate growth to the learners and their parents.

The evaluative techniques and instruments that are useful at each level of the pyramid may be placed in three categories: (1) formal reading tests, (2) informal measures of reading, and (3) teacher observation.

Formal Reading Tests

Formal measures are of three general types: (1) group standardized tests, (2) basal reader tests, and (3) individual reading tests. The first category, group standardized tests, is likely to be the most familiar, for teachers most frequently use these instruments in their attempts to evaluate reading progress.

Standardized Tests   Standardized tests have been discussed frequently in the literature. While the misuse of test results has been a commonly cited reason for terminating formal testing programs, the tests themselves are usually not to blame. Pre-service and in-service training that draws attention to the three most important considerations in the use of standardized tests—the objectives of each test, the consistency with which it measures and its limitations in terms of cost, time required for administration and ease of scoring—can put test scores in their proper perspective. Standardized tests can produce useful though limited information; informal procedures must be used to expand their findings.

Specific application of standardized tests can be made at successive levels of screening in the "inverted pyramid." At the gross-measurement level of total class evaluation, achievement batteries such as the *Iowa Test of Basic Skills* or the *Stanford Achievement Battery* may be used. Typically such batteries provide an estimate of general reading level (usually an inflated measure with regard to the actual level at which instruction should take place) and several subscores such as Vocabulary, Paragraph Meaning, and Study Skills. Specific strengths and weaknesses are not identified by such tests, although classroom teachers could easily study the pattern of errors made by individual youngsters taking them and obtain some diagnostic information. Many achievement batteries yield reliable and useful scores even on subtests. When used in conjunction with a good ability measure, achievement batteries can provide means for determining whether general reading achievement is close to expectancy for each child.

In the first grade, readiness tests provide information that roughly corresponds to achievement batteries for the higher grades. The subtests included in most readiness tests have been found to lack real diagnostic value and are often too short to provide reliable measures of specific skills such as visual discrimination and auditory discrimination (Bond and Dykstra, 1967). The greatest value of present readiness measures is with regard to predicting success in reading and providing some general guidance for grouping in beginning instruction.

At the next level of screening (groups smaller than the whole class), general survey tests, such as the *Gates-Mac-Ginitie Reading Test* and the *California Reading Test,* may be used. These instruments are also group tests but focus specifically on reading. In addition to providing a general reading score, like the achievement tests, survey tests usually yield subscores on such variables as Vocabulary and Comprehension. Administration of a survey test to youngsters who have some irregularity on their achievement battery can provide additional evidence to confirm or refute the earlier scores. In most cases, reading survey tests are longer than the reading section of general achievement batteries and therefore more reliable.

Group diagnostic tests such as the *Stanford Diagnostic Reading Test* and the *Bond-Balow-Hoyt Silent Reading Diagnostic Test* provide a third level of screening. At this level of assessment a profile of scores is obtained for each child (an example profile form is shown in Figure 2). Patterns of scores may indicate areas needing special remediation or point the way to more detailed analysis with specific skills tests (e.g., *McCullough Word Analysis Tests*). Because of the time and cost involved in administering, scoring, and interpreting such tests, not all youngsters will receive this degree of analysis.

Basal Reader Tests   The second general category of formal measures is comprised of basal reader tests. These tests are created to assess the child's readiness for beginning a new book and to provide an appraisal of skills recently introduced and are therefore more directly tied to the instructional program than the tests previously discussed. Basal reader tests seldom have accompanying norms and are usually not administered under carefully controlled conditions. The reliability and validity of basal reader tests are not usually reported. Standardized tests are primarily for student comparisons,

FORM
W

LEVEL
II

Stanford
Diagnostic
Reading Test

BJORN KARLSEN • RICHARD MADDEN • ERIC F. GARDNER

NAME _____
          last   first   initial

BOY ☐ GIRL ☐ GRADE _____ TEACHER _____

SCHOOL _____ DATE OF TESTING _____
                                                                year   month   day

CITY OR TOWN _____ DATE OF BIRTH _____
                                                                year   month   day

STATE _____ AGE _____
                                                                years   months

T E S T	TEST 1:	Reading	Comprehension	TEST 2	TEST 3	TEST 4	TEST 5	TEST 6
	Literal	Inferential	Total	Vocabulary	Syllabication	Sound Discrimination	Blending	Rate of Reading
RAW SCORE			*					
S	9	9	9	9	9	9	9	9
T	8	8	8	8	8	8	8	8
A	7	7	7	7	7	7	7	7
N	6	6	6	6	6	6	6	6
I	5	5	5	5	5	5	5	5
N	4	4	4	4	4	4	4	4
E	3	3	3	3	3	3	3	3
	2	2	2	2	2	2	2	2
	1	1	1	1	1	1	1	1

*Insert Reading Comprehension Total Grade Score here.

HARCOURT, BRACE & WORLD, INC. NEW YORK

Figure 2

whereas basal reader tests are task oriented.

Children often do extremely well on basal reader tests,
occasionally making perfect scores. Since mastery of a skill

is usually being assessed, the focus of the test is on the child's grasp of the skill or set of skills.

The use of basal reader tests within the framework of the successive levels of screening is rather flexible. At times such tests are valuable for whole-class assessment to assist in the formation of instructional groups. At other times such tests may be used to group children for remedial instruction, since the information provided is immediately useful for planning corrective instruction. Within the limits imposed by rather uncertain reliability, the great variety of subtests in the basal reader tests permits some analytic asessment. Basal reader tests are useful primarily for screening on a group basis and identifying areas requiring immediate reteaching.

Individual Reading Tests   The third category of formal measures for evaluating the learner is comprised of individual reading tests. Some individual instruments are primarily oral reading tests; others have an oral reading section but contain additional sections that enable the examiner to gather specific diagnostic information.

Tests such as the *Gray Oral Reading Test* and the *Gilmore Oral Reading Test* are designed to provide a useful supplement to information gathered by silent reading tests but not to serve as a substitute for them. With these tests the teacher notes the child's ability to read orally paragraphs of increasing difficulty and answer questions concerning the content of what is read. The validity and reliability of these tests are usually satisfactory; however, the number of selections that can be read during an administration limits the amount of reading behavior that can be sampled. Since oral reading tests must be administered individually, they are also rather demanding of teacher time. Furthermore, oral reading requires several skills not necessary in silent reading, so the difficulty in assessing silent reading ability is compounded.

Oral reading tests provide an estimate of the child's instructional reading level. Considerable diagnostic information can also be obtained by the skilled examiner who is able to accurately record and interpret reading errors. Such tests can also be adapted to assess silent reading comprehension, and also listening ability, often regarded as a measure of reading potential.

The oral reading test involves an analytic assessment that is appropriate at an advanced screening level; it is not suitable for whole-class administration. Teachers use oral reading tests with children who require more thorough analysis than that which is provided by most group paper and pencil tests.

The individual diagnostic test can be used to assess the status and needs of some youngsters who require detailed study. The individual test focuses intensively on specific reading skills such as knowledge of initial consonants and synthesizing word parts. While relatively few classroom teachers are trained to administer the *Durrell Analysis of Reading Difficulty* and the *Spanche Diagnostic Reading Scales,* knowledge of these tests can be helpful. The techniques used in an individual test can be effectively applied informally by the teacher.

The time required to administer complete individual tests makes them somewhat impractical for the classroom teacher. A reading specialist may be available to provide further diagnosis outside the classroom. It is entirely possible for the teacher to profitably employ parts of these tests, also.

The in-depth approach represented by the individual diagnostic test is the logical extension and culmination of a selective screening procedure using standardized tests.

Informal Measures of Reading

Informal measures are teacher-developed instruments that are designed to assess children's progress in an area of particular interest or concern to the teacher. Such measures are not standardized and, like basal reader tests, are task oriented.

Five categories of informal measures will be discussed: (1) workbook and worksheets, (2) informal reading inventories, (3) cumulative record files, (4) interviews, and (5) checklists and inventories.

Formal measures enable the classroom teacher to meet

several of the principles for diagnosis prescribed by Bond and Tinker; however, several important considerations are unmet. The techniques and instruments grouped under the heading of informal measures serve to expand the evaluation program. Informal measures are particularly important in achieving the continuous assessment that is required to obtain the evidence necessary for prescribing immediate corrective instruction. Whereas most group tests measure broad skill areas, informal measures that assess specific skills can be selected and used with individual children. Furthermore, attitudes, tastes, and interests that are extremely difficult to assess by formal means can be gauged by various informal measures.

Informal measures are useful at various levels in the pyramid of successive screening levels. Information gathered by means of informal techniques and instruments is especially important when the classroom teacher attempts to differentiate instruction according to the needs of individual learners. Such informal measures are regularly used on a whole-class basis. Practically speaking, however, some informal measures are used for intensive diagnosis with only a small percentage of youngsters. This is true because of the limited time available to the busy classroom teacher for such study.

Since informal measures are used at many levels of screening, the following discussion will describe one measure (rather than one level) after another, focusing on the commonest functions of each. The reader is reminded that use of the measures varies with the time and expertise available in a given classroom.

Workbook and Worksheets Although not normally regarded as an evaluative device, a workbook or worksheet, when properly used, can be an extremely effective means for daily evaluation. Following the introduction of a new skill, the teacher can assign appropriate followup exercises in a workbook or provide worksheets on a topic. In addition to providing practice in using the newly learned skill, such an exercise enables the teacher to determine where additional instruction is required and which children need individual attention. Teacher-prepared worksheets can be especially effective since the special needs of a class are considered as the instructor writes an exercise.

Informal Reading Inventories   The Informal Reading Inventory (IRI) has been described in some detail elsewhere (Johnson and Kress, 1964; Austin *et al.*, 1961). Essentially, the IRI is a series of paragraphs that are graded in terms of reading difficulty. The selections are often taken from a basal reader series. The IRI is administered by the classroom teacher to individual children. As the selections are read aloud, errors are recorded and word attack skills noted. Comprehension is usually checked immediately by means of several questions related to the content of the selection read. The level at which the reader enjoys reading—that is, the recreational reading level—the level where instruction can profitably begin, and the level at which the reader is frustrated are often identified with this instrument.

Information gained from the administration of an IRI is especially helpful in assigning appropriate instructional materials for each child. Since selections from basal readers are easily included in an IRI, the material to be used for the instructional program can be employed. Children can also be assigned to instructional or corrective groups on the basis of an IRI assessment. Since detailed diagnosis is not easily conducted by means of this informal technique, the IRI is primarily a general assessment tool. Considerable diagnostic information can be gathered with the IRI by a skilled teacher, however.

Cumulative Record Files   The cumulative record is a particularly valuable source of data compiled in previous years. Because of the limited amount of information gathered prior to grade one, this resource is more useful with grade two and grade three youngsters. The results of formal testing are normally recorded in the cumulative record. More importantly, the observations of a child's previous teacher and pertinent information concerning his health, attendance, and home background are often recorded. The results of referral for special testing or training are also contained in most cumulative records. These data provide the teacher with information about every member of the class. Grouping for instruction and assigning of appropriate reading material are instances in which such data are useful. Successive levels of screening also draw heavily on the information contained in the cumulative record. A case study, for example, often begins with the information contained in the cumulative folder.

Interviews   Ideally, the classroom teacher meets individually with each child in his class on a regular basis. Interaction of this sort permits the teacher to know the child and his needs as no other system can. As a practical matter, one-to-one situations involving teacher and student are rare in the modern classroom. Nonetheless, considering the advantages of personal consultations, teachers should strive mightily to employ this technique.

The child's attitude toward reading, his tastes, and his reading interests can be very effectively assessed in a teacher-pupil interview. A quick review of the books recently read by a child and several penetrating questions concerning his reaction to them will offer insight no paper and pencil instrument can provide. Samples of oral reading spaced over several weeks and months can highlight progress as well as demonstrate needs and deficiencies. The child's pleasant association between reading and working individually with the teacher in a relaxed setting can be instrumental in building positive attitudes toward reading.

Because of the limited time available for interviews, this technique is employed primarily with children who require intensive diagnosis. Case studies in particular should rely heavily on it.

Checklists and Inventories   Checklists and inventories can be developed with many purposes in mind. Information related to a child's home background, travel experiences, interests, hobbies, personal library, and the like can be readily obtained with such devices. The validity and reliability of these instruments are limited by the ability and willingness of the child to provide accurate responses. An example of a checklist appears below.

INTEREST INVENTORY RECORD

What do you like to play best of all? _____

What other games do you like? _____

What things do you make? _____

Do you have pets? _____

Do you collect things? _____

What hobbies do you have? _____

Suppose you could have one wish which might come true. What would it be? _____

What is your favorite TV program? _____

What others do you watch? _____

What is the best book you ever read? _____

What other books have you liked? _____

Do you have any of your own? _____

Who, if anyone, reads to you? _____

Do you go to the library? _____

Do you read comic books? _____

Do you read any magazines or newspapers? _____

What kinds of books do you like best? _____

What kind of work do you want to do when you finish school? _____

Do you plan to go to college? _____

What school subject do you like best? _____

What school subject do you like least? _____

In what subject do you get your best grades? _____

Your poorest grades? _____

Checklists and inventories are valuable for use with the whole class. Data gathered with these devices enable the teacher to adjust the instructional program in a variety of ways to effectively individualize instruction. Knowledge of hobbies, for example, may help the teacher guide a youngster's recreational reading or boost his status and self-esteem with the opportunity to present a special report.

Teacher Observation

Teacher observation provides a third means for evaluating the learner. Authorities regard teacher observation as the single most important element in an evaluation program (Bond and Wagner, 1966; Smith, 1963). In a single day the classroom teacher has countless opportunities to appraise the progress and needs of each learner. The teacher also has the opportunity to synthesize the diagnostic data gathered from all other sources and adjust his observations to gather missing information. With the press of daily responsibilities, however, teacher observation often fails to yield the information desired.

This disparity between the potential and the actual value of teacher observation can be largely overcome by three valuable techniques: (1) systematic observation, (2) anecdotal records, and (3) sample products.

Systematic Observation The variety of activities occurring during a reading lesson plus the number of children in a typical classroom combine to form a complex set of interactions for the teacher to observe. Therefore it is essential that specific purposes for observation be outlined ahead of time. The teacher must decide which child or children he will focus on and during which activities. These factors are determined by the particular need for information that exists. For example, if test data, workbook performance, and an interest inventory all point to a specific instructional need for a given child, the teacher may wish to confirm these data with his own observations. By planning in advance, systematic observations can be conducted. Haphazard observation on an incidental basis usually provides little evaluative information.

Systematic observation is a technique that provides information on specific children and should be used with each child in the room. The technique is not restricted to any given level in the screening model. The type of information gathered with the procedure varies with the purposes for which it is used and the expertise of the teacher.

Anecdotal Records Teacher observations can be further systematized by use of a rather simple anecdotal record-keeping procedure. Pertinent observations concerning an individual child, gathered in either a systematic or incidental manner, are entered in a notebook or noted on file cards. During the press of daily duties, a word or phrase can be noted on a slip of paper to aid in recall. Later, more explanation and detail can be written into a child's record. Patterns of behavior may emerge in such records, and careful documentation relieves the teacher of trying to recall all significant related incidents. Such records are often useful on a broader scale than reading instruction.

Sample Products   Samples of the child's work collected over a period of time can be especially valuable in evaluating the learner. Patterns of errors can be readily identified by this procedure, and progress can also be documented. Samples of work should be gathered in specific skill areas or spread across a broad range of skills, depending on the progress of an individual child. The simplest procedure for assembling a collection of products is to maintain a folder for each child. Periodically, a product from every member of the class can be filed; at other times, a particularly revealing or timely product can be filed for individual children.

The objectives of the primary grade reading program should be the criteria against which the progress of the learner is judged. A variety of evaluation techniques and instruments for gathering the necessary data have been described here as well as a successive screening procedure for conducting evaluations. The classroom teacher must bring these components together in order to develop an effective program for evaluating the learner.

The individual child is assessed by means of general screening procedures including achievement tests, basal reader tests, informal reading inventory, performance in his workbook, checklists, and teacher observation to determine his progress toward the objectives of the primary reading program. His ability to recognize words independently, for example, is assessed by all these means. When adequate progress is being made, general assessment continues, and the child moves on through the program.

However, should inadequate progress be discovered, more analytic procedures are undertaken. Diagnostic tests, oral reading tests, specially prepared worksheets, interviews, and systematic observation are utilized. Analysis continues in greater detail until the route to improvement is identified.

In sum, evaluation of the learner is essential in order to check progress toward program goals and formulate immediate procedures for overcoming difficulties.

EVALUATING TEACHING

In contrast to evaluating the learner, techniques and instruments for the evaluation of teaching are somewhat limited in number and scientific rigor. Basic to the difficulty encountered in the assessment of teaching is disagreement about what constitutes good teaching. Depending on which authority is consulted, various attributes might be listed as being characteristic of affective teaching. Because evaluation must proceed with reference to some goal, the following description of good teaching found in Boy and Pine (1963) will be used as a basis for discussion.

THE TEACHER'S PROPER FUNCTIONS

1. Engage in quality teaching, i.e., teaching which reflects depth of knowledge and which is based upon the empirical evidence of research. The teacher develops a learning atmosphere in which students can achieve and learn with optimum effectiveness and realize their full potential.

2. Function as a curriculum specialist in his specific subject or at his particular grade level. By virtue of his training and experience the teacher should be recognized as a curriculum specialist in his subject area.

3. Conduct research designed to measure the effectiveness of his teaching and to improve instructional materials and methods. The professional teacher will also be aware of and make use of the research findings applicable to his subject and level of instruction.

4. Motivate students to learn by using imaginative and creative teaching and learning approaches, and by developing instruction and curriculum which is meaningful to the student and which meets his needs.

5. Keep abreast of current developments and new knowledge in his subject field and his chosen profession of education. This will be accomplished through attendance at professional meetings and conferences, memberships in appropriate professional organizations, reading, independent study, and course work.

6. Prepare instruction and up-to-date teaching materials and tools.

7. Function as a resource consultant to other professional personnel in providing services to meet the needs of each individual student.[2]

An obvious but somewhat limited evaluation procedure is measuring the growth of student performance on tests. This approach is especially unsatisfactory at the elementary school level, where the development of attitudes and rational thought are primary instructional goals. Furthermore, as indicated in the Coleman Report (1966), innate and environmental differences among learners often account for much of the variation on tests, making them a poor measure of teaching.

Although precise evaluation of teaching is not yet possible, several possible means for assessment do exist. Evaluation techniques and instruments for assessing teaching may be classified into two major categories:[3] (1) external means and (2) introspective means. External means have the disadvantage of measuring only what is visible and quantitative. Introspective means rely entirely on personal judgments and are therefore not likely to be objective. Due to the uncertain reliability and validity of all measures of teaching quality, evaluation programs ought to employ a variety of techniques and instruments so that patterns of behavior may emerge.

External Means for Evaluating Teaching

Three approaches to the evaluation of teaching by external means will be examined: (1) interaction analysis, (2) observation by a supervisor, and (3) closed-circuit television.

Interaction Analysis   Procedures have been developed by Flanders (1965), Amidon (1967), and others for assessing the nature of classroom interaction. Basically, the interaction

---

[2] Angelo V. Boy and Gerald J. Pine, "Needed for Teachers: A Role Description," *The Clearing House* (September, 1963), p. 8.

[3] Few evaluation devices for assessing teaching are strictly external or internal, most being a combination of both, but this dichotomy is helpful for purposes of discussion.

analysis technique requires that an observer classify the types of activities present in a classroom according to who is speaking (e.g., teacher, student, or silence), the nature of the talk (e.g., lecture, giving directions, or asking directions), and the nature of the interaction (e.g., acceptance of feelings, praise or encouragement, criticism, or acceptance and use of ideas of students).

The data yielded by interaction analysis must be interpreted in part subjectively, but they generally reveal the degree of dominance exhibited by the teacher in classroom activities and the kinds of intellectual tasks that children are asked to perform. In general, most educators can agree that children learn more when the teacher plays a minor role in directing their discussions. However, disagreement occurs when specific cases are cited. Most educators can also agree that higher-level tasks such as interpretation and synthesis are preferable to memorization and simple recall. Again, disagreement would be found on the type of thinking desirable in a given instance.

Despite these limitations, interaction analysis can be an effective tool for appraising a teaching-learning situation. It is quite simple and highly desirable for the classroom teacher to tape record his own lessons and conduct an interaction analysis of his own teaching. Having assessed the type of classroom interaction taking place, a teacher can judge the desirability of his teaching and make efforts toward improvement. A set of guidelines for good teaching such as those by Boy and Pine quoted earlier are necessary, however, so that performance can be compared with accepted objectives.

Observation by a Supervisor   The responsibilities of a supervisor typically include the observation and evaluation of teaching. Structured tools such as an interaction analysis, checklist, and evaluation form are frequently used. The exact nature of the evaluation may vary enormously, and all possibilities cannot be explored in this discussion. One contribution of the supervisor is that, as a second party, he can bring some degree of objectivity and freshness to the task of evaluation. Follow-up discussions permit exchange of ideas and the opportunity to see a situation through the eyes of another.

Just as evaluation of a child should focus on means for improvement and not take the form of passing judgment, evaluation of a teacher by his supervisor must not dwell solely on negative factors or irrelevant aspects of personality. It is essential that evaluation focus on progress toward a set of stated objectives for good teaching. Supervision ought to be conducted with the intent of improving instruction; observation in the classroom must be focused on that goal as well. With this focus, observation by a supervisor can make a genuine contribution to the reading program.

Closed-Circuit Television   Closed-circuit television (CCT) and the use of video tapes can be powerful tools in self-evaluation of teaching. The opportunity to get out of one's own skin and see a lesson as an observer has several advantages. First, the teacher can focus on different aspects of the teaching situation and see the lesson a number of times. Second, with the press of teaching responsibilities removed, the teacher can observe his own behavior with a degree of detachment not possible while a lesson is in process. For example, the number of students participating in a discussion and the quality of the voice can be noted. Such a technique enables the teacher to judge his performance against a chosen criterion and effectively plan a program of self-improvement.

Introspective Means for Evaluating Teaching

All teachers are constantly in the process of evaluating their performance by introspective means. As a lesson proceeds, the degree of attention exhibited by the class is noted and serves as feedback for self-evaluation. Other examples of daily introspective self-evaluation could be cited. The sensitive and concerned teacher depends heavily on this useful but haphazard approach to evaluation.

A more systematic and exhaustive method of conducting introspective evaluation is to use checklists such as the one that follows.

CHECKLIST FOR TEACHER SELF-EVALUATION
OF THE READING PROGRAM

Looking at My Classroom

   I. Are there evidences of my reading program around the room?

   A. Charts

   1. Primary: Are there evidences of experience charts?

   Are there charts relating to specific reading lessons?

   Are there vocabulary charts?

   Are there sound charts?

   Teacher-made?

   Pupil-made?

   Are there attractively arranged displays of pupil language efforts?

   2. Intermediate: Are these charts to guide development of writing and speaking skills?

   Example: paragraphs, reports, letters

   Are there pupil-teacher–made summaries?

   Example: social studies, science, health

   Are there charts to develop word meanings and concepts?

   Are there charts to illustrate principles of word analysis?

   Are there attractively arranged displays of pupil effort?

   B. Additional Materials for Independent Reading

   1. Are there books of *varying levels* related to *different topics* and of *diverse types* (text-books, biographies, travel books, stories, etc.) attractively arranged and easily available to the children?

   2. What provision do you make in your planning for
      a. helping children develop an interest in independent reading interest?
      b. building cooperatively general but meaningful purpose for this reading?
      c. sharing the ideas, information, and enjoyment children gain from this activity?

  II. Does my classroom environment lend itself to individual and group work in reading?

A. Is there a library or reading corner which
  1. displays books in an enticing manner?
  2. provides space for book reviews, book information, and pupil comments?
  3. provides a comfortable reading in terms of chairs, tables, adequate lighting?
B. Is the room so arranged that the group working with the teacher
  1. is compact enough to enable all to hear without using a loud voice?
  2. is far enough from those working independently so that it is not disturbing to the others?
  3. has sufficient space to work comfortably?
  4. is planned so that graphic materials used by the teacher are readily visible to all members of the group?
  5. is planned so the teacher has writing space available if the situation demands additional visual material?

Looking at My Class

I. Is each person in my room at the same proper reading level?
  A. Have I accurately assessed each child's instructional reading level and independent reading level through
    1. studying the reading record card?
    2. analyzing objective test results?
    3. reading former teacher reports?
    4. administering needed informal inventories?
  B. Have I utilized the above information in planning
    1. other language activities?
    2. social studies?
    3. science, health, safety?
    4. mathematics?
II. How have I provided for the group working independently?
  A. Are the independent activities
    1. reading- or language-centered?
    2. differentiated according to pupil abilities?
    3. related to previously taught reading skills?
    4. the result of a directed reading activity follow-up?
    5. an outgrowth of independent reading?
    6. so constructed that there is an identifiable learning purpose in them?

Looking at the Lesson

I. Are my directed reading activities (developmental reading lessons) a strong part of my reading program?
   A. Are the introductory phases planned so that they include
      1. definite, precise, specific, attainable teacher purposes?
      2. adequate (neither too little nor too much) readiness in terms of theme, background knowledge, vocabulary, and concepts?
      3. necessary vocabulary presentation in context?
      4. a check of individual pupil mastery of needed concepts and vocabulary?
      5. challenging, interest-provoking, attainable purposes set for the individuals in the group?
      6. silent reading to achieve purposes set?
      7. a culminating activity in oral or written form?
      8. an appropriate length of time for the particular group?
      9. suitable distribution of time among the various elements of such a lesson?
   B. Are follow-up lessons constructed to contain
      1. teacher-guided pupil recall of purposes?
      2. activities appropriate to purposes set and material read?
      3. opportunities for use of vocabulary and concepts introduced in the original presentation?
      4. carefully constructed, pre-planned questions, statements, or challenges to stimulate pupil reaction to materials?
      5. a balanced program of written and oral responses?
      6. approaches other than question and answer?
      7. provision for ample opportunities for pupil self-evaluation and teacher-pupil evaluation?
      8. reasonable time for these activities?
   C. Are reading skills presented so that
      1. one specific skill is developed in a lesson?
      2. children are helped to discover principles and generalizations *for themselves?*
      3. children are helped to understand how and when the skill is applied in reading material?
      4. sufficient practice items are used with the group?

     5. Individual written practice follows the group presentation?
     6. situations are provided in which the skill is applied?
     7. the proper amount of time is devoted to each phase?

II. Are oral reading activities given their proper place in the total program?
  A. Are oral reading activities planned so that
    1. children acquire the proper concepts concerning the value and place of silent reading and oral reading?
    2. the time devoted to oral reading is minor in scope and used for a specific purpose?
    3. of those included, a major portion involves
      a. an audience situation in which only the person reading has the book?
      b. reading to prove a point?
      c. reading to find a point of information?
      d. choral speaking?
      e. sharing poetry?
      f. dramatizations? [4]

The items on a checklist vary from straightforward questions requiring little or no subjective judgment, e.g., Are reading skills presented so that one specific skill is developed in a lesson?) to very subjective questions requiring much self-analysis (e.g., Are follow-up activities constructed to contain a balanced program of written and oral responses?). The greatest value of such checklists is that many aspects of the reading program are explored which might otherwise be forgotten or ignored. Introspection is highly susceptible to self-delusion. The teacher who wants to be completely satisfied can rationalize and explain away nearly any negative aspect of his teaching. The teacher intent on objective self-evaluation can learn much from introspective means.

    A concern that spans the entire matter of evaluating teaching is achieving the objectives of the primary grade reading program. Ultimately any teaching strategy, method, or technique must lead to the realization of the instructional

[4] Reprinted by permission of the Reading Center, State University College, Fredonia, New York, John E. Connelly, Director.

goals stated earlier. Closed-circuit television enables the teacher to observe his own interaction with students, but excellent interaction is meaningless unless the children are building positive attitudes toward reading, learning fundamental skills, and establishing reading tastes and interests.

EVALUATING MATERIALS

The evaluation of materials for reading instruction has become increasingly important as literally thousands of new items have been placed on the market within the past decade. The availability of special funds for purchase of materials, due largely to Title III of the Elementary and Secondary Education Act, has been a prime reason for this influx. The importance of providing materials that meet the needs of individual learners has also been a major factor. Whatever the causes, educators have recognized the need for a means to evaluate the wealth of materials currently available.

Two main avenues to the evaluation of instructional materials are presently open (1) field testing and (2) armchair analysis. Very little large-scale effort has been made in the direction of field testing because of the time and expense involved. An additional factor is that uncontrolled variables such as teacher effect can contaminate the findings.

The second approach to evaluation of materials for reading instruction is armchair analysis. In this approach school personnel, usually part of a curriculum committee, organize themselves for the purpose of deciding which instructional materials will be adopted. Few evaluation instruments are available to guide such groups. Various techniques have been employed; it is impossible to determine their reliability and validity. Systematic evaluation based on carefully drawn criteria is more helpful than haphazard judgments based on emotion and personal bias.

Educators involved in the evaluation of materials for reading instruction might well follow a three-step procedure:

1. Define the reading program objectives
2. Assess the local needs of teachers and students

3. Systematically appraise the candidate materials against the objectives and needs of the local situation

Goodman, Olsen, Colvin, and Vanderlinde have developed a text (1966) which may be useful in the evaluation of materials for reading instruction. The book lists 218 questions that can be applied to reading materials; depending on the needs of a given school district, a greater or lesser number of the questions will seem relevant. The authors stress that only when the evaluators have defined their needs and philosophy of teaching reading can the appropriate questions be chosen. Their questions are grouped into the following categories:

1. Psychological Principles
2. Sociocultural Principles
3. Educational Principles
4. Linguistic Principles
5. Literary Principles

Specific questions include: To what extent do phonics constitute a formal, systematic program of instruction? Does the type face interfere with legibility? Do reading materials contain the common language structures of oral language? Is there balance among topics? [5]

After materials have been adopted, their use in the schools becomes a form of field testing. The performance of students who use the materials becomes an empirical test of their appropriateness. Test results and teacher reactions serve as two major means for further evaluating the materials.

The key to evaluation of materials for reading instruction in the primary grades is systematic assessment with reference to carefully chosen criteria—criteria that are ultimately linked to developing favorable attitudes toward reading, systematic skill development, and broad interests and tastes in reading.

EVALUATING THE ENTIRE PROGRAM

Evaluation of the primary grade reading program depends in part on the results of separate evaluations of learners, teacher,

[5] K. S. Goodman *et al., Choosing Materials to Teach Reading* (Detroit: Wayne State Univ. Press, 1966), passim.

and instructional materials. The program must also be assessed on a wider scale—on a district basis. Needless repetition, serious omissions, improper sequence, and necessary revisions in the reading curriculum can only be discovered by evaluating the entire reading program of a school district.

The goals of the district reading program provide a standard against which to measure various aspects of the program. Several typical categories of goals are directly related to the reading achievement of the learners:

1. Learners develop positive attitudes toward reading
2. Sequential skill instruction is provided
3. Lifelong reading interests are initiated
4. High standards of taste are developed

Other goals are associated with teaching:

5. On-going evaluation is conducted with a variety of techniques and instruments
6. Corrective and remedial instruction is provided immediately
7. Instruction is individualized
8. In-service education is provided

The goals include the importance of materials:

9. An adequate supply of facilities, equipment and materials appropriate to the needs of each learner are available

Finally, goals related to the entire program are included:

10. Parents and the community at large are well informed about the program
11. The program objectives are specific and clearly defined
12. Experimentation with and evaluation of new and innovative ideas are conducted.[6]

A variety of techniques and instruments are available for assessing progress toward achieving these and other goals related to the entire reading program. The following will be

[6] Adopted from Roger Farr, James Laffey, and Carl Smith, "Taxonomy of Evaluation Techniques for Reading Programs," Indiana University, U.S. Office of Education Contract 0-8-980812 (November, 1968).

discussed: (1) comparison to national norms, (2) comparison to local norms, (3) use of libraries, and (4) checklists, inventories, and questionnaires.

Comparison to National Norms

Many commercially prepared standardized tests are accompanied by national norms. Some assessment of the effectiveness of the district reading program can be based on comparisons between the achievement of local youngsters and the norming population. Scores of all students in the district on subtests as well as total achievement scores can be contrasted with the published norms to give a pattern of strengths and weaknesses. The district performance may compare favorably with the norms or deviate significantly.

Some caution is necessary in comparing districtwide achievement with national norms. First, norms represent average achievement for a particular group of youngsters. Local youngsters may be distinctly different from the bulk of the norming population. Suburban children from professional and white-collar homes might be expected to easily surpass published norms. The achievement of inner-city children, on the other hand, often falls below published norms. Despite these limitations, however, districtwide trends in achievement can be noted with this procedure.

A second limitation of comparisons between local achievement and national norms is that the local program may have objectives which are not entirely compatible with the design of the test used. Phonic analysis, for example, may be an essential skill for high performance on a given test. If a local program does not emphasize phonics until a later date, its students will score poorly on the test. Naturally, tests are chosen partly on the basis of compatibility between the instructional program and test items, but some inconsistency is unavoidable.

Districtwide comparisons between local achievement and national norms provides useful information for program evaluation. Careful analysis is necessary to avoid inaccurate interpretation of the results.

Comparison to Local Norms

Local norms provide a means for evaluating districtwide reading achievement that is not subject to the major criticism raised with regard to national norms. Since students from one year to the next in a given district are probably quite similar, comparisons between successive groups become quite meaningful. Developed over a period of years, local norms can provide a reliable point of reference that accurately reflects reasonable expectations for a given group of children. Unless extensive program changes are instituted, even discrepancies between local objectives and test objectives become less crucial. If the sequence of the local program is responsible for a weakness shown by one year's group on a standard test, roughly the same weakness should be evident in the test scores of the groups of other years.

Comparison with local norms therefore adds a unique and valuable facet to an evaluation of the districtwide program. Program performance this year is compared to performance in earlier years.

In the case of both national and local norms, it is important to remember that norms represent only average performance, not standards to be achieved. This distinction is too often forgotten, with the result that reaching a certain norm becomes an end in itself.

Use of Libraries

An evaluation program that began and ended with a study of how community and school libraries were being used by children would be incomplete, but it would probably be more meaningful and significant than many evaluation programs which gather data from dozens of other sources. The "finest" reading program possible with regard to teachers, materials, tests, facilities, and the like should be regarded as a failure if local youngsters do not read widely for information and recreation.

The number of books circulated by a library per week provides an additional index of how successful the reading program has been in stimulating reading. Caution must be exercised in regarding data on book circulation as an absolute measure of recreational reading because borrowing a book does not guarantee that it is read. Furthermore, in some districts children may have excellent personal libraries at home and depend very little on school and public libraries. Despite these factors, raw circulation data can be analyzed to gain insight into the reading habits of children in a school district.

The number of books circulated is an important matter. Comparisons from month to month and year to year are useful as a measure of the amount of reading taking place. By categorizing the types of books being borrowed from libraries it is possible to study the nature of children's reading selections. The circulation of fiction and nonfiction books can be compared, and figures can be compiled on how many award-winning books and children's classics are taken out. These data are helpful in assessing the reading tastes of children. The teachers in a district or school may adjust their instructional program to feature certain types of books if circulation data indicate they are being overlooked. For example, nonfiction books such as biographies may be chosen for display in the reading corner and read aloud to the class by the teacher if data on their circulation suggest a need for greater interest in them. In sum, these checks can help determine what aspects of the total reading program need attention. But unless simple circulation figures indicate a healthy flow of books into the hands of children, this more fundamental issue should be considered first.

Checklists, Inventories, and Questionnaires

The primary value of checklists, inventories, and questionnaires lies in their comprehensiveness. Aspects of the reading program not normally evaluated can be brought to the evaluator's attention by a specially prepared inventory. For example, a tally sheet of instructional materials, divided into categories such as audio aids, visual aids, games, boxed developmental kits, enrichment readers, and trade books will show the number and types of instructional aids available in a district. The varied learning styles of children make necessary the availability of several types of materials. From the questionnaire, it is possible to assess the variety of materials and identify needed additions.

Objectives of the entire reading program not easily assessed by other means can be partially explored by means of checklists, inventories, and questionnaires. An example of a checklist to assess the total program is provided below.

CRITERIA FOR EVALUATING READING PROGRAMS

Teacher: Questions

1. Are the teachers ambitious, energetic, and eager to do an appropriate and effective job of teaching reading?
2. Are they willing to keep up to date in the field by reading professional materials and by attending helpful workshops?
3. Do they give critical attention to the individual needs of each child?
4. Do they locate reading deficiencies and immediately supply the appropriate instruction?
5. Provision for individual differences
6. Do the teachers have knowledge of the total reading process?
7. Are records and progress charts kept on each youngster?
8. Does the teacher have a good background in reading?

Content Area: Questions

1. Are other subjects taught in a way that encourages use of reading abilities?
2. Are textbooks used at each level accurate as well as written on various reading levels so they match the abilities of the children?
3. Does it encourage each child to become a discriminating, independent reader? Are there literary materials to help develop individual tastes?
4. Does the reading program emphasize reading for understanding and aim to develop flexibility in comprehension and rate in accordance with the student's abilities and purposes and different levels of materials?
5. Are there special provisions for the culturally deprived?
6. Is it a continuous program extending K–12, taught on all levels in all subject areas by all teachers to provide instruction and guidance in reading skills?
7. Does the reading program provide experiences essential to reading at all areas of development?

Materials

1. Are many materials provided, basal and supplementary, which include definite lessons in how to read as well as highly interesting and varied reading selections to be read and discussed?
2. Are there materials that children can identify with?
3. Do teachers know the materials available in the school?
4. Is the reading program a continuous program beginning at each learner's current level and attempting to lead him at his own success rate to his maximum achievement? (Are there plentiful reading materials that cover a wide range of difficulty and interest?)
5. Are they utilizing all the resources—human, community and governmental—available in order to (benefit) realize specific objectives?

Fundamentals

1. Are lessons taught with the following things in mind?
   a. selections from the reader
   b. training in reading for various purposes
   c. establishing independence in identifying new words
   d. improving reading through skillful teaching in various content areas
   e. developing independence in coping with meaning difficulties
   f. locating and removing each pupil's reading deficiencies
   g. measuring pupil achievement
2. Is the reading program an all-school program with carefully identified educational goals? Does it support the cooperation of the entire staff?
3. Are the objectives clearly stated and understood so that the program has direction?

Time

1. Is a definite period of time assigned, each day, to the teaching of the fundamentals of reading at each intermediate grade level? (Reading should be taught in every period of the day.)

Environment

1. Physical
2. Emotional
3. Is there an abundant supply of supplementary material?

4. Is there evidence of pupil progress and pupil participation (skills checklist, progress charts)?
5. Is the reading program coordinated with the pupil's other communicative experiences?
6. Is there a cooperative effort and interest on the part of all teachers and administrators?
7. Does it differentiate instruction to meet the individual needs of each child and at the same time does it integrate the commonality of interests and abilities of the group?
8. Is reading related to all areas in the curriculum?

Measurement

1. Does measurement and evaluation parallel the instructional program?
2. Is there continual, careful measurement and evaluation of student's progress, which provides the basis for further instruction?
3. Does the reading program have the support and cooperation of the entire staff?
   a. The reading program should be considered as a process rather than a subject.
   b. Reading should be taught on all levels in all subjects. Special care should be given to teaching skills with thoroughness in the fields of social studies, arithmetic, and science.
4. Is there a clear statement of objectives to indicate the direction and scope of the program?
5. Is there continuous measurement and evaluation of the effectiveness of the program? [7]

The information obtained with a questionnaire of this sort is evidently quite varied in nature. Some questions provide objective data; others are very subjective and provide largely opinion. For purposes of evaluation, the responses concerning a given goal of the total program must be pulled together and studied for possible trends. In concert with information from other sources, districtwide patterns should be apparent. For example, a questionnaire of the type presented above may reveal that various respondents in a district find that materials for phonics instruction are inadequate. Verification of this trend can be gained by studying pupil performance

[7] Reprinted by permission of the Reading Center, State University College, Fredonia, New York, John E. Connelly, Director.

on achievement tests. Poor performance on items requiring knowledge of phonics would support the questionnaire data. Thus several sources of information appear to support an investment in additional materials for phonics instruction.

SUMMARY

The classroom teacher must constantly be evaluating the status and needs of her students in order to provide them with the appropriate instruction. The objectives of the primary grade reading program guide the instructional activities of the teacher and provide standards for progress. A comprehensive evaluation program includes assessment of the learner, teaching, instructional materials, and the total reading program.

The learner is evaluated through formal reading tests, informal measures of reading, and teacher observation. Teaching is evaluated by external means including interaction analysis, observation by a supervisor, and closed-circuit television, and by introspective means. Instructional materials must be evaluated in terms of the reading program objectives and the needs of teachers and students. Evaluation of the total program employs such techniques as comparing local achievement with national norms, establishing local norms for purposes of measuring performance over time, studying the use of school and public libraries, and using checklists, inventories, and questionnaires to survey often overlooked aspects of the reading program.

Without careful and continuous evaluation and attempts to improve, a reading program lacks focus and a sense of priorities. Clearly stated objectives provide the goals for instruction and the standards against which to assess progress.

References

Amidon, Edmund, and Hough, John. *Interaction Analysis: Theory, Research and Application*. Reading, Mass.: Addison-Wesley, 1967.

Austin, M. C., Bush, C. L., and Huebner, M. H. *Reading Evaluation*. New York: Ronald Press, 1961.

Bond, Guy L., and Dykstra, Robert. "The Cooperative Research Program in First-Grade Reading Instruction," *Reading Research Quarterly* 2 (Summer, 1967) : 5–142.

Bond, Guy L., and Tinker, Miles A. *Reading Difficulties: Their Diagnosis and Correction.* New York: Appleton-Century-Crofts, 1967.

Bond, Guy L., and Wagner, Eva Bond. *Teaching the Child to Read.* New York: Macmillan, 1966.

Boy, Angelo V., and Pine, Gerald J. "Needed for Teachers: A Role Description." *The Clearing House* (September 1963) : 7–12.

Chall, Jeanne. *Learning to Read: The Great Debate.* New York: McGraw-Hill, 1967.

Coleman, James. *Equality of Educational Opportunity.* (U.S. Department of Health, Education, and Welfare, OE 38001. Washington, D.C.: U.S. Gov't. Printing Office, 1966.

Flanders, Ned A. *Teacher Influence, Pupil Attitudes and Achievement.* U.S. Department of Health, Education, and Welfare. Superintendent of Documents, Catalog no. F.S. 5.225 :25040, 1965.

Farr, Roger, Laffey, James, and Smith, Carl. "Taxonomy of Evaluation Techniques for Reading Programs," Indiana University, U.S. Office of Education Contract 0-8-980812. November, 1968.

Goodman, K. S., Olsen, H. C., Colvin, C. M., and Vanderlinde, L. F. *Choosing Materials to Teach Reading.* Detroit: Wayne State University Press, 1966.

Johnson, Marjorie, and Kress, Roy. *Informal Reading Inventories.* Newark, Del.: International Reading Association, 1965.

Riessman, Frank. *The Culturally Deprived Child.* New York. Harper & Row, 1964.

Smith, Nila Banton. *Reading Instruction for Today's Children.* Englewood Cliffs, N.J.: Prentice-Hall, 1963.

Tiedt, Sidney W., ed. *Teaching the Disadvantaged Child.* New York: Oxford Univ. Press, 1967.

Witty, Paul A., ed. *The Educationally Retarded and Disadvantaged.* Sixty-sixth Yearbook, Part I. National Society for the Study of Education. Chicago: Univ. of Chicago Press, 1967.

10

Evaluating Secondary Reading

WALTER HILL

The following quotes are from a staff conference on the improvement of a secondary reading program:

An English teacher: "How am I supposed to know which kids can and cannot handle the assigned readings of the class?"

A school counselor: "Show me a secondary reading test which really does the job!"

A reading specialist: "How can we expect to evaluate a secondary reading program when most secondary teachers do not know enough about the reading process to evaluate correctly one pupil's reading performance?"

A school administrator: "Everyone, including me, is for the improvement of secondary reading and the evaluation program which goes with it, but you haven't told me where we are going to get the money!"

Each of these comments suggests a real problem of evaluating reading at the secondary level. The evaluation of human behavior is never an easy task nor an exact science. Successful evaluation of secondary reading is dependent upon staff knowledge of the reading process and the evaluation process in education. Further, it is enhanced by clearly stated program

PRINTED here for the first time with the permission of the author.

objectives, by sufficient funds to support evaluation activity, and by teacher concern about reading development at the secondary school level.[1]

This article does not assume that all the problems of secondary reading evaluation can be immediately resolved. It does assume that secondary reading evaluation can be improved and that students, professional staff, and society will benefit from such improvement. Specifically, it accepts these premises: (1) We are legitimately concerned with improving reading performance at the secondary level, and, therefore, we are obligated to evaluate student reading behavior and the program in which it develops. (2) All human behavior, including reading, is capable of measurement and evaluation, even though our present skills and knowledge are less accurate than we should wish. (3) We can and will improve such evaluation only as we work at improving it. (4) Our present knowledge and skill include much that we can use, much that is practical and can provide both student and teacher with much that is helpful, even if it is not perfect. The article suggests that the secondary reading program and its closely related evaluation program are both in the state of *becoming* rather than *being*.

The following pages will examine the proper functions of secondary reading evaluation, its relationship to instruction, basic evaluation procedures, the measurable dimensions of reading performance, types of evaluation, and a sequence for reading evaluation. Attention is first focused on what is usually done. From such a perspective, improvement will seem no overwhelming task.

TYPICAL PATTERNS IN SECONDARY
READING MEASUREMENT

Despite a recent increase of concern among secondary teachers, reading as an instructional entity has been largely ignored at the secondary level. It is not surprising, therefore, that the

[1] Walter Hill, *Secondary Reading Programs*, rev. ed. (Newark, Del.: International Reading Association, 1969), p. 2.

attendant evaluation program has been neglected. Relatively few schools have a broad workable program of secondary reading evaluation in operation. Most schools limit themselves to obtaining normative scores for the reading subtests of survey achievement test batteries that they administer annually or biennially. In some schools, these reading subtest results are supplemented with reports of informal classroom evaluation and, even less frequently, with diagnostic assessments of the notably retarted readers.

The Standardized Achievement Battery Subtests

The typical reading subtests of standard achievement batteries provide the school with two measures: one for vocabulary and one for comprehension. The vocabulary score is really a measure of the recognition of word meanings and reflects the student's breadth of conceptual background as well as his use of word recognition techniques. The comprehension score typically results from an objective test of what the student recalls after reading a paragraph or short multiparagraph selection. These scores are normative; a grade equivalent or a percentile rank corresponding to the raw score obtained by the student is generally given. Teachers frequently claim that a grade equivalent score is more meaningful than a percentile ranking (a statement that a certain per cent of a student's peers throughout the nation surpassed him on the subtest). However, a grade equivalent score is based on a comparison of the student's raw score with the scores made by students in various grades; it does not indicate the level of textbook or reading material that the student can handle for independent or instructional purposes. (The general rule of thumb is that a standardized grade equivalent score overestimates by two grades the secondary student's functional reading level as measured by an informal reading inventory procedure. Another limitation of these scores is that they are *time-limit* measures; they should be interpreted as normative measures in rate-of-reading vocabulary and rate-of-comprehension over short selections.

In spite of such limitations, the subtests of standardized achievement tests can be defended as one part of a complete program in reading evaluation. They are economical; their expense is charged to the general achievement testing program of the school. They are there; why not use them! The scores obtained are useful as comparative estimates even though they are lacking in specific validity. Since most general achievement batteries have been developed and normed in a reliable and valid manner, the reading subtest scores tend to be accurate measures of the student's power in reading relative to other students in his class, grade, and national peer group. Collectively, the scores provide a school with some idea of the reading power of its students compared to that of students in other schools. Individually, as part of a screening procedure, the scores can help identify students with poor reading ability. And, since reading scores seem to have a moderately high predictive power for general academic success at the secondary level, they may help in making general academic decisions about the student.

Some of the reading subtests of general achievement batteries provide greater diagnostic insight than others. The *Iowa Test of Educational Development,* for example, provides reading subtest scores for social studies, science, and literature. The reading subtest of the *Tests of Academic Progress* provides a manual key for identifying comprehension patterns.

Informal Reading Assessment

In some secondary settings, the achievement battery subtest scores are supplemented by informal teacher evaluation. Most teachers obtain some indirect evidence of student reading performance when they mark worksheets, assigned problems, and unit tests. Too often, such assessments are concerned with the student's mastery of content rather than his ability to analyze and learn from reading. The informal observations of classroom teachers seldom find their way into reading evaluation folders except in the form of course grades. Nevertheless, informal teacher assessment has great potential as a source for improved secondary reading evaluation. It awaits the stimulation of an effective in-service education program and a program of gathering and channeling the observations made.

Other Types of Evaluation

Additional measurements of the reading skills of selected students are likely to be taken if the secondary school has a reading program or a reading specialist as a staff member. When the specialist functions as a remedial reading teacher, the additional measures will tend to be diagnostic tests. If the reading program is part of regular classwork, the additional reading measures may be standard survey tests in reading. Such tests can provide confirmation for the results of the school's general reading testing. Depending upon the test selected, it may provide some broad skill assessment of diagnostic value. If the reading class is taught by a teacher with some training in the field of reading, this survey test will be supplemented by various informal measures, possibly including an informal reading inventory of class or individual skills. An individual reading case study is developed occasionally for a student with the most serious reading and adjustment problems.

In spite of growing sensitivity to reading problems at the secondary level, special programs of instruction and diagnosis are not yet common. Consequently, the "vocabulary" and "comprehension" scores from the general school achievement battery remain the most common form of secondary reading evaluation. The following pages, by stressing what might be effected in the future, should point up the limitations of this minimal current approach to secondary reading evaluation.

READING EVALUATION: THE BROAD VIEW

Some Definitions

Reading evaluation is concerned with curriculum and instruction as well as with the behavior of students and incorporates the functions of measurement, assessment, and diagnosis. Evaluation necessarily involves judgment—an appraisal of behavior in terms of how it compares with some desired objective. This would hold regardless of whether we were evaluating a student, a group of students, the curriculum they followed, or the procedures and materials which figured in their instruction.

Reading *evaluation* would include all activities meant to gather data about pupils or programs as well as the data analysis process leading to a clear statement of the present functional or comparative status of pupil, pupils, or program. Reading evaluation is dependent upon reading *measurement* for the quantification of reading and reading-related behaviors. One of the frequent tools employed to quantify this behavior is the *reading test*. The reading test may take various forms, but fundamentally it is a mechanism designed to elicit a valid and reliable sample of the individual's reading related behavior. To be useful, the reading test should present a uniform or consistent task to each person taking the test and provide a means of comparing the responses made on the task to either some functional or normative standard.

As used here, reading *assessment* includes nonstandardized observations of student reading performance as well as testing results. For example, it would include teacher checklists, autobiographies (personal histories), observed work on reading-related projects, and progress charts. Reading *diagnosis* ordinarily is reserved for students with suspected limitations in reading; it places emphasis upon the analysis of reading subbehaviors, makes use of testing and assessment procedures, and requires practitioners with training and experience in special diagnostic techniques.

In practice, reading evaluation, measurement, assessment, and diagnosis cannot be meaningfully separated. Evaluation eventually calls for diagnosis. Diagnosis presumes a hypothesis that certain objectives of performance are desirable. Testing and other reading assessment is sterile unless it is linked to objectives, programs, and the need for diagnosis. In this article, these elements of evaluation are viewed as interrelated and interactive.

Major Functions of Reading Evaluation

The main function of reading evaluation is to evaluate the behavior of individual pupils and class groups. Too frequently, this concern at the secondary level is narrowly interpreted as the need to assign grades. While there can be little doubt that grades can sometimes help motivate and reinforce learning, too much emphasis on the function of grading may result in the neglect of other types of evaluation and may create a negative student set toward the reading program.

The broader functions of reading evaluation at the secondary level include:

1. providing the student with feedback about the adequacy of his responses, to improve his learning,
2. establishing and modifying instructional objectives and content,
3. identifying group and individual reading skill status and progress, and
4. contributing to our society's general bank of evidence about the processes of reading and learning to read at the secondary school level.

More specifically, reading evaluation serves to: (1) compare the reading achievement of individual students, the class, or the school with the achievement of other students, classes, peer groups, and schools, both locally and nationally; (2) assess the progress made by the individual or group at regular intervals; (3) identify areas of skill weakness which need to be emphasized in the program; (4) determine appropriate instructional levels of materials for individuals and class groups; (5) screen the pupils to locate underachievers and others with reading problems; (6) diagnose student reading-learning problems; and (7) refer pupils with special learning needs to special programs.

Evaluation and Instruction

An intimate circular relationship exists between pupil learning and the evaluation of that learning. This is seen most immediately and directly in the day-to-day contact between teacher and student. The teacher sets up a stimulus learning situation, and the student responds to that situation. The teacher assesses the effectiveness of that response (for example, the pronunciation of a word, the location of a specific detail, the identification of a key idea, or the critical evaluation of a writer's purpose) and feeds back to the student the evidence of his response accuracy or the degree and type of his response error. Using this feedback, the student adjusts his next response performance. In the daily interaction between teacher and students, it is nearly impossible to differentiate between instruction and evaluation.

The same degree of intimacy between instruction and evaluation should obtain in the broader reaches of the reading program. Basically, the essential steps in reading instruction are these:

1. The development of major objectives in terms of desired general changes in reading behavior.
2. The development of enabling objectives which translate the general objective into specific changes in reading behavior.
3. The organization of the instructional sequence including the selection and creation of teaching strategies and materials calculated to produce each desired specific behavior change.
4. The evaluation of the pupil response to this specific learning experience.
5. The adjustment or progression of the learning sequence depending upon whether the behavioral change was successful.

An effective program of reading combines day-to-day evaluations of pupil motivation and ability with periodic unit and course evaluations. Foremost among the standing questions which the program is obligated to answer are: (1) To what degree are the general objectives of the reading program being met? (2) To what degree are the enabling objectives being met? (3) Should adjustments be made in the general or specific objectives? (4) How effective were the specific learning sequences, teaching procedures, materials? (5) How effective was the program of evaluation?

The common and constant goal of instruction and evaluation is to produce pupil learning of a desired nature. To this end, nothing should escape the scrutiny of the evaluation program. Surely, this includes the examination of broad program objectives, the evaluation of the evaluation program itself, and the careful assessment of both pupil and teacher behavior. Pragmatically, the relationship between evaluation and instruction is a natural one; the sensitive teacher will integrate the two, if not restricted by an artificial curriculum and a defensive administration.

Guidepoints for Reading Evaluation

An effective broad program of reading evaluation seldom happens by chance. Like any other operation, it must be guided by objectives to maintain consistency and creative momentum. The following principles would seem particularly appropriate to the secondary program of reading evaluation.

Secondary reading evaluation should: (1) reflect the general and specific objectives of the secondary reading program; such evaluation considers the total scope of the program: both by levels (for example, developmental, remedial, and college-preparatory) and by program phases (for example, basic instruction, functional application, and recreational reading); (2) be a planned, sequential, and continuous program; (3) be an integrated part of the instructional program; (4) reflect the cooperative efforts of the classroom teacher, the student, the reading specialist, the administrator, and other pertinent school personnel; (5) draw upon multiple and varied procedures for observing reading behavior; (6) work at a continuing compromise between the need for efficiency in gathering and processing data and the desire for complete information on every student; (7) consider its primary objective to be the improvement of pupil reading performance either directly through feedback to the pupil concerning his performance or progress or indirectly by producing changes in the curriculum, methods, materials, organization, or the evaluation program itself.

KEY DIMENSIONS OF SECONDARY
READING PERFORMANCE

Educational appraisal, to be meaningful, must be related to the educational objectives that guide the current classroom instructional segment or unit as well as those set for the total program. It is a common practice to state the specific objectives of a reading program in terms of the individual skills to be developed. The skill objective is more effective when stated in the form of a student behavioral outcome (for example, "to be able to identify the topic sentence of a paragraph") than when stated in terms of a teacher action (for example, "to teach the recognition of topic sentences").

Too often, reading objectives are stated in the form of an outline of a large set of reading skills. Such an outline has several disadvantages. First, it tends to overwhelm the teacher; he is tempted to spread his instructional firepower superficially over too large a target. Second, the outline is easily interpreted as a list of incidental instructional activities rather than as a list of behaviors which the student should master in the course of instruction. Third, the outline encourages both teacher and student to view the learning or use of a reading skill as a unilateral rather than a multidimensional behavior. The unilateral objective oversimplifies instruction and evaluation. The effect is that the student does not receive in-depth instruction and practice. This deficiency frequently goes unnoticed until he encounters serious problems in academic adjustment.

Let us take a reading skill objective as described by an outline and examine it. Here is a typical example: "to understand main ideas." Now, when will the student have satisfied this objective? The main ideas in what size reading unit? In paragraphs, in stories, or in books? In what level and subject of material? What will be an indication of his effectiveness? His percent of accuracy? His speed? Does the objective describe performance on a test or in independent study? Does it mean he can locate a main idea, interpret a main idea, or recall a main idea?

Figure 1 and its accompanying list of elements attempt to convey something of the complexity of secondary reading skill behavior.[2] Neither evaluation nor instruction of secondary reading is likely to be satisfactory unless the evaluator and teacher both have a basic understanding of the complexity of the reading process.

The point is not that every teacher or test must cope with every dimension of a reading skill. However, the program, *in toto*, should reflect the most important elements in the reading process.

[2] Since the model in Figure 1 is directed at the broad normative reading behaviors typical of the secondary reader, one preliminary phase, that of grapho-phonemic correspondences, has not been included.

The clear implication of the model is that both instructional and evaluational objectives should specifically reflect the
dimensions of the skill in question. The reading skill objective

**Figure 1.   Dimensions in the Instruction and Evaluation
of a Secondary Reading Skill**

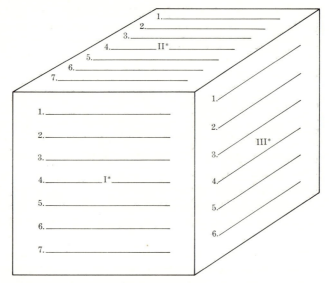

*I—Syntactical-Contextual Dimension
II—Cognitive-Operational Dimension
III—Qualitative Performance Dimension

criticized above should be replaced with a more specific formu-
lation: for example, "to locate with speed and accuracy the
main ideas of selected typical paragraphs in science and social
studies textbooks of 'instructional level' difficulty."

Dimension I: Syntactical-Contextual Units

   1. Words
   2. Sentences
   3. Paragraphs
   4. Multiparagraph selections
   5. Articles, chapters, stories, essays, etc.

6. Books
7. Multiple sources (correlative and comparative)*

Dimension II: Cognitive-Operational Functions

1. Location of appropriate data
2. Literal interpretation of data
3. Inferential interpretation of data
4. Recall of data
5. Organization of data
6. Critical analysis of data
7. Problem-solving application of data

Dimension III: Qualitative Performance Elements

1. Accuracy of perception and interpretation (comprehension unit)
2. Rate of perception and interpretation
3. Level of material (readability)
4. Flexibility (adjustment of purpose to material)
5. Self-direction (successful independent effort)
6. Habituation (attitude plus knowledge)

BASIC INSTRUMENTS AND PROCEDURES OF SECONDARY READING ASSESSMENT

This section identifies and provides brief comment on ways to assess secondary reading performance. While the procedures require varying degrees of sophistication, most are within the scope of the secondary teacher who is willing to invest a reasonable amount of energy to the task. Each procedure can provide the classroom teacher as well as the reading specialist with practical information. The procedures complement each other. Used in combination, they can provide a broad and fairly detailed profile of secondary level reading.

Special measures of reading capacity, such as individual intelligence measures, are not described here; neither are the

---

* An example of the use of multiple sources in literature might include comparing the central character's reaction to adult authority, figures in the following sources: Salinger's *Catcher in the Rye*, Updike's *Olinger Stories*, and Saroyan's *My Name is Aram*.

analytical tests of language and learning patterns employed
by the psychologist or reading specialist with cases of severe
reading difficulty. The procedures discussed here emphasize
the interpretation and application phase of reading, since these
elements of the process are of greater interest to secondary
personnel. The assessment of basic word skills, useful in some
secondary situations, will be examined in a later section.

Cumulative Student File

The student's personal school record, usually collected and
filed in the pupil personnel office, can provide valuable background data on reading and learning patterns. General and
special testing results, particularly when traced from the
primary grades, provide a developmental view of the student's
language progress. From such data a rough comparison can
be made of reading achievement with estimates of learning
potential and achievement in other academic areas. Serious
reading problems generally become evident in the early primary grades.

Collectively, the test scores, school grades, health and
developmental history, and teacher comments in a folder can
help to distinguish a general pattern of learning difficulty from
a specific reading problem. Junior and senior high school
grades for courses involving substantial reading assignments—
English literature, social studies, and the general sciences—
should be compared with those which are less dependent upon
reading for success. Differential or sporadic success patterns
within such "reading content" courses are sometimes significant clues that a student's problem is reading difficulty rather
than general academic adjustment.

Unfortunately, the cumulative student record frequently
is neglected as a source of vital pupil data. Records do not
always follow a pupil who transfers or graduates into new
schools. Within a school, records are not always kept up to
date. Teachers often fail to submit significant observations.
Some school systems overcome many of these problems with a
special pupil reading folder which follows the student through
his instructional years and which contains space for teacher
observations, a profile of skill growth, and pertinent test data.

Some secondary schools have found it practical to assign the responsibility for student files to the pupil's counselor or adviser. The cumulative record can be a valuable source of reading evaluation—when it is diligently maintained.

The Standardized Reading Survey Test

Some of the strengths and weaknesses of the reading subtests of the standarized achievement batteries were discussed in an earlier section. Most of that discussion is appropriate to the consideration of standardized reading survey tests, for the tests are very similar.[3] Indeed, some survey reading tests—for example, the *ITBS Silent Reading Comprehension Test*—are little more than achievement battery reading subtests abstracted and sold as an individual package.

Some reading survey tests are part of a vertical battery or ladder of reading tests. The *Gates-MacGinitie* tests, published by Columbia University, consist of consistently normed tests for each school level. Such batteries tend to provide alternate test forms, useful for pre- and past-testing functions of various sorts.

Some survey tests are subdivided into subtests which validly measure different reading tasks, thus providing additional diagnostic insight. Most survey tests give three scores (vocabulary, comprehension, and total reading) ; some add a separate measure of reading rate; and several produce additional diagnostic information. One such reading battery is the *Diagnostic Reading Tests* developed and published by the Committee on Diagnostic Reading Tests. The DRT provides a systematic sequence for group reading diagnosis. The sequence starts with a survey test of the traditional type, which may be administered to the entire secondary reading population being evaluated. If certain students fall substantially below their expectancy level in vocabulary, comprehension, or rate of reading, they can be grouped and given the second or third group diagnostic tests for the areas of their suspected deficiency. This system is efficient and yields some information useful for

---

[3] Oscar Buros (ed.), *Reading Tests and Reviews* (Highland Park, N.J.: Gryphon Press, 1968), p. xx.

ping students for corrective reading instruction, but it is more accurately considered a diagnostic screening battery than an in-depth reading diagnosis.

Some reading survey tests (for example, the *SRA Reading Record*) provide as many as six reading subtests within an instrument that can be administered within the time limit of one class period. This is an attractive package, but the prospective user should realize that each subtest is of limited length, and the reliability and thus the validity of the subtests may suffer accordingly.

Two other ways in which diagnostic information may be gained from standardized screening tests should be mentioned, if only to provide some idea of the variety of these tests. The *Iowa Tests of Educational Development*, a secondary achievement battery, contain separate subtests that measure the student's ability to interpret passages drawn from social studies, science, and literary materials. When these subtests are compared to the content knowledge subtests of their respective areas, they provide both a profile of relative reading strengths in the three major content areas and a differential comparison of accumulated background with the ability to learn through reading in that content area.

The reading comprehension subtest of the *Tests of Academic Progress* may be used to provide yet a different diagnostic insight. Published by Houghton Mifflin, the TAP has been normed on the same population used for norming the *Lorge-Thorndike* group intelligence tests. While group tests of reading and intelligence suffer enough weaknesses to suggest they are best employed as screening rather than absolute measures, the use of comparable norms in the TAP and Lorge-Thorndike tests avoids one major problem of intelligence-reading comparisons. These comparisons are important in separating underachievers from slow learners—a step usually vital to making the best use of corrective-remedial resources.

Work-Study Skill Measures

There is a notable difference between being able to interpret reading material and being able to use that content to learn or to solve problems. There are several standardized measures of reading work-study skills which are available for the seventh through ninth grade populations. These tests usually emphasize the locational skills in reading and cannot be considered an adequate sample of functional study or problem-solving processes in reading.

The ability to locate, study and learn, and apply information obtained from printed sources is highly functional to high school, college, and life tasks. Assessing a student's strengths and weaknesses in this phase of reading is therefore important. A student's weaknesses in work-study skills may be due to lack of knowledge, lack of flexible applicational skill, lack of polished habit, or lack of positive drive. Hence, assessment in this area will require more than the limited sampling provided by standardized work-study skills tests. Standard published study habit checklists or inventories like that developed by Preston and Batel [4] add another assessment dimension. Probably the most useful additional evaluation in this area will come from such informal measures as examining worksheets based upon an assigned problem requiring the use of reading, and from informal questionnaires or interviews on reading study habits.

The Informal Reading Inventory

In common measurement parlance, an "informal" test means a teacher-made or nonstandardized performance measure. Many procedures and forms are used in the informal assessment of reading behavior; they are quite necessary to fill in the wide gaps of information left between standardized sources of data.

However, an "informal reading inventory" (i.r.i.) refers to one of several specific types of reading assessment devices. Basically, these devices are sequential level reading power measures which derive much of their value from the fact that the selections form a graded ladder of reading content. While the typical i.r.i. is an individually administered device, with certain adjustments it can be used in group situations.

The original and most common form of the i.r.i. is com-

[4] Ralph Preston and Morton Batel, *Study Habits Checklist* (Chicago: Science Research Associates, 1957–67).

posed of three equivalent sets of reading segments drawn from sequential basal readers from preprimer through eighth-grade levels. Ten or more questions measuring significant literal and inferential facts and ideas are prepared for each of the three graded sets of selections. One set is read to the student to determine his functional listening level—the highest level at which he can answer 75 per cent of the questions correctly. The second set is read silently by the student; a comprehension score of 75–90 per cent is considered appropriate for "instructional" purposes, while a comprehension of 90 per cent or better is considered adequate for "independent" level reading. The third set of selections is read orally by the student. An experienced teacher of reading, using an error coding system, can study the student's word pronunciation and oral reading patterns at the several levels and gain insight into his grasp of sound-letter correspondences and his syntactical strengths and weaknesses. Oral reading fluency and comprehension can be used to confirm functional reading levels.

The value and validity of the individual informal reading inventory is highly dependent upon the ability of its constructor and administrator. In the hands of a skilled teacher, it can be a valuable diagnostic tool for use with secondary students with a basic reading deficiency. One of the better sources of information available on this assessment technique is *Informal Reading Inventories* by Johnson and Kress.[5] Best results are obtained when teachers have had supervised practice with the i.r.i. technique before they use it in their own classes.

A form of this procedure which can be employed in secondary schools by personnel with little background in reading diagnosis is the group silent content reading inventory. This inventory consists of a set of selections, each two to four paragraphs in length and drawn from the textbooks or source books which will figure frequently in the instruction of the content area. If possible, these selections should be arranged according to reading difficulty or complexity. A series of ten to fifteen questions should be developed that reflect both the stated and the implied content of the selection and call for organizational

---

[5] Marjorie Johnson and Roy Kress, *Informal Reading Inventories* (Newark, Del.: International Reading Association, 1965).

and critical analysis. When administered early in the school year, this group reading inventory will aid the teacher in identifying students with functional reading difficulty, in the differential assignment of study materials, and in identifying comprehension-thinking skills which need to be developed during the course.

Other Informal Means of Reading Assessment

The varieties of informal procedures for reading evaluation are nearly unlimited. Any device or procedure that produces useful information concerning student reading-learning needs, abilities, interests, attitudes, and experiences is, by definition, appropriate. Some of the most common are listed here. Space does not permit a thorough description; the reader is referred to general studies of reading assessment, secondary reading, and educational measurement that provide models and suggested uses.[6] Informal assessment is greatly enhanced when the teacher's observations are guided by the use of a reading behaviors checklist and systematically collected.

Informal Word Inventories These can be based on graded reading lists such as the *San Diego Check Test,* or a sample can be drawn from the glossaries of textbooks. The student pronounces and defines the word. Errors provide an indication of word skill deficiency, level of reading power, and vocabulary weaknesses.[7]

Reading Assignment Worksheets The systematic construction of reading worksheets and the comparison of the students' performances give useful insight into comprehension and study problems. These worksheets usually take the form of reading-study guides or informal tests for the assign-

---

[6] Mary C. Austin *et al., Reading Evaluation* (New York: Ronald Press, 1961. Ruth Strang, *Diagnostic Teaching of Reading* (New York: McGraw-Hill, 1964). Robert Thorndike and Elizabeth Hagen, *Measurement and Evaluation in Psychology and Education,* 3d ed. (New York: Wiley, 1969).

[7] Margaret LePray and Ramon Ross, "The Graded Word List: Quick Gauge of Reading Ability," *Journal of Reading,* Vol. 12 (January, 1969), pp. 305–07.

ment of reading selection. They may concentrate upon any of a number of reading skills, substantive understandings, or reading-study processes. A broader version of the study guide worksheet would treat (1) unknown or difficult vocabulary to be encountered in the selection, (2) the development of general purposes for the initial survey of the selection, (3) specific problems to be solved through the use of the information gained, (4) practice on specific comprehension techniques, and (5) recall or application of the vital content. A systematic use of the dimensions of Figure 1 in developing worksheet questions will provide the teacher with diagnostic data on student learning problems as well as evidence of learning progress.

Teacher Observation   The regular observation of student reading behavior in class and analysis of work done out-of-class is helpful.

Student-kept Records   There are three advantages, at least, to involving students in the assessment of their own reading performance. The practice may save the teacher some time, but the system works best when the teacher consults with each student over his records on a regular basis, so the advantage of the practice is not time saved so much as time used to better effect. When the records take the form of a progress chart, regularly kept, they enhance motivation. When such records take the form of a diagnostic checklist thoroughly explained at the beginning and used as a basis for progress conferences, the student seems to learn a good deal about the nature of reading and its application to problems. One note of caution; the use of such self-kept records as a basis for grading generally defeats the other purposes of the process.

Evaluating Reading Interests and Attitudes   Many approaches are available to the teacher. Common techniques are student checklists, incomplete sentences forms, interest inventories, sociometric games, and reading autobiographies.[8] One

[8] A detailed description of these techniques may be found in Albert J. Harris, *How to Increase Reading Ability* (New York: Longmans, Green, 1961). An example of the Incomplete Sentences Test appears on page 484 of that textbook.

technique found to be practical in secondary classes is a largely blank sheet titled "What I'd Like to Tell Mr. Hill About the Reading Involved in This Course." The papers could be turned in unsigned and contained, along with some witty, brutally frank, and emotionally releasing comments, insightful and helpful information and advice about improving test materials, improving interest, and, quite rightly, improving teaching performance.

MEASURING BASIC WORD SKILLS
AT THE SECONDARY LEVEL

Students who have made normal progress in reading will have mastered the basic word analysis and word acquisition skills by the time they reach secondary school. Approximately one-fifth of the typical seventh-grade class will show some insecurity in using word skills, however, and since weakness in these fundamental skills can undermine independent reading practices, some screening is useful, particularly at the junior high school level, to identify students with word skill difficulties.

Basic Word Skills

Following is a list of basic word skills over which the student should have adequate control by eighth grade.

1. A meaning vocabulary large enough for him to understand 95 per cent of the nontechnical words in his textbooks.
2. A sight vocabulary (instant recognition) that permits him to read recreational materials appropriate for his age and interests in a fluent manner and that enables him to readily recognize 85 to 90 per cent of the nontechnical vocabulary of his textbooks.
3. The sight perceptual skill to recognize familiar words with high accuracy at one-fourth of a second.
4. The ability to use sentence context to anticipate the meaning of familiar words as well as to help analyze the meaning of unfamiliar words.
5. Skills of individual word analysis and synthesis that in combination allow the student to unlock the pronunciation and meaning of unfamiliar words. These skills include:

a. Phonic skills: the association of speech sounds with letters, phonograms, and syllabication.

b. Structural skills: the analysis and synthesis of a word by its meaningful parts—for example, roots, prefixes, suffixes.

6. The effective use of reference works such as dictionaries and thesauri to obtain the pronunciation and meanings of words.

Word Power Measures

There are a number of traditional techniques for the evaluation of word power. At the secondary level, the most commonly used measure is the standardized reading vocabulary test, a broad survey measure which combines a measure of word meaning with word recognition and analysis. A low score on such test may indicate that general word reading difficulty is the source of a student's general reading problems. However, a low score on the standardized vocabulary test may result from a number of different causes: (1) limited intelligence, (2) limited language background, (3) restricted experiential background, (4) lack of wide personal reading, (5) visual difficulty, (6) slow reading (if a time-limit test was used), (7) inaccurate word recognition techniques, and (8) inadequate word analysis techniques. Some of these possibilities can be eliminated by checking the available data on the student. It is always possible that more than one factor contributed to the problem. It is usually advisable to further screen students with low vocabulary test scores with a group standardized test of word perception and analysis skills. Students who perform poorly on this group screening measure may then be selected for some type of individual diagnosis of word skills.

Some of the more useful instruments and procedures for identifying and analyzing word ability problems are presented below. With the exception of the group standardized tests, these evaluation procedures work best when they are employed by a professional with experience in reading diagnosis and familiarity with word skills and their functions.

Standardized Vocabulary Subtest This is a subtest of a general achievement test battery such as the *California*

Achievement Tests or the *Sequential Tests of Educational Progress.* These subtests have already been discussed.

Standardized Vocabulary Test This is a specific measure that may or may not be a part of a special series of reading tests. It provides a more extensive sampling of word recognition and meaning than the battery subtest. In some cases, the test may be divided into different vocabulary areas and will provide differential normative scores by vocabulary area—for example, English, science, social science—as well as a total or general score.

Word Pronunciation Lists These are selected word lists that the student pronounces aloud from sight recognition or analysis if the word is unfamiliar. The examiner marks the number and type of errors. There are two major patterns in the construction of such lists: the functional word list and the screening levels list. An example of the first would be the Dolch list of *220 Basic Sight Words* which figure heavily in the running service vocabularies of most content textbooks. An example of the second is the *San Diego Quick Word Test,* whose words have been selected on a try-out basis and arranged to correspond with reading levels. One or two errors on the various levels of the San Diego list provide a fairly accurate estimate of which reading material level is appropriate for independent and instructional purposes. Most word pronunciation lists lend themselves to analysis of error patterns in word recognition and word analysis.[9]

The Informal Word Recognition Inventory This is a teacher-made word pronunciation list. The teacher takes a representative sampling of words from a series of readers or content textbooks and asks the student to read the list. The procedure gives the teacher a quick indication of which instructional materials are most appropriate for his various students.[10]

Oral Reading Most ancient of word assessment tools, oral reading is still a useful way to determine the quality of

[9] LePray and Ross.
[10] Johnson and Kress.

a student's word recognition and analysis skill. When the reading selections are arranged in sequential order of difficulty as in
an informal reading inventory, the oral reading exercise also
provides a good indication of the student's appropriate levels
for independent and instructional reading. Experience has
shown that students will have difficulty reading independently
in those materials in which they make more than one or two
word errors on one hundred running words. More than five
errors per hundred causes serious difficulty with materials
even when the instructor aids in the reading of a selection.

Standardized Word Abilities Batteries   These are commercially published tests that consist of a series of subtests
which measure various word skills—for example, vocabulary,
word recognition skills, and word analysis skills. Some are
silent word skills tests and are appropriately administered to
small groups. Examples include the *Silent Reading Diagnostic
Tests* (Bond-Clymer-Hoyt), the *Doren Silent Diagnostic Tests,*
and *McCullough Test of Word Skills.* All of these tests may be
used as tools of individual diagnosis. These tests are quite
useful as general screening measures of word difficulty.

Diagnostic Reading Batteries   While these individually
administered tools of reading diagnosis are intended to measure multiple aspects of student reading ability, they include
subsections directed at the assessment of word skills. They
are used most effectively when the instructor has had special
training in their use.

Informal Word Analysis Measures   One informal word
analysis measure is the worksheet. Students identify words
with varied endings as the teacher presents them on flash
cards. A more structured form is the word analysis inventory,
a sampling of a student's command of word skills progressing
from the very simple (knowledge of letter names) to the complex (pronouncing multisyllable nonsense words arranged by
structural units).

A PLAN FOR THE PROGRAM
OF READING APPRAISAL

As we have seen, there are many functions to be served by the program of reading evaluation. The assessment of student performance is the pivotal point upon which it all turns. Ideally, we should like to see every secondary school student receive a thorough individual analysis of reading skills. Realistically, this is not possible. The objective must be a compromise which maintains efficiency within the limits of necessary economy and yet provides individual evaluative attention where it is most needed.

The following plan provides one approach to this needed compromise. As Figure 2 indicates, the plan employs a series of successive screenings. All students would encounter screening at Level I. Average and good readers would be screened out at this level of reading appraisal, since they are in least need of further special assessment. It is assumed that their reading-learning needs and reading progress will be appraised through the informal procedures of the regular instructional program. At each successive screening level, only the most serious and needful reading problem cases would be passed on to the next and more expensive (in time and energy) level of assessment.

It will be noted that the several diagnostic levels are tied into referral channels to aspects of the hypothetical reading program. No screening or diagnostic system is perfect, hence flexibility in assessment, referral, and instruction must be maintained. This flexibility is represented in Figure 2 by the two-headed arrows, which connect program and assessment and program and program.

A brief description of the specific nature and function of the five levels of appraisal is provided here:

Level I: Regular School Achievement Assessment The major functions served are: to use on-going testing program results as first screening of reading difficulty cases, to compare individual and group reading progress with other skills progress, to provide gross measurements of achievement-capacity differentials.

Level II: Reading Skills Survey   The major functions
served are: to screen further for reading disability, to verify
previous reading achievement results, to add to skills profile
—particularly in silent reading comprehension.

Level III: Individual Skills Analysis   The major functions served are: to gain detailed skills assessment with individual tests and observations, to identify nonlimiting reading
disability and recommend correction procedures or programs,
to screen further for serious cases of reading disability.

Level IV: Reading Case Study   The major functions
served are: to gather and collate data about the student's
personal development and school adjustment pertinent to his
reading disability (will include individual skills analysis), to
verify questionable findings of previous diagnostic levels, to
identify skill disorders and general learning conditions which
inhibit reading progress, to develop and effect a remedial program for cases of serious reading (learning) disability and
underachievement.

The remedial or reading specialist usually is responsible
for developing the reading case study. However, the specialist
will call in other professional persons for needed diagnoses not
within his own personal skills or authorized area of operation.
The professionals most frequently involved are the school
counselor or psychologist (for diagnoses of individual intelligence and personal adjustment), speech pathologist (speech
and hearing), school nurse and family physician (general
health data), teacher (classroom learning behavior), and parent (family relationships and general developmental history).

Level V: Depth Case Study   Since this is the most time
consuming and expensive of the various diagnostic levels, it
should be reserved for those problems which require intensive
and specialized attention. Ordinarily, a youngster requires a
full or depth case study when the reading case study fails to
identify his needs or identifies special learning problems that
are not amenable to remedial instruction by the reading specialist even when well motivated and therapeutic conditions
exist. Reading disability may be a part of this youngster's

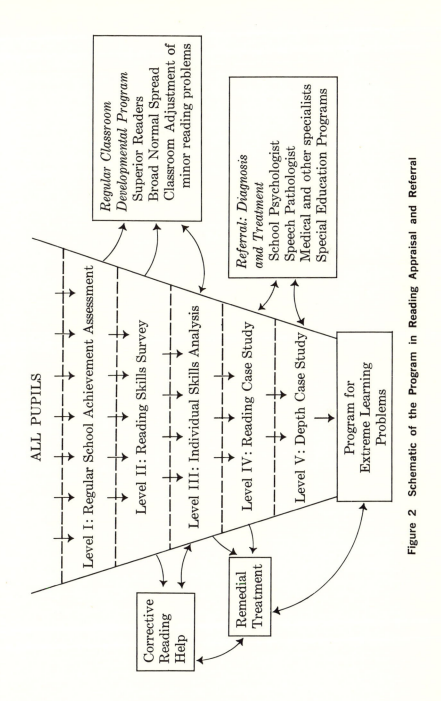

Figure 2 Schematic of the Program in Reading Appraisal and Referral

problems, but it is likely that the problem is more serious and more generalized than this. The client of the depth case study is hypothesized to be a candidate either for a special program for those with extreme learning problems or for one of the traditional phases of a special education program.

The depth case study is likely to be an operation effected by a team of professionals including the reading specialist as one member. Other members are likely to include the professionals that the reading specialist sometimes calls in in making a reading case study, as well as medical specialists, social case worker, and a psychiatrist.

CONCLUSION

This article has attempted to combine a broad survey of needed areas of improvement in secondary reading evaluation with some suggested procedures for effecting such improvement. Much remains to be said. Much remains to be learned about valid and practical ways of evaluating secondary level readers and reading programs. More importantly, much remains to be done, and much could be done even at our present state of imperfect knowledge. The success of the evaluation of secondary reading is tied to the success of the secondary reading program. They are interdependent elements, and both are highly dependent upon the staff and, thus, upon the individual teacher —his knowledge, his skill, but, most importantly, his attitude and drive. In this article, the evaluation program is viewed as a changing thing—a matter of *becoming* rather than *being*. No less can be expected of the teacher upon whom the evaluation program ultimately depends.

References

Austin, Mary C., *et al. Reading Evaluation.* New York: Ronald Press, 1961.

Barrett, Thomas C., ed. *The Evaluation of Children's Reading Achievement.* Newark, Del.: International Reading Association, 1967.

Buros, Oscar, ed. *Reading Tests and Reviews*. Highland Park,
    N.J.: Gryphon Press, 1968.
Hill, Walter. *Secondary Reading Programs*. Rev. ed. Newark,
    Del.: International Reading Association, 1969.
Johnson, Marjorie, and Kress, Roy. *Informal Reading Inven-
    tories*. Newark, Del.: International Reading Associ-
    ation, 1965.
LePray, Margaret, and Ross, Ramon. "The Graded Word List:
    Quick Gauge of Reading Ability." *Journal of Reading*
    12 (January, 1969) : 305–07.
Strang, Ruth. *Diagnostic Teaching of Reading*. New York:
    McGraw-Hill, 1964.
Thorndike, Robert, and Hagen, Elizabeth. *Measurement and
    Evaluation in Psychology and Education*. 3d ed. New
    York: Wiley, 1969.

11

Measuring the Reading Ability and Potential of Adult Illiterates

DON A. BROWN

Many adult residents of our inner cities are seriously debilitated by inadequate formal education or, more specifically, lack of ability to read and write. The extent of illiteracy in this country is difficult to measure, yet the seriousness of the problem is underlined by the fact that some 23 million adults, aged twenty-five and older, have completed less than eight years of schooling. Of these, 8 million have completed less than five years of schooling, and are, accordingly, defined as functionally illiterate. In New York state alone it is estimated that 800,000 adults are functionally illiterate.

Functionally illiterate people are frequently dependent on others for financial support; they are often unable to handle their own financial affairs, particularly in matters of budgeting. They are severely limited in social mobility and in cultural participation. Functional illiteracy circumscribes the individual to more and more limited means to cope with a society of ever increasing achievement. Instructional programs must be improved if the needs of these people are to be met, and the keystone to the improvement of these programs lies in better means of measurement and evaluation.

PRINTED here for the first time with the permission of the author.

There are three general populations of adult illiterates. One is the dropout population. These persons are usually young men and women who have dropped out of school before completing requirements for a high school diploma. Many of them are unable to read above the fifth-grade level, even though they may have completed eight or more years of schooling. Many federal and state programs are aimed at educating and preparing these young people to support themselves in adulthood.

The second population consists of foreign-born illiterates. A person in this group may be able to read and write quite well in a language such as Spanish, Italian, Polish, or German. He must master some English before he will be ready to learn to read, but given a reasonable amount of help, those who are literate in another language and learn to speak English will be able to learn to read and write their new language in a relatively short time.

The third population consists of native-born disadvantaged illiterates, most often Negro or "Appalachian poor white." This population causes the greatest concern and shows the least amount of promise. Its members are often part of the "hard-core unemployed," the last to be hired and the first to be fired. In a civilization that is becoming more technically oriented all the time, they are badly equipped even to maintain their present situation in society, let alone begin to improve it.

Numerous programs have been inaugurated to attempt to teach disadvantaged adult illiterates the basic requirements of reading, writing, and arithmetic. These programs, which are expressions of social concern for those who have so long been relegated to a position of unimportance and unconcern, are under understandable pressures to demonstrate convincingly the effectiveness of the instruction they provide. This is not easy for them to do, first, because the job of training illiterates to read is enormously difficult and slow, and, second, because no suitable evaluation instruments exist.

Unfortunately but perhaps inevitably, many groups concerned with education in the United States, including publishers, teachers, private organizations, and public supervisory bureaus, have virtually demanded that outstanding growth result from the dollars that they have invested. One reason for such demands may be that to some it seems "logical" that an illiterate adult ought to learn to read more quickly than a first-grade child: the greater experiential background of the adult, they think, should have increased his chances of profiting from instruction. They do not stop to consider the possibility that adults who have proceeded through life for twenty to sixty years without learning to read may have developed an extremely poor opinion of their academic ability and chances of success. A first-grade child usually approaches beginning reading instruction with enthusiasm and self-confidence, whereas the adult illiterate usually feels that learning to read will be hard, and he is not at all sure that he will be able to accomplish this miracle.

The great difficulty of teaching adult illiterates to read might have been recognized sooner if proper measurement devices had been available for adult beginning readers. Unfortunately, they were not available, and without proper instruments of measurements and evaluation, it was impossible to tell where the students were when programs were begun, where they were when the programs ended, or even what their potential for profiting from instruction might be. The tests that did exist had mostly been prepared to measure the reading gains of small children, or to test the learning potential of literate adults. (Today, a few adult-oriented beginning reading tests are available; how they compare with children's reading tests, how scores on the tests compare with results from an informal reading inventory, and how they compare with each other are questions that remain to be answered.)

A major problem in measurement and evaluation of adult literacy gains is the lack of agreement and understanding about what constitutes the equivalent of a grade level for adult basic education. It is so difficult to apply elementary school grade level markings directly to adult literacy programs that many programs have apparently attempted to ignore such classifications altogether. This has resulted in a great deal of confusion. At the Buffalo Literacy Research Center a study was made of supposedly "beginning" level reading materials presently in use for adult literacy training. Through the use of readability formulas, rough estimates were made of the level of difficulty of the materials. Although some materials began as low as upper first-grade level, other materials inaugurated "beginning" reading instruction at the fifth-grade level. In some textbook series, the first book of the series was more difficult than the second in terms of the readability formulas. And in several cases, the reading difficulty at the end of the first book was higher than at the end of the second book in the series. In other cases, the reading difficulty increased so rapidly from one lesson to the next that, in the course of the completion of one workbook, a student would supposedly have had to increase in reading ability several grade levels in order to keep pace with the reading material. On the other hand, one beginning reading level workbook made no appreciable gain in difficulty from the first page to the last.

Defective materials of the kind studied result from our lack of practical experience in adult literacy training. Practical experience with children's elementary programs has slowly, and in some cases by accident, given us an understanding of the way materials must be paced for children to learn properly. Without such a background of experience in adult literacy training, many publishers are producing materials which are too difficult and are poorly and improperly paced.

DIFFICULTIES IN MEASURING THE APTITUDE AND ACHIEVEMENT OF ADULT ILLITERATES

Since measurement and evaluation are crucial to the improvement of instruction, it is necessary to take a critical look at tests presently being used in the development of better curricula for adult basic education. Until recently adult basic educators have had no choice but to use children's tests as both placement and achievement measures. Measures of potential were drawn from tests available for use with adult *literates*. None of these measures were constructed specifically for use with adult illiterates.

One difficulty in using the same standardized reading tests for adults as for children is that an adult uses a different vocabulary from that which a child uses. Many of the standardized reading tests use such terms as "run," "jump," "play," "baby," "doll," and "wagon." Adults are presumably more interested in learning to read more utilitarian words such as "job," "work," "bus," "payday," "house," and "check." The use of children's tests with adults tends to provide invalid results.

A second difficulty in using children's tests with adults is that the subject matter concepts in the tests are different from those in the reading materials most enthusiastically accepted by adults in literacy training programs. In a study of the reading interests of adult illiterates at the Buffalo Literacy Research Center, adults were found to be most interested in reading materials concerning their own personal and family improvement, jobs, religion, and health. They were least interested in reading children's stories and, in general, the kinds of things contained in basal readers in use in most elementary school reading programs. Unfortunately, adult literacy programs that capitalize on this interest by using special materials are penalized when their students' progress is measured by children's tests, since the tests measure the learning of children's words and concepts.

Perhaps this helps to explain why some programs that are enthusiastically received by adult illiterates, are based on their interests, and are paced to their needs, often produce no more significant reading gains than those programs which simply make use of children's basal readers. Most of the standardized tests in use at the present time are built on the vocabulary and concepts contained in basal readers and, naturally, do not attempt to measure much of the vocabulary and concepts of adult-oriented programs.

A third difficulty with the tests presently being used to measure achievement for adult illiterates is that populations of children are used for standardization. Largely because it is unclear what constitutes a grade equivalent level for adult basic education, test-makers rely on grade school populations to establish norms for most tests. Even for some "adult" beginning reading tests, a perusal of the manuals shows standardization has been carried out using children populations rather than adult populations.

A fourth difficulty in using children's tests with adults is the format of the tests. Some of the elementary reading tests are quite childish in their appearance. This is not the greatest disadvantage of such tests, but the format of adult tests presently in use or under development is certainly preferable. The self-respect and feeling of personal worth of the adult illiterate must be safeguarded; the format of the materials he uses should not suggest that he is a child.

The general format of test books and answer sheets should reflect the fact that adults often have had almost no instruction on how to take a test. We begin testing elementary school youngsters almost as soon as they enter school, and by the time they are in the third grade, we expect them to know how to handle an answer sheet and how to proceed through the test booklet. Adults "look" as though they ought to be able to handle the situation also. As a matter of fact, however, they have had little or no preparation as to how to take a test. They suffer particularly from confusing answer sheets. One of the more promising adult basic tests recently on the market makes use of an answer sheet that has been found to be quite difficult for many of the students in adult literacy programs.

The adult illiterate often has more difficulty than the first-grade child in handling a pencil and paper. Although an adult may not squirm as much as a first-grade child, prolonged testing sessions are highly uncomfortable for him, and he has difficulty maintaining interest and attention over a long period of time. He often suffers from visual problems that are undiscovered until he is required to do close work. In addition, he has more difficulty following directions than his maturity would indicate.

It is altogether too easy to assume that adults can handle the task of test-taking without any problems. The wise examiner will realize that they have had little or no instruction and that they may wonder whether they are to proceed down or across the page, whether they are to turn the page and continue the test or should stop, what they should do when they come to an item and do not know the answer, and so on. Part of the burden of getting good test results lies in teaching adult illiterates explicitly what one must do in order to take the tests.

Assessing Reading Gain

The evaluation of programs and materials is often made largely in terms of reading gain as measured by pre-testing and post-testing. Good testing practices are therefore a prerequisite to the accurate evaluation of programs and materials. The following guidelines to testing should be helpful.

Tests ought to be used that are compatible with the general level of performance of the students. The writer visited one literacy program that was having difficulty in assessing the abilities of its students. He found that although most students in the program were unable to read above third-grade level, they had been given a test designed to measure reading ability for students with fifth- to seventh-grade abilities. The test must be fitted to the student. Sometimes a preliminary screening test will yield a rough approximation of the ability of the student to be tested, thus permitting the teacher to choose the proper level of test.

Test scores must be carefully interpreted. Tests don't measure certain kinds of reading progress; they also do measure gains that are not true reading gains. Many adult illiterates must go through the process of developing readiness to profit from reading instruction before they will make satisfactory gains in their ability to read. Readiness tests are rarely given to adults, however. Students who need readiness training will usually score at a low first-grade level when they are tested by a standardized reading measure. A test given after the end of the period of instruction may show that there has been little or no gain, when in reality there may have been considerable progress in developing *readiness* to profit from instruction. The lack of gain on the standardized tests is discouraging to the student, discouraging to the teacher, and discouraging to the administrators of the program—even though the student is actually profiting from instruction, and no one ought to be discouraged.

In the course of the Buffalo study of reading interests previously mentioned, a number of students recorded little or no progress during the first year of instruction but quite satisfactory gains during the second year. In the opinion of the research staff, these scores indicated that, during the first year of instruction, the students had been acquiring the underlying abilities or readiness that they needed to be able to profit from reading instruction. Pre-test and post-test scores during the first year of instruction, however, showed little or no gain.

Tests not only fail to measure some forms of reading progress; they measure some forms of progress that are actually not true reading gains at all. When an adult illiterate takes his first test, he is often still unfamiliar with the school, unaccustomed to test-taking, and has not begun to recall skills that at one time he had learned but that now have fallen into disuse. His performance on the first test will therefore understandably be much poorer than his performance on the second taken at the end of the program. Many programs that report sizable gains for the truly low-level illiterate need to investigate their pre-testing techniques to be sure that they are not giving the first test under stressful conditions and that they have allowed enough time for the student to become adjusted to the school situation.

Illusory reading gains also may result from the use of different tests for pre-measurement and post-measurement. One school visited by the writer tested all incoming adult illiterates with the *Gray Oral Reading Test* within a few minutes of the time that they arrived in the school building. The student was taking a strange test from a person in authority whom he did not know, in strange surroundings, creating a most stressful situation. The results of the test were later compared to the results of another test, a standardized reading test designed for third graders, administered at the end of the school year. The two tests tested different abilities: the *Gray Oral Reading Test* measured oral fluency and word recall, while the standardized reading test measured ability to recognize word meanings and understand paragraphs while reading silently. The tests were given under totally different circumstances and were standardized on different populations. Yet the results were reported as though the differences between the two represented true gains in reading ability. This was obviously a faulty practice.

Occasionally the inadequacy of existing tests will lead an evaluator to attempt to assess a program's effectiveness simply by tabulating the levels of material through which the students have progressed. He may cite the fact that the students began at "Level One" and proceeded through "Level Eight" as evidence that they have gained eight grade levels in reading ability during the course of the program. Although such statements of progress are heartening to the administrators and funders of the programs, they are highly inaccurate.

It is most difficult to produce gains in reading ability when the students are adults with less than third-grade reading achievement. There is little evidence to suggest that any program teaching adult illiterates with reading ability below the third-grade level can raise the mean level of the class in excess of three years in two hundred hours or less of reading instruction. Larger recorded gains are usually erroneous. Perhaps the students began reading at the first-grade level although they actually were able to read fifth-grade or sixth-grade material. Or perhaps their "success" in the program was that they were judged to be reading in fifth-, sixth-, seventh-, or eighth-grade level material without the confirming evidence produced by any sound evaluative instrument—either (1) a standardized test properly administered or (2) the instructional level on an informal reading inventory (discussed below). Simply moving through "levels" does not constitute gain any more than being measured once while stooping and a second time while standing on a chair changes a man's height.

Although not commonly used, informal reading inventories offer one of the better means of assessing reading gains. The informal reading inventory is a sequence of reading materials of increasing complexity; the examiner uses it to determine the highest level at which his students may read instructionally or independently. The advantage of this technique is that the inventories may be based on the reading material that the student is actually using. The disadvantage of the technique is that we have no well-established levels of performance for adults comparable to the grade levels for the elementary school. This makes it difficult to get a sequence of materials of increasingly difficult levels.

New tests are badly needed that are built on adult-oriented interests, standardized on adult populations, and complete with different forms and different levels. Progress has recently been made; it is hoped that these early efforts will continue and the products will be improved.

ASSESSING POTENTIAL

Potential is assessed by measuring manifestations of a person's ability to learn from his environment. Basic to this is the assumption that all persons to be tested must have experienced a somewhat similar environment containing somewhat similar opportunities to learn. Unfortunately, a sizable proportion of adult illiterates does not share the pool of common experiences on which most tests of potential are based. This means that these tests do not measure ability to learn from one's environment *for these people.* Their low test scores do not mean, therefore, that they are unable to learn, but only that they have never had the opportunity to learn the information needed to do well on the test.

For example, if an adult illiterate has never been taught that the sun rises in the east and sets in the west and that if he faces west, north is to his right and south is to his left, he would not be expected to know the directions. If we then try to test his potential for learning by saying, "If you walk north one block, then turn left and walk another block, what direction would then be to your left?" we are not able to assess his intellect or potential. We cannot say he has no potential because he did not have an opportunity to learn the elements on which we based the test of potential. (If he had had such an opportunity and had not learned, then we might be able to say something about his learning ability.)

To repeat, most tests of potential for adults presume that the individual has acquired certain common skills and information. The subtest of coding in the *Wechsler Adult Intelligence Scale* presumes that each person taking the subtest has had an opportunity to learn how to use a pencil and paper and to follow verbal directions. If, in fact, a person has not had that opportunity, the test can give no indication of his intelligence. Equally suspect as intelligence measures are tests of common knowledge such as the following items from the WAIS information subtest: "Where does rubber come from?" "Name four men who have been President of the United States since 1900." "Longfellow was a famous man. What was he?" The WAIS vocabulary subtest asks the individual to define a number of words such as "fabric," "conceal," and "enormous." Such questions and tasks measure academic learnings that adult illiterates, whatever their intelligence, have rarely had an opportunity to acquire.

The basic means by which adults gain information today is through reading. Adult illiterates are at a disadvantage because they simply cannot use the avenue most adults use to instruct themselves. Generally speaking, tests of intelligence for adults tend to discriminate heavily against illiterates, and instead of testing their potential for profiting from instruction, they simply measure the extent to which they have been unable to receive instruction—most of which they have been unable to absorb because of their illiteracy.

Proof that present-day tests of potential do not identify learning abilities within the adult illiterate population lies in the fact that not even the WAIS, considered to be a paragon of such measures, was able to satisfactorily discriminate between adult city-core illiterates who made gains in learning to read (demonstrating their potential to learn) and those who did not make gains (indicating lesser potential in terms of learning ability).[1]

Scores on tests of adult learning potential are sometimes advanced as "proof" that the poor education of adult illiterates or various minority groups is attributable to intellectual inferiority. Since tests of adult potential are commonly based on academic learning which many adult illiterates could never have acquired, such a conclusion is unwarranted.

The poor quality of existing aptitude tests does not mean that the potential of the adult illiterate is absolutely unfathomable. During the Buffalo study, certain factors were identified as indicative of ability to profit from reading instruction. They included:

1. Expressed preferences for certain book titles
2. Ability to grasp analogies illustrated with common items
3. Ability to see missing parts in common, simple pictures
4. General reading ability of the subject's family

[1] Don A. Brown and Anabel P. Newman, *A Literacy Program for Adult City-Core Illiterates*, Final Report for Project No. 6-1136, U.S. Dept. of Health, Education, and Welfare (Buffalo: State Univ. of New York at Buffalo, 1968).

5. Ability to arrange pictures in logical sequence
6. Ability to trace a path through a maze
7. Understanding certain functional information such as handedness and directions.

An item analysis of the numerous variables presented to the subjects during the study will perhaps yield the information necessary to create a test able to show the potential of adult illiterates to profit from reading instruction. Certainly an accurate aptitude test is vitally needed by the teachers of adult illiterates.

For Further Reading

Emans, Robert. "Teacher Evaluations of Reading Skills and Individualized Reading," *Elementary English* 42 (March, 1964) : 258–60.

McDonald, Arthur S. "Factors Affecting Reading Test Performance," *Research and Evaluation in College Reading*. Ninth Yearbook of the National Reading Conference for College and Adults, pp. 28–35. Fort Worth, Texas: Texas Christian Univ. Press, 1960.

Michaelis, John U., and Tyler, Fred T. "A Comparison of Reading Ability and Readability," *Journal of Educational Psychology* 42 (December, 1951) : 491–98.

Mills, Robert E., and Richardson, Jean R. "What Do Publishers Mean by 'Grade Level'?" *Reading Teacher* 16 (March, 1963) : 359–62.

Russell, David H., and Fea, Henry R. "Validity of Six Readability Formulas as Measures of Juvenile Fiction," *Elementary School Journal* 52 (November, 1951) : 136–44.

Simpson, Ray H., and Camp, Kenneth L. "Diagnosing Community Reading," *School Review* 61 (February, 1953) : 98–100.

Spache, George. "A Comparison of Certain Reading Tests," *Journal of Educational Research* 43 (February, 1950) : 441–52.

Woodbury, Charles A. "The Identification of Underachieving Readers," *Reading Teacher* 16 (January, 1963) : 218–23.

Section Three

IMPROVING CLASSROOM EVALUATION OF STUDENT READING POWER

The diagnosis and evaluation of student reading abilities should be continuous and contiguous with classroom instruction. This means that classroom teachers need to develop techniques they can apply as part of their daily reading instruction.

These teacher evaluation techniques should be closely related to the objectives of the reading program and to the materials being used for classroom instruction. The first three articles in this section describe classroom diagnostic procedures. In Article 12, Sheldon outlines the broad scope of classroom diagnosis and suggests how and when this diagnosis should take place. Gallant discusses, in Article 13, the development of a diagnostic reading test. The procedures he outlines should be especially useful to teachers as they plan their diagnostic teaching of reading. In Article 14, Johnson reviews the steps in developing a classroom informal reading inventory and points out how such an inventory can be used to improve classroom instruction.

167

The last two articles offer thought-provoking general studies of classroom diagnosis. In Article 15, Bennett challenges the hypothesis that today's classroom teachers and reading specialists can make use of diagnostic information. He concludes that, if classroom diagnosis is to take place, teachers must be trained for diagnostic teaching. Article 16, by Daniel, compares the validity of various reading evaluation devices in determining instructional groups for reading. Daniel suggests, as other researchers have before him, that "in general" the grade placement scores of standardized reading tests are about two years above students' actual instructional reading levels. His observations should make educators wary of planning instruction solely on the basis of standardized reading tests.

The following questions should aid in the evaluation of what the articles say about procedures and problems in conducting classroom diagnosis:

1. Are classroom teachers adequately trained to carry on the diagnostic teaching of reading?
2. What are the essential ingredients for a classroom reading diagnosis?
3. How do standardized reading tests aid in the process of classroom diagnosis? How do these tests compare to informal classroom assessment?
4. Should each classroom teacher develop his own classroom diagnostic package? If so, how can such a package be developed?
5. What are the limiting factors in conducting valid and reliable classroom diagnosis?

12

Specific Principles Essential to Classroom Diagnosis

WILLIAM D. SHELDON

The classroom teacher usually recognizes that children vary in reading skills and in their ability to learn to read. Although most teachers are familiar with various tests and ways of assessing reading status, they also need to understand certain basic principles of diagnosis and how to apply these principles in the classroom.

SPECIFIC PRINCIPLES OF DIAGNOSIS

The following specific principles of diagnosis need to be understood by each teacher:

1. Diagnosis is an essential aspect of teaching and is a preliminary step to sound instruction.
2. Diagnosis should be continuous because child growth in reading depends upon the sequential development of skills, which is promoted through the teacher's knowledge of each child's progress.
3. Diagnosis is an individual task and reflects the fact that each child is different.

REPRINTED with permission of William D. Sheldon and the International Reading Association. "Specific Principles Essential to Classroom Diagnosis," in *The Reading Teacher*, vol. 14, no. 1 (September 1960), pp. 2–8.

4. Diagnosis of reading status demands far more than an assessment of reading because reading difficulties are symptomatic of many causative factors.
5. Because reading is but one aspect of language, teachers must understand the listening, speaking, and writing status of children to fully understand their reading abilities.
6. Because the instruments of diagnosis have not been perfected, the limitation of each instrument must be thoroughly understood.

After considering the principles of sound diagnostic procedures many teachers throw up their hands in despair and say that they cannot diagnose. They suggest that diagnosis is beyond them. It is our contention that teachers can and must diagnose if an analysis of reading problems is to be accomplished.[1] We shall consider each principle and develop ways in which the principles can be applied in practice by every teacher.

DIAGNOSIS AN ESSENTIAL PRELIMINARY

Diagnosis is an essential aspect of teaching and is a preliminary step to sound instruction. Diagnosis as a first step in lesson planning suggests two things:

1. Lessons in reading must be planned with a specific understanding of each child's limitations in reading in mind. This means that formal and informal tests are needed to pinpoint the actual level on which each child can profit from instruction.

2. As teachers gain precision in evaluating the reading status of children, instruction will tend to become more specific, and instructional groups will be limited in size. Specific teaching means that provision will be made within each lesson for the reintroduction in a new context of words not mastered in previous lessons or a reemphasis on the learning of an analytic skill which is not applied properly in new lessons. There is also considerable flexibility in such teaching. Instead of following completely a pre-planned lesson, teachers

[1] Sheldon, W. D. "Teachers Must Diagnose," *Education, 78* (May, 1958), 1–2.

adjust to pupils' learning of each new skill and provide for more review of difficult skills than would ordinarily be provided to more able readers.

For the ordinary child whose reading is developing in a more or less normal manner, four aspects of reading must be assessed:

1. *Understanding of concepts* related to each specific lesson. Teachers can assess concept development by giving each child an opportunity to discuss the new ideas in a lesson. It is especially important that pupils be allowed to relate the new ideas to their own understanding by recounting experiences they have had which are similar to those in the story. Sometimes children indicate their understanding of concepts by supplying synonyms for the word or phrase which has fixed the concept.

2. *Understanding of specific meanings* of known words as used in the new lesson and a clear understanding of new words met for the first time in the lesson. An accurate understanding of word meaning is basic to good comprehension. It is particularly important for teachers to explain words which have a different meaning in a new context. Arousing the curiosity of children about specific word meaning contributes also to the development of critical thinking in reading.

3. *Ability to attack new words* through one of the analytic techniques. Most reading lessons develop an eclectic approach to word analysis. This means that whenever opportunities for using phonetic or structural analysis or contextual clues arise that teachers should lead children to use the varied analytic skills. In so doing teachers increase skill and flexibility in word analysis. For more mature readers it is wise to encourage whenever appropriate the use of glossaries and dictionaries in analyzing new words.

4. *Ability to comprehend* the material read and to answer questions about it. It is important that a constant check be made of the pupils' understanding of what they read. Such aspects of comprehension as understanding the main idea and related details, interpreting the author's meaning and reacting critically to what is read must be developed in daily instruction.

In summary then, the first principle of diagnosis is recognized when teachers plan their daily lessons to meet the reading needs of each child in a precise manner.

DIAGNOSIS CONTINUOUS

Diagnosis should be continuous because child growth in reading depends upon the sequential development of skills, which is promoted through the teacher's knowledge of each child's progress. Continuous diagnosis indicates a need for evaluating children carefully before instruction begins and then continuing the diagnosis on a daily, weekly, and term basis. First steps in diagnosis can involve the rather routine practice of studying the records which previous teachers have made on each child. At the first-grade level scores from reading readiness tests are usually available. Also of value in the appraisal of each pupil are measures of mental maturity. Often the most important contributions to first-grade teachers is the knowledge obtained from the written comments of kindergarten teachers concerning the observed over-all learning status and capacities of each child.

The next step in diagnosis involves careful and studious reaction to each child as first lessons are taught. When children find new concepts difficult to deal with in their reading, stumble over words taught in previous lessons, fail to isolate a simple main idea or detail, then the sensitive teacher is aware in general of the need for instructing the children in less difficult material. Sometimes children have specific problems which can be resolved by careful reteaching. Careful diagnosis during initial teaching is of the greatest importance. It is our contention that poor reading is actually encouraged when teachers instruct children on too difficult a level. Many reading specialists feel that if each child were taught on his instructional level, with this instructional level frequently reassessed, reading failures would be reduced substantially and children would enjoy reading.

While teachers can do a day-by-day diagnosis during actual teaching by listening to children read and connecting their written reactions to reading, it is also important that more elaborate periodic checks be made of progress. Certainly no book or reading level should be deemed mastered until a thorough check is made of vocabulary studied, word analysis skills learned, and comprehension of materials is assessed. This testing or evaluation is best done through informal tests which are based on the books read and the lessons taught.

For example, after a certain book is read, a check could be made of each child's recognition of every fifth new word in the book. A short test of the child's ability to actually apply newly learned word analysis skills can be made from the skills taught in the lesson. The recognition of the silent letters in vowel digraphs might be reviewed, or the ability to note differences between long and short vowels can be checked. If a new rule of syllabication has been taught, a check can be made of it in practice.

A more elaborate diagnosis can be made at the end of a term. The instruments used can consist of teacher-made tests based on actual materials read, informal inventories such as those described by Betts,[2] Dolch,[3] Harris,[4] and others. Formal inventories such as the Durrell Analysis of Reading Difficulty,[5] McKee's Phonetic Inventory,[6] and other tests of this type can be used. An even more formal assessment can be made by the use of standardized reading tests which, although limited in terms of the diagnosis of individuals, have certain values as gross gauges of progress.

DIAGNOSIS AN INDIVIDUAL TASK

Diagnosis is an individual task and reflects the fact that each child is different. To diagnose, the teacher must consider the individual child. This means that time must be set aside for

[2] Betts, Emmett A. *The American Adventure Series Handbook.* Chicago: Wheeler Publishing Co., 1956.
[3] Dolch, Edward A. "Testing Reading With a Book," *Elementary English,* XXVIII, No. 3 (March, 1951), 124–125.
[4] Harris, Albert J. *How to Increase Reading Ability,* 3d ed. New York: Longmans, Green, 1956.
[5] Durrell, Donald D. *Durrell Analysis of Reading Difficulty* (New Edition). Yonkers: World Book Co., 1955.
[6] McKee, Paul. *The McKee Inventory of Phonetic Skill.* Boston: Houghton, Mifflin.

diagnosis both during the daily lesson and at the end of such time periods as those suggested above. Informal reading inventories such as those suggested by Betts,[7] can be the most important diagnostic instruments in the classroom teacher's kit.

The informal inventory can be constructed by selecting passages from graded reading books which have not been read by children prior to the testing. Two selections of 100–150 words in length can be selected from each reader, or a selection can be written using the vocabulary of specific readers. One selection is used to test oral reading while the other is used as a measure of silent reading. Teachers note the kinds of errors children make while reading orally and use the errors as a guide for corrective instruction. Such errors as omissions, substitutions, reversals, repetitions, ignoring punctuation, incorrect phrasing are all noted during oral reading.

Comprehension of the materials read silently is measured through questions asked following the reading. These questions demand an understanding of the main idea, related details, the sequence of ideas, and the understanding of ideas not directly stated by the writer.

Teachers can receive from the suggested references some guidance in evaluating the level on which children read. However, the decision as to whether a child is frustrated by what he reads, is not challenged by the material, or needs instruction to read successfully is left up to the judgement of the teacher.

DIAGNOSIS MORE THAN READING ASSESSMENT

Diagnosis of reading status demands far more than an assessment of reading because reading problems are symptomatic of many causative factors. It is important that classroom teachers realize that many resources outside the classroom are needed for a complete assessment of children. Teachers need to know the nature of the reading problem if children are showing signs of distress during reading instruction. An

[7] Betts, Emmett A. *The American Adventure Series Handbook.* Chicago: Wheeler Publishing Co., 1956.

ability to classify readers as corrective or remedial, as differentiated from the normal or developmental, can be strengthened through reading.[8,9,10,11]

Kress[12] describes the child with a corrective problem as one who

> may be retarded in reading anywhere from a few months to several years below his expected grade level of achievement, as estimated by an individual intelligence test. For this child, the principal deterring factor, which inhibits progress in reading, is the inability of his classroom teacher to instruct the child on a level within his present range of word recognition and comprehension skills. The child's problem may involve inadequacies in experience background, concept development, word recognition, and/or word comprehension, but there is no basic neurological or psychological learning difficulty present.
>
> The remedial reader is quite a different type of learning problem. If the difficulty is identified early, the extent of retardation in reading may be no greater than that found in mild corrective problems. However, the child with a remedial problem, in addition to being faced with the same inhibiting factor as found in the corrective category, is handicapped by a basic neurological or psychological difficulty.
>
> A child in this category has an associative learning problem. When the usual teaching techniques are employed, the child cannot relate meaning from his own experience background to the symbols-words which he is trying to learn.

A teacher is well on his way to sophistication in diagnosis when he recognizes that a child has serious problems needing corrective or remedial treatment rather than a simple problem

[8] Betts, E. A. *Foundations of Reading Instruction.* New York: American Book Co., 1956.
[9] Harris, *How to Increase Reading Ability,* 3rd ed.
[10] Johnson, Marjorie S. "Factors Related to Disability in Reading," *The Journal of Experimental Education,* XXVI (Sept., 1957), 1–26.
[11] Stauffer, Russell G. "Reading Retardation and Associative Learning Disabilities," *Elementary English, 26* (March, 1949), 150–157.
[12] Kress, Roy A. "When Is Remedial Reading Essential?" *Education, 80* (May 1960), 540–544.

which would respond to more carefully presented developmental lessons. While the teacher might not know how to diagnose the more serious difficulties nor know how to treat them, he should be able to recognize when children have serious problems.

Classroom teachers can look to the school physician and psychologist to provide help in the diagnosis of general health and emotional status. A thorough diagnosis by experienced clinicians can also provide more clues of the child's intellectual and neurological status. The classroom teacher is not expected to perform the diagnostic functions of the physician, psychologist, or neurologist, but we can expect the teacher to be well enough acquainted with children to know when the severity of a reading problem warrants a more complex diagnosis than he can provide.

READING AND LANGUAGE ARTS

Because reading is but one aspect of language, teachers must understand the listening, speaking, and writing status of children to fully understand their reading abilities. The relationship among the various language arts must be thoroughly understood by teachers before they can fully appreciate the child's problem in reading. Corrective or remedial reading instruction is a questionable procedure when the basic problem of a child is his inability to listen adequately or speak our language with fluency.

It is probable that the isolated teaching and diagnosis of reading has been due to the emphasis upon reading instruction that has not taken into full consideration the place of reading in the development of language. Certainly a meager listening and speaking background will account for much of the difficulty children have in reading. An inability to write adequately is also related to a general language problem. Certainly an understanding of the structure of our language gained through both listening and reading will be reflected in the child's ability to write in a correct manner.

Teachers should make a special effort to assess the listening abilities of children. The assessment can be made through informal means, such as reading to children and then observing their reactions. If a child can re-tell or dramatize a story which has been read to him we can gain some appreciation of his ability to listen. The teacher might also give commands or directions and observe the child's ability to respond. A more formal assessment of listening ability can be obtained through the STEP Listening Test.[13] Early primary teachers have been provided many excellent measures of listening through lessons found in so-called readiness booklets.

It is of first importance that teachers of bilingual children, or children who come from deprived homes, study the listening ability of children to make sure that the words introduced in reading are part of the listening vocabulary.

Speaking ability can be determined through daily contact with children. However, a word of caution is in order here. It has been our experience that a few children often monopolize the speaking opportunities in a group or class. Records kept by teachers of the conversation of children in their classes frequently reveal that a relatively few children monopolize these discussions. An informal assessment of speaking ability has been devised by Sylvia Jones.[14] She has selected a series of colorful action-filled pictures of scenes with which most first-grade children are familiar. Mrs. Jones has given these pictures[15] to individual children and asked them to tell her about the pictures. The notes of what each child has said not only indicate the fluency of the children but the wide range of their concepts, vocabulary, and general understanding.

Informal tests of writing are also needed to round out the understanding of the general language skills of children. A knowledge of the listening, speaking, and writing ability of children will not only give teachers a better understanding of the reasons for reading disabilities, but will also serve

[13] *Cooperative Sequential Tests of Educational Progress, Listening.* Princeton: Cooperative Test Division, Educational Testing Service, 1957.
[14] Jones, Sylvia. "A Sampling of the Vocabulary of Fourteen First Grade Children" (Unpublished study), Syracuse University Reading Center.
[15] Durrell, *Durrell Analysis of Reading Difficulty*, 1955.

to focus attention on the fact that reading cannot be taught in isolation. Reading must be presented in a general language development setting.

LIMITATIONS OF DIAGNOSTIC TESTS

Because the instruments of diagnosis have not been perfected, the limitation of each instrument must be thoroughly understood. It is recommended that teachers study the tests they use to assess the status of children in order to become fully aware of uses and limitations of the tests. If a test has been reviewed in Buros' *Mental Measurement Yearbook*,[16] then it is helpful to read the critique of the test in this volume. The more sophisticated test expert often pinpoints limitations of tests and indicates strengths or weaknesses not always obvious to the teacher.

In using informal inventories in which comprehension is checked by rather simple questions of detail, it is interesting to discover how many questions children answer correctly without fully understanding the material.

The range of scores which can be obtained by giving two or three different reading or intelligence tests to the same child should also be noted.[17] Some teachers have discovered that certain formal reading tests have a limited ceiling and are not adequate as a measuring instrument for the more able children in a class. Teachers have found that other tests yield reading scores which might represent a grade placement one or two years higher than that on which children can read with understanding.

It is important that teachers become well acquainted with the formal and informal tests used in the assessment of children. The limitations of tests should be understood in terms of the children being tested. Teacher judgment also needs

---

[16] Buros, Oscar (ed.), *Fifth Mental Measurement Yearbook*. Highland Park, N.J.: The Gryphon Press, 1959.
[17] Sheldon, W. D., and Manolakes, George. "A Comparison of the Stanford-Binet, Revised Form L, and the California Test of Mental Maturity (S-Form)," *The Journal of Educational Psychology*, 45 (Dec., 1954), 499–504.

critical examination. If tests measure inadequately, it is the teacher who must detect the inadequacy, and it is the teacher who must provide a further measure of skill.

If children are to be properly taught they must be diagnosed accurately. Teachers can diagnose the reading status of their children to a limited degree by adhering to a few basic principles. When the limited diagnostic ability of teachers needs supplementing, then teachers must be well enough informed to call in the necessary help in order to obtain a more accurate estimate.

13

The Development of
a Diagnostic Instrument

RUTH GALLANT

There is no substitute for the observant and qualified classroom teacher in the handling of reading problems, both from
a preventive and a remedial standpoint. Such teachers, whose
sensitivity to all elements of the reading program is reinforced
by a working knowledge of diagnosis and remediation, are
essential to any effective plan for the reduction of reading disabilities.

That there will continue to be children who have problems in learning to read seems inevitable as long as differences
in children continue to exist. Developing the abilities of the
classroom teacher as a diagnostician and remedial teacher
offers no panacea—it could, however, become a major force
in reducing the quantity and scope of the disabled reader
problem. The advantage lies in the unlimited opportunity
which the classroom teacher has to observe day-by-day learning, to spot incipient problems, to administer the proverbial
ounce of prevention, or to distribute with regularity and
consistency the needed pound of cure.

What are the hard-core demands placed on classroom
teachers who attempt to identify and give special assistance to

REPRINTED with permission from *Indiana Reading Quarterly*, vol. A
(April 1968), pp. 25–31.

children with reading problems? They may be roughly cate-
gorized as three fold: (1) identification with a reasonable
degree of precision those basic skills which underlie the reading act and establishment of a tentative learning sequence;
(2) construction of tasks which are measures of competence
for each basic skill and administration of the measurement
device; and (3) selection of materials and procedures for use
by the learner in eliminating the identified areas of weakness.

Most teachers, having received as a part of their undergraduate education a sketchy overview of the total reading
process, focus on that portion of the reading skills continuum
which the basal reader series assigns to their classroom. Admittedly, teachers learn the "nuts and bolts" of teaching in
the classroom; for most of them this means that they know
the classroom procedures for teaching reading for one or two
grade levels, supported by some hazy notion of what is involved
at the other levels. Under these conditions, the attempts of
classroom teachers to help children falling outside the area of
their assigned grade level lack the clarity and precision needed.

The plight of the teacher is further complicated by the
kind of reading test data made available to her. Given the
usual school record of an achievement test score in reading,
the teacher knows, for example, that a fifth grade boy has a
grade equivalent score of 2.5 in reading on a standardized
test. She does not know precisely what it is that this fifth
grade pupil can do that enables him to score even at a second
grade level. And, equally as important she does not know
which tasks among the multiple ones involved in the total
reading act, he *cannot* do.

Concern with the problems facing the classroom teacher
who attempts to diagnose and remedy reading problems led
the investigators to serious consideration of ways in which the
classroom teacher could be helped to meet the hard-core demands. A logical starting point seemed to be the construction
of an instrument which would measure mastery of those
skills essential to progress in learning to read. This instrument would have built-in ease and efficiency of administration
and interpretation so that teachers could prepare themselves
in its use and it would tap the classroom teacher's knowledge
of a specific child as well as her opportunity to observe him

in many situations. It would differ from instruments currently available in its stress on teacher observation and judgment, its avoidance of grade equivalent labels except where labels would serve as guides in the selection of instructional materials, and its emphasis on ease and efficiency of use by the teacher in the classroom.

The balance of this article deals with the problems involved in constructing an instrument which would meet these criteria. In addition, certain principles applicable in the construction of any measurement device are presented.

FACTORS AFFECTING THE SCOPE OF THE INSTRUMENT

The original intent was to measure reading abilities over a series of increasingly more complex steps: these would range from identification of the letters of the alphabet to the use of critical reading skills at advanced elementary grade levels. But a pupil who can read factual (as opposed to story type) material at upper third grade reading difficulty level and retell it reasonably well reaches the ceiling of the present instrument. Why this drastic change between the intent of the investigator regarding the scope of the instrument and the completed instrument?

In working with groups of children whose range of reading problems covered the total continuum, a distinction between the processes involved in mastering the mechanics as opposed to those involved in the refinement and expansion of comprehension became evident. Falling into the first category were those children who had not learned a basic sight vocabulary nor internalized a workable system of word-attack and who could not, therefore, gain meaning from primary materials. Oral reading which reflected reasonable fluency and full grasp of the meaning of materials at approximately third grade level of difficulty became the criterion of success for this group. The ability to *comprehend* material of approximately third grade reading level when read silently became a second criterion.

Ability to read silently was taken as indicative of the learner's mastery of mechanics to the point of independent utilization of these skills. Silent reading comprehension served also as a measure of pupil concentration on the reading task and attention to meaning when the overt control exerted by the listener was removed.

Pupils falling into the second category, needing refinement and expansion of comprehension ability, were those who had mastered the mechanics of reading, who could read simple primary materials; but who could not handle the more complex language and concept load of advanced materials. Making this gross distinction among problem readers seemed to clarify the task of the teacher in working with either category of problem as well as providing more distinct guidelines for diagnosis and instruction.

On the basis of this view of reading problems, the decision was made to limit the test instrument to the measurement of the tasks involved in category one, development of the basic skills of reading. This was the first limitation placed upon the scope of the instrument.

A further limitation was that imposed by the user, the classroom teacher. Concern for the multiple demands placed upon the time and energy of elementary teachers precluded the use of a lengthy, detailed, wholly individualized instrument. Maximum return of useful information for minimum investment of teacher testing time was a decisive factor in the selection of and procedure set for each task. Ease of administration and interpretation were prime considerations also.

In summary, the scope of the instrument was affected by three factors: the function of the instrument, that is, pinpointing the learner's reading difficulties; the view of reading held by the investigators, that learning to read has two distinct problem categories, one being the mechanics of the process and the second being an expansion of comprehension; and the examiner-examinee population for which the instrument was intended.

SELECTION AND REFINEMENT OF TASKS

Measurement of the extent to which a learner had mastered the mechanics of reading was the primary function of the instrument. Attainment of this mastery required evidence in three areas: (1) basic sight vocabulary, (2) word-attack, (3) oral and silent reading. For each of these areas a criterion of success had to be set and a task or series of tasks devised to measure the progress of the reader in meeting the established criterion. A discussion of the criteria and rationale supporting the standards set by the criteria follows. Examination of the three criteria serves also to distinguish those factors affecting this phase of test construction.

Criterion for Area One, Sight Vocabulary

The learner gives evidence that he recognizes by sight the vocabulary common to basal reader materials, up to and including third grade reading difficulty level.

Third grade was selected as the cut-off point in that most materials designed for primary grades normally use a vocabulary common to the oral language of children of this age group. The investigators were agreed that the use of words as test items whose meaning and pronunciation were both unfamiliar would present, therefore, a problem more pertinent to the category of comprehension refinement and expansion than to mastery of the mechanics of reading.

Tasks which demanded quick recognition of familiar words in isolation were prepared. An order of difficulty for the words selected had to be established and the assignment of difficulty level had to be consistent with that used in the classroom. The basal reader is the main instructional tool used in the majority of the schools in the United States;[1] it follows then that in an instrument designed for use in these classrooms, the vocabulary items selected and the difficulty level assigned to them had to be based on current basal ma-

---

[1] Austin, Mary C. and Morrison, C. *The First R: The Harvard Report on Reading in Elementary Schools.* New York: Macmillan, 1963, p. 54.

terials. A research study by Stone and Bartschi[2] listed by grade level those words common to five of the most widely used basal series and proved an excellent resource. The list was used in the preparation of both the oral and silent reading tasks and the sight vocabulary task.

Criterion for Area Two, Word-Attack

The learner gives evidence of competence in handling the many sub-parts or components of word-analysis and utilizes a system of word attack which works for him.

The many skills comprising the complex interrelated process of word-attack had to be identified and a judgment made as to their relative value to the learner. There was danger here of enmeshing the examiner in a maze of data unless attention was focused on only the most essential of the many identifiable components. In addition, a means of summarizing the data was needed which would show, in readily accessible form, exactly what needed to be learned. The investigators therefore attempted to build into this portion of the instrument some direction in teaching-learning sequence.

Lists of word-attack skills and a suggested teaching sequence are available in most basal series. As a basis for the decision as to which skills to include in the instrument, the investigators relied heavily upon their own classroom and clinical experience with problem readers.

Several of the tasks appearing in the first trial edition were discarded as feedback accumulated from teachers and graduate students who were using the materials as part of a diagnostic battery in the reading clinic. In addition, Indianapolis schools returned test protocols used in their summer reading programs. Inspection of these data showed that some tasks failed to provide sufficient additional learning disability evidence to justify their inclusion. The classroom teachers further suggested that every valid means of cutting back on testing time be utilized, and pointed out sections which were

[2] Stone, David and Bartschi, Vilda. "A Basic Word List From Basal Readers." *Elementary English*, April, 1963, pp. 420–427.

particularly time-consuming. Acting upon the suggestions of these teachers, tasks judged essential were re-examined and where practical, designed to permit either small group or individual testing. Tasks which could be by-passed on the strengths of success in previous tasks were so marked.

In instructions to the teachers the purpose of each task was stressed. Teachers were urged to observe and record behavioral clues, to take the initiative for additional probing in areas where they found a need for more feedback or clarification of the pupil's level of mastery. They were encouraged to re-word directions, to use additional sample items in order to clarify directions, to expand a task to include new or repetitive test items, and to re-arrange test conditions so that the tension of formal testing was removed. (Undergraduate students using the instrument as part of a clinical tutorial program proved to be most ingenious in devising re-test materials of high interest appeal. Reduction of pupil tension under these conditions was immediately apparent.)

Criterion for Area Three, Oral and Silent Reading

The learner gives evidence of reasonable accuracy of comprehension in oral and silent reading of materials of third-grade or higher reading difficulty level.

The oral reading section consisted of seven paragraphs with a difficulty range of primer to third grade. As previously stated, the vocabulary was selected from a listing of words familiar to five of the most widely used basal series. Reading difficulty level was determined for each paragraph through application of the Spache Readability Formula.[3]

Directions to the examiner were that he continue with this task until the pupil reached the frustration level, the point at which errors were of such a quantity and number that meaning was lost or distorted. As a general rule, a cut-off point of five gross errors in one paragraph was selected as being indicative of frustration.

The decision to use seven brief paragraphs arranged in

[3] Spache, George. *Good Reading for Poor Readers*. Champaign, Illinois: Garrard Press, 1962, pp. 129–139.

a hierarchy of difficulty as a measure of oral reading ability was made in terms of the specific function of this portion of the instrument. The information gathered from this section on oral reading was not focused on determining pupil's reading achievement level. This instrument had far too limited a sampling of reading items to be a valid measure of achievement level. The function of the oral reading task was to provide a setting for the observation of the kinds and patterns of errors, the manner in which the reader handled an encounter with an unfamiliar word, and to provide an estimate of the degree to which mastery of the basic skills had been established.

The silent reading portion consisted of three paragraphs, written at third and beginning fourth grade difficulty levels. Directions stated that the silent reading task be used only if the pupil could read without difficulty the oral paragraphs at the second grade level. The decision of the investigators to include a section on silent reading but to limit it to this very narrow reading difficulty range was based again on their view of the reading process and the function of this portion of the instrument.

The purpose of the silent reading task was not to determine the pupil's level of achievement; the same limitation of inadequate sampling was applicable here also as it was in the oral reading task. The sole purpose of the silent reading task was to permit the examiner to observe the extent to which the pupil could utilize independently, without the overt controls which are imposed by the examiner in an oral reading situation, the mechanics of the reading process.

To ask a pupil to demonstrate this independence unless he gave evidence in oral reading of mastery of the basic skills seemed wasteful of examiner time. Exceptions would have to be made, of course, in instances where extreme tension or other disabilities were judged to be adversely affecting the pupil's performance in the oral reading. This was an example of the extent to which teacher observation and knowledge of children would largely determine proper and best use of the instrument.

The investigators made no attempt to measure silent reading ability beyond beginning fourth grade level since it would be doubtful if a pupil reading this well would have any difficulty with the mechanics of reading. Under these circumstances, the source of the pupil's reading problem, assuming that he had one, could not be identified by this instrument.

INSTRUCTIONAL PRACTICES AFFECTING TASK CONSTRUCTION

A re-examination of the discussion of the establishment of criteria and selection of tasks in the areas of sight vocabulary, word-attack, oral and silent reading shows that the same three general factors controlled this second round of decision making. The purpose of the instrument, the view of reading held by the two investigators, and the user population were overriding considerations. Distinguishing this second stage from the first were the pragmatic decisions made on the basis of current classroom instructional practices.

A clear-cut example of this refinement may be seen in the procedure used in selecting items for the basic sight vocabulary sub-test. While the investigators, in principle, might take the stand that the present restrictions on vocabulary in primary reading materials are unrealistic and unnecessary, they know that in practice these controls do exist. Basal reader materials are what classroom teachers have available and, in many situations, are required to use. Therefore, an evaluation instrument, the purpose of which is to guide the classroom teacher in her current teaching situation, must accommodate itself to this particular limitation or run the risk of being irrelevant.

A second example of a decision based on pragmatic as opposed to theoretical considerations is seen in the technique used to estimate reading difficulty level. The Spache formula utilizes two factors, sentence length and number of hard words. (Hard words are defined here as those not appearing on the Dale List of 769 Easy Words.) Complexity of sentence structure, familiarity of language patterns, and concept load are factors which also affect reading difficulty level. Their impact may, in fact, override the importance of sentence length and vocabulary, in that a very complex abstract idea, even though stated in simple terms and short sentences, still presents a difficult reading task. But measurement of these additional factors presents multiple unsolved problems. The investigators therefore chose to measure the more accessible elements of sentence length and vocabulary and to attempt to control the subtle, less measurable factors through editing and re-writing as the paragraphs were tried with children.

PREPARATION OF EXAMINER'S MANUAL

Emphasis on teacher observation and teacher judgment set the tone for the examiner's manual. The need for clear-cut forceful expression of this view, a view which expressed the underlying strategy of the whole instrument, was made apparent as each new group of examiner-users returned the test protocols. Teachers, accustomed to the formal procedures used in administering standardized achievement tests, were reluctant to make judgments, re-state directions, expand subtests, all of which involved decisions that the investigators believed could be done only by the examiner. It was the intent of the investigators to point up, through this instrument, the value of systematic observation of the reading skills, the need for teachers to look at learners, to listen, to probe and explore the when, how, and why of incorrect responses.

Another area which the manual deliberately left open for examiner judgment and decision-making was in the evaluation of the responses to the two comprehension questions which follow each oral reading paragraph. Suggested answers had to be deleted from the manual in order to focus examiner observations on individual pupil responses. Early trial editions had shown that given the "right answer," examiners failed to explore the near hits, much less the occasional wild irrelevancies in which lay clues to reading errors. No answer proved to be better guides than several alternative rights.

Summary record pages, designed to bring together all of the information from the several subtests or tasks, were repeatedly revised in an effort to sharpen the focus on the instructional needs of the pupil. Here again minimizing demands on teacher time was an essential concern. The summary record sheets had to be so organized that pertinent information was easily and quickly recorded, and equally as easily and efficiently interpreted by anyone working with the pupil.

SUMMARY

Attacking remedial problems in the classroom places demands on classroom teachers which can only be met by the majority of teachers when materials for diagnosis and remediation are placed at their fingertips. The construction of an instrument for reasonably easy identification of weaknesses in the mastery of the mechanics of reading was undertaken as a first step in this direction. A manual of recommended materials and procedures should follow.

Three factors governing decisions as to the scope of the instrument and the selection of tasks to be included were: the selected function of the proposed instrument; the theoretical view of reading held by the investigators; and the limitations imposed by the examiner-examinee population of users. Instructional practices currently dominating elementary classrooms had to be considered also if the instrument was to be of practical value to today's teachers.

Co-investigator in this project is Mrs. Isabel Craig, Associate Professor and Director of the Reading Clinic, Indiana University.

14

Reading Inventories
for Classroom Use

MARJORIE SEDDON JOHNSON

Good teaching is dependent on understanding of those to be taught. Planning for reading instruction is, therefore, impossible without thorough investigation of each pupil's present level of achievement and his specific strengths and weaknesses. The classroom teacher must make an evaluation, in all of these areas, of each pupil in his group. He can accomplish this task most efficiently through the use of informal inventories.

NATURE OF INFORMAL INVENTORIES

Standardized tests rate an individual's performance as compared to the performance of others. By contrast, an informal inventory appraises the individual's level of competence on a particular job without reference to what others do. It is designed to determine how well *he* can do the job. Materials of known difficulty are used to find out if he can or cannot read them adequately. Inventories can be administered on an individual or a group basis. For general classroom use the group inventory is most desirable, except for those pupils whose

REPRINTED with permission of Marjorie Seddon Johnson and the International Reading Association. "Reading Inventories for Classroom Use," in *The Reading Teacher*, vol. 14, no. 1 (September 1960), pp. 9–13.

status cannot be appraised adequately without a complete clinical inventory. For them, the evaluation may depend on an individual word recognition test and reading inventory.

In either case, the child reads material at known levels and responds to questions designed to measure his understanding of what he has read. When group procedures are used, material at one level only is usually employed for each test. When an individual inventory is administered, materials at successively higher levels are read until the pupil reaches the point at which he can no longer function adequately. In both cases specific abilities can be evaluated at the same time that information is obtained on the appropriate difficulty level of materials for independent reading, instruction, and listening activities. Getting all this information through group inventory techniques may require a number of sessions with reading at various levels. However, with either procedure the teacher has an opportunity to determine levels and needs in the only logical way—by seeing how the pupil functions in an actual reading situation.

PURPOSES

If instruction has the object of helping the child improve his performance, it must begin at his present functioning level. The first purpose of the inventory, therefore, is to find the correct level for instruction. Does the particular pupil need to begin work at primer, third reader, sixth level? Where is the point at which he has needs which require instructional help and at which he can profit from it?

Not all work which the child does should be dependent on instructional aid. He should have opportunities to apply the abilities he has acquired, to function under his own direction, and to practice so that he can develop a more facile performance. All of this must be done at a level where he can achieve virtual perfection without assistance. A second purpose of the inventory, then, is to determine the highest level at which the individual can read well on his own, his independent level.

Reading ability is not an entity, but rather a composite of a large number of specific abilities. Improvements in reading performance, therefore, can be brought about only as the individual gains greater grasp of needed abilities. Before plans can be made to help a pupil, the teacher must determine what causes him trouble, etc. A third purpose of the inventory is to get this information on each child's specific assets and liabilities in the total picture of his reading ability.

Many factors, in addition to the language and thinking abilities, influence the child's performance in reading. How well is he able to attend and concentrate? What does he expect to get from reading? How does he respond to ideas presented by others? How much background of information and experience does he have to bring to the reading? How efficiently does he use his background? A fourth purpose of the inventory is to find answers to these and other related questions.

PROCEDURES

For evaluating in group situations the first step is to make an estimate of the possible instructional level of each child. Many kinds of data can be gotten from cumulative records, former teachers, and observations of daily performance. From these sources comes the information on which the hypothesis about instructional levels is made. Perhaps in a sixth-grade class, for instance, a teacher decides tentatively that he may have one group ready for instruction at fourth level, another at fifth, a third at sixth, and a fourth somewhere above sixth. In addition, he feels that four of his pupils are quite far below the others in achievement, but is uncertain about definite levels.

He might proceed by selecting a good piece of reading material at sixth level and preparing himself thoroughly for using it as an inventory. This preparation would include all of the attention to vocabulary, word recognition problems, thinking abilities, etc., which would be given to a piece of material to be used for an instructional reading activity. When his preparation is complete, he is ready to begin the inventory for those whose instructional levels are approximately at sixth reader.

When this group is assembled for the inventory, the over-all plan for the activity will vary little from that for any good instructional reading activity. The differences lie in matters of emphasis. The objective is not to teach, but rather to find out if this material would be suitable for teaching. The basic question to be answered for each pupil is this: "Can he profit from instruction in this material?" Each phase of the reading activity, therefore, must be slanted toward evaluation. Actual teaching would be done only to see how well various individuals can respond to instruction given at this level. Thus any instruction given in the inventory situation is actually for purposes of further evaluation.

During the readiness or preparatory period of the group inventory the teacher may use a variety of techniques and materials. His objectives are the following: to evaluate the pupils' background of relevant experiences and their ability to use these experiences, to see how many relevant concepts they have at their disposal, to determine whether or not they have a grasp of the vocabulary used in this material to express essential concepts, to evaluate their ability to perform whatever thinking processes are involved in understanding the selection, and to determine the degree of interest they show. These same objectives guide the evaluation phase of an instructional directed reading activity. In both inventory and instructional activity these objectives will be achieved only if the teacher allows freedom for the pupils to reveal themselves —their interests, concepts, vocabulary, experiences, thinking abilities, attention, etc. As the teacher guides the activity he must not become the dispenser of information, the judge of ideas presented. He may stimulate group discussion through use of what he knows about the children's backgrounds, materials read previously, pictures accompanying the material to be read currently, concrete objects rich in stimulus value, or countless other things related to the chosen material.

In the inventory no attempt would be made to fill all the discovered gaps. For some of the pupils taking the inventory, deficiencies in experience, vocabulary, concepts, or thinking abilities, for instance, might be so severe that instruction in this material would be impossible. For them the essential question has already been answered—sixth reader is too high for instruction. Depending on the total classroom situation at the moment, they might be dropped from the reading inventory to go on with some other activity or continue in it even though no more evaluation of their performance at this level is necessary. If they continue, the teacher is obligated to see that it is not a frustrating experience for them and that their inability to function is not evident to all to a debilitating degree.

For those pupils who seem able to proceed with the material the preparatory phase would continue with some developmental work. Clarification or development of concepts, introduction of essential vocabulary, guidance in thinking processes, etc., might be undertaken. Students would be guided toward the establishment of purposes for reading. All this would be done to further the evaluation—to see how well they can profit from this help and apply it during the rest of the reading activity.

Once the preparation has been completed and purposes for reading established, the second phase of the activity begins. Pupils read the material silently to satisfy the purposes they set up. Now the teacher has an opportunity to observe their performance. Some may proceed with no difficulty—reading at an acceptable rate, reflecting their understanding in their expressions, stopping when they have achieved what they set out to do. Others may exhibit various symptoms of difficulty—frowning, lip movement, finger pointing, requesting frequent help, and many others. Some may take an inordinate amount of time as they struggle along. All the things the teacher sees and hears during this silent reading period will become part of the data on which he bases his final evaluation. If pupils want to ask questions, he will be available. From the questions they ask and the comments they make to him he may discover a great deal about the strengths and weaknesses in their performance.

When the silent reading has been completed, group discussion will focus on the purposes established for reading. Here the teacher will have an opportunity to discover how well various individuals satisfied these purposes. Rereading, both oral and silent, may occur spontaneously or be done on request. Appraisal can be made of oral reading performance, ability to locate information, ability to determine relevancy of ideas, etc. Questions other than those raised in the original purposes can be asked to allow for more nearly complete evaluation of each individual's understanding of the material and his handling of the word recognition problems.

By the time the preparatory phase, silent reading, discussion, and rereading have been completed, the teacher should have clear evidence of each child's ability or inability to profit from instruction at this level. About those who can function adequately with his instructional aid, he should have a great deal of additional information. He may have noted that one had difficulty getting meaning from a context clue expressed in an appositional phrase. Another may have needed help with handling the *ti* element in words like *partial*. A third may have had trouble with two vowels together when they are in two separate syllables. A fourth may have trouble with a sequence based on order of importance. In other words, the teacher may have discovered a great deal about the specific needs of these pupils he is going to instruct at sixth level. At the same time, he undoubtedly learned much on the positive side as he observed the things they were able to do well and the readiness they had for additional learnings.

About those who handled everything independently, spontaneously, and virtually perfectly at sixth level, the teacher may know only that he must check them at a higher level. He has not seen their needs because they are not evident at the independent level. About those for whom this material was much too difficult, he may know little more than that he must check them at a lower level. He could not appraise their skills and abilities because they were in so much trouble that they were unable to apply even those they had. Evaluation of specific needs would have to wait for the inventory at the instructional level.

During succeeding periods the same procedures would be followed with other groups and other materials. Those for whom sixth reader materials had been too difficult might become part of groups being checked at fourth or fifth. Those for whom sixth had been too easy might be checked at seventh or eighth. Even after all the group inventories are completed, additional information might be needed on some pupils. It would be to to these that individual inventories would be administered. This might well mean making special arrangements outside the classroom setting.

MATERIALS

For both group and individual inventories materials must be ones of known difficulty level. Each piece of material should be a meaningful unit, not a disjointed portion of a longer selection. It should offer the possibility of evaluating important skills and abilities. It should not be material with which the pupil is already familiar.

Many types of material can be used. Selections from basal readers, graded texts in the content areas, "news papers" designed for pupil use—all these and many others are among the choices. For the group inventory in the classroom one might well use selections from the very texts being considered for use. In this way a direct answer can be gotten to the immediate question—"Is *this book* suitable instruction material for *this child?*"

If a science teacher wants to determine his pupils' instructional levels for science work, he needs good science material for his inventory. The question, however, might be this: "What level should this child be using for his light, recreational reading?" In that case, the inventory should be done with story-type material. In other words, the material must be pertinent to the purpose for which the evaluation is being made.

SUMMARY

Reading needs can be diagnosed only through observation of reading performance. Instruction can be planned effectively only on the basis of such diagnostic study. Through group reading activities conducted with the stress on evaluation the good classroom teacher can determine appropriate levels for independent and instructional work. Having found the right level for instruction, he can appraise each child's strengths and weaknesses and plan to meet his needs. All this can be accomplished with classroom materials by any alert, sensitive teacher who knows his pupils, knows a reading program, and knows his materials for the informal inventory.

15

The Diagnostic Proficiency of Teachers of Reading

RICHARD W. BURNETT

Much of the public controversy in the field of reading has resulted from the extolling of one particular method of reading instruction above all others by advocates who are almost evangelistic in their zeal. Phonics has had its day of intensive publicity and currently, an individualized self-selection method is widely promoted as a panacea.

Reference to the more enduring and restrained authoritative works in the reading area discloses that one point of view has maintained a consistent position as an approach to reading instruction. That is the point of view which puts the teacher in the role of a classroom diagnostician who has command of various instructional methods and techniques which can be adapted to the peculiar learning problems presented by a class as a group and as individuals in a class. For a teacher to practice a diagnostic type of teaching as opposed to practicing an inflexible cookbook method of instruction, it is necessary to assume that he or she has the skills to carry on diagnostic problem solving.

More and more, as mounting research evidence seems to indicate that there is no one best way to teach reading to every individual, emphasis has been placed on making every teacher

REPRINTED with permission of Richard W. Burnett and the International Reading Association. "The Diagnostic Proficiency of Teachers of Reading," in *The Reading Teacher*, vol. 16, no. 4 (January 1963), pp. 229–34.

a "diagnostic" teacher. Bond and Tinker[1] state that diagnosis of reading problems is an essential part of classroom instruction. Sheldon, in *The Reading Teacher* for September 1960,[2] emphasizes that diagnosis is an essential aspect of teaching and a preliminary step to sound instruction. Harris[3] points out that the distinction between remedial teaching and classroom teaching has become less sharp because teachers have incorporated into their daily procedures the principles which are fundamental to good remedial work. In another treatment of diagnostic teaching procedures, Harris[4] describes diagnosis as a systematic exploration carried on by an individual who has the theoretical background and the practical experience to (1) know what questions to ask, (2) select procedures which supply the needed facts, (3) interpret the meaning of the findings correctly, and (4) comprehend the interrelationship of these facts and meanings so as to come out with a clear, correct, and useful understanding of the problem situation.

BACKGROUND OF THE STUDY

In an effort to develop an instrument to measure a teacher's skill in using diagnostic procedures, a diagnostic problem solving test in reading was conceived. The research strategy underlying the construction of such a test was based upon the work of Turner and Fattu,[5] in which it is proposed that the study of teacher problem solving proficiency provides a useful approach to creating instruments to assess classroom teaching

[1] Bond, Guy L., and Tinker, Miles A. *Reading Difficulties: Their Diagnosis and Correction.* New York: Appleton-Century-Crofts, 1957.
[2] Sheldon, William D. "Specific Principles Essential to Classroom Diagnosis," *The Reading Teacher,* 14 (1960), 2–8.
[3] Harris, Albert J. *How to Increase Reading Ability.* New York: Longmans, Green, 1961.
[4] Harris, Albert J. "Diagnosis and Correction of Reading Disabilities." In *Corrective Reading in Classrooms and Clinic,* pp. 80–87. Compiled and edited by Helen M. Robinson. Supplementary Education Monographs. Chicago: University of Chicago Press, 1953.
[5] Turner, Richard L., and Fattu, Nicholas A. *Skill in Teaching, A Reappraisal of the Concepts and Strategies in Teacher Effectiveness Research.* Bulletin of the School of Education. Bloomington: Indiana University, 1960.

skill. In order to study teacher problem solving behavior outside of the classroom, these authors say that it is necessary to construct problems, develop a way to assess performance on these problems, and show that the problems are useful for talking about the problem solving behavior of teachers. A value in this approach is that it is possible to compare how well teachers perform in relation to each other by presenting a controlled situation in which the problems are the same for every teacher.

The principal task was to construct a test which would be valid in terms of discriminating levels of proficiency at problem solving in the teaching of reading, and would as well hold some promise of providing insight into why individuals differ in proficiency.

The first step in establishing validity for the test rested on the conceptual framework underlying the problems. This framework required that the problems be similar in type to those met in a classroom, that the operations called for in solving the problems be similar to the operations undergone by the problem solver in an actual situation, and, finally, that the scoring criteria be logically defensible. A significantly high performance by a group of recognized experts in solving the problems would not be the basis for judging the correctness of solutions, but would support the conceptual validity. Showing that the instrument discriminated among groups who differed in training and experience at solving problems would be an additional support of the test's validity. Another validation factor would be to demonstrate that discriminations made by the instrument are made consistently and in line with other research findings.

DESCRIPTION OF THE INSTRUMENT

After examining tests used in the area of medical diagnosis and electronic troubleshooting, it seemed possible to design sets of problems to measure five levels of operation in the use of diagnostic procedures in reading. The first level problems call for the examinee to pick critical information from a pool of data. The second level problems require selecting a means of securing additional data. The third level requires the examinee to interpret the data with which he has been provided. At fourth level, recommendations for improving instruction must be made which are based on the information accumulated up to that point. Finally, at fifth level, all of the available data are supplied the examinee and he must re-evaluate his fourth level recommendations in the light of new information.

On the test, the examinee is called upon to rank four responses at each level in terms of how well they meet the specifications called for in the problem. For example, one set of directions calls for ranking four explanations of a child's reading problem on the basis of how well the explanations fit the information that has been presented. The response pattern is as follows: responses which make use of the most data, responses which use only part of the data, responses which over-generalize from the available information, and responses which are irrelevant and based on no supplied facts.

The test which was used in the research contained two sets of five problems, each set testing all five levels of operation. The two sets are based on the records of two children who had been reading clinic referrals. Both children, a third grade boy and a fifth grade girl, present problems not unlike those which any elementary teacher could normally expect to encounter in the classroom. The school records, recorded test data, and anecdotal records present data in much the same way they would be available to any classroom teacher.

A total score from zero to forty points was possible on the test. Choices were so weighted that to a considerable extent the total score reflects consistency in the way the examinee ranks his choices. An examinee who was unable to use data would tend to be inconsistent in his analysis of the problem situation from one level to another and would score low on the test. An examinee who tended to ignore the data and follow a method of teaching regardless of the information provided would also score low on the problems.

PROCEDURE

Three groups differing in training and experience were tested.

One group consisted of seventy-five students enrolled in undergraduate elementary education courses in a large state university. These students were tested before receiving any training or experience.

The second group was made up of ninety-three elementary teachers. The teachers were from grades one to six and represented an experience range from a few months to over thirty years. Thirty-nine were from school systems near or within a small city of under 25,000 population, while fifty-four were teaching in a large urban area of over 500,000. Nearly equal numbers of private and public college graduates were in the sample. Only teachers who held at least a bachelor's degree were included in the teacher group.

The third group included nineteen reading teachers, consultants and supervisors who met International Reading Association suggested specifications for certification as reading specialists.[6] These qualifications call for completion of a prescribed set of courses and/or five years of specific experience in the field of reading.

All three groups were given the research instrument. ACE test scores were available for thirty-one of the undergraduate students, and Co-op C2 level of reading comprehension scores were available for fifty-one of the students. Correlations were done of the scores on these two tests with the scores on the research instrument.

FINDINGS

It was found that the nineteen reading specialists significantly outscored the ninety-three experienced teachers. The teachers significantly outscored the seventy-five undergraduate students. As shown in the table, the mean differences were significant beyond the .01 and the .05 levels, respectively.

All variances compared in the study were tested for homogeneity by the F test and found to be homogeneous at the .01 level. All tests reported are two-tail tests.

Each of the two sets of problems was shown to result in mean score differences in the same direction, although not at

---

[6] Letson, Charles T. "IRA Membership Standards." *The Reading Teacher*, 13 (1959), 78–81.

Comparison of Scores for Undergraduate Students, Experienced Teachers with College Degrees, and Reading Specialists

Group	N	Mean	Variance*	t	Level of significance
Students	75	13.85	26.66		
				2.08	.05
Teachers	93	15.85	49.37		
				4.96	.01
Reading specialists	19	24.10	46.87		

* Single classification analysis of variance disclosed that significant variations do exist among the criterion groups ($F = 19.56$).

equal levels of significance among students, teachers, and reading specialists.

Reliability estimates based on a split-half technique using odd and even items resulted in a coefficient of .76 for the sample of experienced teachers and .84 for the reading specialist sample. A low reliability of .33 obtained for undergraduate students when contrasted with the higher coefficients, suggests that the instrument is of the proper difficulty level for teachers, but it is too difficult to result in consistent performance from undergraduate students.

The correlation between the ACE test scores and the scores on the diagnostic problem solving test was .02. The correlation between the Co-op C2 level of reading comprehension scores and the research instrument was also .02. Limited significance could be attached to these coefficients, however, because of the near chance level of performance on the research instrument for the student group providing the scores.

Within the teacher sample, exclusively primary or intermediate level teaching experience was not found to result in significant mean score differences on the problems. Teachers who taught in large city school systems were not shown to significantly outscore teachers in small city school systems. Teachers who were graduated from public teacher preparatory institutions when compared with teachers graduated from private institutions were found to make a higher mean score with the difference significant at the .05 level. Teaching experience beyond the third year was not shown to result in increased scores for either private or public college prepared teachers. Possession of a master's degree was not associated with significant performance gains for either private or public college graduates. Age was not found to be a significant variable.

Experienced teachers with private college undergraduate preparation were shown not to differ significantly in mean score from public college undergraduates. The performance difference in favor of those with public college undergraduate training was found to persist in the sample of reading specialists with a difference significant at the .01 level. The finding of a performance difference between public college prepared teachers and private college prepared teachers is consistent with findings in reported research on the problem solving proficiency of teachers in teaching arithmetic.[7]

IMPLICATIONS

This research was limited in that it sought only to explore the validity, reliability, and eventual utilization of tests of diagnostic problem solving proficiency in reading. Other instruments could well be modeled after this one. A revision of this test with alternate forms is already in the process of validation. The implications for subsequent utilization of such instruments, once they are refined and thoroughly validated, are numerous. A possible use envisioned for the test is as a device to assist in the screening of applicants for advanced course work in clinical methods in reading.

Broader uses of reading problem solving instruments present themselves as a result of the report of the 1961 Harvard-Carnegie reading study.[8] This report has served to focus attention on teacher preparation practices as the key to improving the quality of reading instruction in the nation's

[7] Turner, Richard L., and Fattu, Nicholas A. *Skill in Teaching, Assessed on the Criterion of Problem Solving.* Bulletin of the School of Education. Bloomington: Indiana University, 1961.

[8] Austin, Mary C., and others. *The Torch Lighters, Tomorrow's Teachers of Reading.* Cambridge: Harvard University Press, 1961.

schools. The recommendations in the report are concerned with the content of basic reading courses as well as areas of administration and instruction in the teacher preparatory program. One of the problems, however, in appraising the value of such large-scale research efforts as the Harvard-Carnegie study in improving the quality of teaching is that adequate and objective means of measuring teacher classroom behavior are unavailable. One of the strengths of a diagnostic problem solving test in reading is that it and similar tests could make possible controlled studies of the variables operating to produce better classroom teachers. Pretest and post-test studies of various student teaching practices, methods courses, and in-service training programs are waiting for the construction and validation of instruments which assess how teachers react when faced with problems peculiar to their profession.

16

The Effectiveness
of Various Procedures
in Reading Level Placement

JOHN EMERSON DANIEL

INTRODUCTION

The attempt, in the public schools, to more nearly meet the individual reading instructional needs of elementary school pupils through the division of classes into graded reading groups, has substantially contributed to the emergence of reading placement tests. The development of these tests has progressed, along with the burgeoning of the multi-group reading idea, in a variety of ways. They have been used as devices to measure achievement, intelligence, aptitude, personality, and quite probably other human characteristics. This study is not concerned with the validity of these many uses of reading tests, but only with their use as indicators of the instructional placement of the individual in classroom reading groups. As such, it has been the experience of the investigator that there is much confusion among teachers as to the application of the test results. The source of this confusion is about as varied as the number of individuals concerned and, consequently, the nature of this study has been limited to an investigation of several commonly used reading placement tests in an effort to

REPRINTED from *Elementary English*, Vol. 39 (October, 1962), pp. 590–600, "The Effectiveness of Various Procedures in Reading Level Placement" by John Emerson Daniel. Reprinted with the permission of the National Council of Teachers of English and John Emerson Daniel.

ascertain what the differences are among these tests in providing grade placement scores.

POPULATION

In order to achieve this goal, it was deemed necessary to take one established group of children and administer a battery of tests to them, thus allowing for an investigation of the several placement scores of each child on a relative basis. The group that was subsequently chosen was a third grade class of 18 girls and 17 boys, all of the white race living within the jurisdiction of the Nazareth Area Joint School System, a surburban community near Bethlehem, Pa. The class ranged in chronological age from seven years, eight months to nine years, four months with a mean age of eight years, two months. The mean mental age was nine years, one month, with a range of seven years, seven months to eleven years, nine months, according to the results of the *California Test of Mental Maturity*.

In October of 1960, a school official administered the *California Test of Mental Maturity, S-form,* 1957, to this class, from the results of which this final delimitation of the population was obtained. The class has a mean IQ of 111, with a range of scores from 91 to 138. A Chi-square test of the normality of the distribution of the class members indicated that the class did not approximate the normally expected distribution but was skewed slightly above the normal expectancy, i.e., $x^2 = 12.1$ p 1%.

GROUPING

Some of the problems of dividing this class into instructional reading groups are apparent thus far. However, as it happened, the second grade teacher made the recommendation to the third grade teacher, that she continue, at least initially, her grouping. The third grade teacher did this and had not changed the three groups up to the time of testing. Therefore, the situation is essentially that this class was divided into the same three reading groups for at least five months by two different teachers. It would appear at this point, that whether or not the teachers were right in their grouping they at least agreed upon the efficacy of their grouping. This fact points up the significance of teacher's grouping as it is related to this study. This investigation is not necessarily concerned with evaluating the teacher's grouping although inferences can be drawn from the results of the investigation. The question is concerned with how well the tests agree with the teacher in a more or less typical situation.

Not only the investigator but the teacher herself recognized that three groups for a class of thirty-five is totally inadequate for dealing with individual reading needs. However, because of a number of typical problems associated with having more groups, the time factor being primary, she reluctantly settled for three groups. In an effort to overcome the possible statistical effect of this functional misplacement of individuals, the teacher was asked to regroup her pupils as she thought they should be grouped for them to benefit from instruction in reading, irrespective of practical considerations.

TESTS

During a five day period in the month of December of 1960, the described population submitted themselves to the battery of tests selected for analysis. The first test administered was the *Gates Advanced Primary Reading Test for Grade 2 (second half) and Grade 3*. This test consists of two printed booklets which were handed out in sequence with the instructions being given orally. On the first booklet, *Word Recognition*, the student was asked to circle the one word out of four which went best with the picture. There were forty-eight pictures, each having four words beside it, and the words appeared to increase in difficulty. The second booklet, *Paragraph Reading*, consisted of a series of thirty-two directions that had to be completed in connection with the twenty-four associated pictures. The words in this part appeared to increase in difficulty and both parts were largely guided by the *Thorndike* lists. The first part was administered in the morning session and the second part was administered in the afternoon session.

Although there was a time limit on the tests, only one child did not finish well within the limit. Both parts of the test provided a grade placement score which, when averaged provided a grade placement score used for the purposes of this investigation.

The next test administered was the first part of the *Bucks County Reading Test*. This is a group test of selected words, organized on the basis of grade levels followed by a series of three or four words, one of which is opposite in meaning to the selected word. The students were given oral directions and asked to underline the word which was opposite in meaning to the first word on the line. The instructional level was established when the number of correct responses fell below 70% on two successive levels.

In order to save time and to avoid a repetitive interruption of the class routine, the second part of the *Bucks County Reading Test* was administered immediately prior to the administration of the *Informal Reading Inventory*. This testing was accomplished under ideal conditions in that a large closet, immediately adjacent to the classroom where the other testing had been performed, was utilized. This private situation provided a familiar surrounding, thus allowing for expediency in establishing rapport with each individual student.

This second part of the *Bucks County Reading Test* consisted of a graded series of twelve groups of words which the student was asked to read. The instructional level was established when the number of word recognition errors exceeded 30% on two successive levels. This latter score, when combined with the score on the word opposite test provided a single grade placement score.

Upon completion of the second part of the *Bucks County Reading Test*, the *Kilgallon Informal Reading Inventory, Form I* was administered to each individual child. This test consisted of a series of graded reading selections from Preprimer to Grade Nine, with each selection having from five to ten groups of questions dealing with the stories at each level. Each level has two such stories, with their corresponding questions, thereby providing for an analysis of both the oral and the silent reading skills. Although this test is commonly used as a diagnostic technique, providing the criteria for establishing four reading levels, capacity, independent, instruction, and frustration as well as allowing for diagnostic analysis, it was limited in this testing to determining only the instructional and the frustration levels. This was considered a necessity, not only because of the time element but because the other information would be superfluous to the nature of the study. These individual reading tests were administered by a trained clinician who was familiar with the test as it is described in the *Foundations of Reading Instruction* by Emmett A. Betts.

All of these tests, except the *Informal Reading Inventory,* provided a single grade placement score which included a fractional breakdown at each level. *The Informal Reading Inventory* criterion did not provide this fractional breakdown but only provided a single grade placement score. To provide this type of score, it is obvious that a fairly rigid scoring criterion would have to be applied to the test results. In an effort to determine if the application of a more liberal, range-type of criterion, providing a fractional breakdown, would make this a more finely discriminating instrument, the Modified * criterion, devised by Dr. Mazurkiewicz, was applied to the test results by Dr. Mazurkiewicz.

* The Modified Criterion

	Word recognition Acceptable range	*Comprehension* Acceptable range
Instructional level	90–97%	70–79%

STATISTICS

A number of statistical techniques were applied to the test scores and the complete interpretive results are listed in tabular form where each related problem is discussed.

The first technique employed was the Pearson Product moment method correlation. This was done to observe the relationships between the various tests. It is important to note that those correlation coefficients between test scores and reading groups are discussed separately. This differential treatment is predicated on the assumption that the Pearson method is ideally used in comparisons of individual test scores. It was felt, that, in spite of this, a unilateral comparison of these coefficients could provide some revelatory information.

The second technique employed was the analysis of variance. This was applied on the basis of three groups as well as on the basis of the five groups that the teacher had devised as her best estimate of instructional placement. The variance formulas were used to observe the discriminative powers of the tests.

The third technique employed was the comparison of the mean scores of each group on each test. This was done first on the basis of three groups and then later, on the basis of the five groups. This was done, primarily, to observe which test agreed most nearly with a three-group reading program. The comparison of the mean scores on the five-group basis was performed to observe the effect, an increase in reading groups has, on the ability of the procedures to place children for instructional purposes.

The fourth technique employed was the computation of the standard deviation, which was done to establish the degree of variability of the class performance.

The final technique computed was the "t" test of the significance of the difference of the means. This was done in order to ascertain the validity of the other statistical computations when applied to the individual.

RESULTS AND CONCLUSIONS

The results of the statistical analysis reveal a number of conclusions that are pertinent to the nature of this investigation. First, by observing the coefficients of correlation in Table I, it becomes apparent that the *Gates Test* and the *Bucks County Test* are more nearly alike than any of the other tests. Therefore, it may be inferred that the individual portion of the *Bucks County Reading Test* may lack grade placement significance because the test as a whole equates well with a group standardized test. In addition, the correlation between the two parts of this test, with a coefficient of .69, indicates that a substantial portion of the two parts is getting at the same thing. These factors raise a serious question concerning the necessity for the two parts since it would appear that for use as a screening device, one of the parts would perform the task

Table I The Coefficients of Correlation Between the Test Scores Showing the Relationships Between the Gates Advanced Primary Reading Test, the Bucks County Reading Test, and the Instruction, Frustration and Modified Instructional Criterion of the Informal Reading Inventory

	B^*	I^*	F^*	M^*
G^*	.81	.76	.77	.75
B^*		.69	.71	.70
I^*			.76	.95

* In order to facilitate structuring the tables, the following abbreviations are utilized here and throughout the remainder of the report.

G   Gates Advanced Primary Reading Tests
B   Bucks County Reading Test
I   Informal Reading Inventory, Instructional Level
F   Informal Reading Inventory, Frustration Level
M   Informal Reading Inventory, Modified Instructional Criterion

as well as both. In light of the other findings, it would be logical to assume that the word recognition portion of the *Bucks County Reading Test* could well be, that one part.

The moderately high correlation between the frustration and instruction levels of the *Informal Reading Inventory* is to be expected. Only if the correlation were low would there be a need for further analysis.

The exceptionally high correlation between the Modified criterion and the established criterion on the Informal Reading Inventory would suggest that there may be little value, in terms of instructional level placement, in adopting the Modified criterion.

Finally, it would appear from analysis of Table I, that any of the tests could be used as a reading level placement criterion.

Secondly, by observing the coefficients of correlation in Table II, it becomes apparent that the *Gates Advanced Primary Reading Test* has a slightly higher coefficient than the other tests. This would suggest that the Gates Test would agree with the actual groupings more nearly than any of the other

Table II The Coefficients of Correlation Between Test Scores and the Teacher's Reading Group Placement

	G	B	I	F	M
The Teacher's reading group placement	.63	.54	.61	.58	.54

Table III   The Analysis of Variance Between Test Scores Based on a Three Group Status

	G	B	I	F	M	1% Confidence level
Test F score	12.76	8.46	9.83	9.78	8.24	5.34

tests. Again it must be remembered that these correlations are between individual scores and groups.

Thirdly, by observing Table III, it becomes apparent that, although all of the procedures arrange the students in a sequence similar to the actual groups, the Gates test, being the most significant, is clearly the best of the procedures for such sorting.

Fourthly, by observing Table IV, which was computed on the basis of the five groups recommended by the teacher, it becomes obvious that as the groups increase in number, the Gates test and the *Informal Reading Inventory,* Instruction Level, increase their sorting abilities. It is also valuable to note that the *Bucks County Reading Test* and the *Informal Reading Inventory,* Frustration Level, lose some of their discriminative ability with an increase in the number of groups while the Modified criterion of the *Informal Reading Inventory* remains virtually unaffected by the number of groups.

Fifthly, by observing Tables V and VI, which are compilations of mean scores and standard deviation on the basis of three and five groups respectively, it becomes obvious that the Modified criterion on the *Informal Reading Inventory* more closely approximated the group levels than any of the other tests on both Tables. This fact, when coupled with the greater ability of the *Gates Test* to sort the children, leads to the conclusion that the *Gates Test* is not accurate in establishing instructional levels. However, further observation of the mean scores and standard deviation reveals that when the constant, 2.0, is subtracted from the *Gates Score,* the remaining figure

Table IV   The Analysis of Variance Between Test Scores Based on a Five Group Status

	G	B	I	F	M	1% Confidence level
Test F score	15.92	7.25	12.01	7.64	8.49	4.02

Table V   The Mean Scores and Standard Deviations of the Several
Procedures When Examined on a Three Group Status

Reading groups	G	SD*	B	SD	I	SD	F	SD	M	SD	G−2	SD
2.0	3.6	1.6	2.3	1.1	0.8	1.33	2.3	1.0	1.3	1.06	1.6	.55
2.5	4.7	2.3	3.6	1.3	1.9	1.1	4.0	2.0	2.5	1.17	2.7	.68
3.0	5.1	2.3	3.8	1.2	2.6	1.2	4.5	1.9	3.1	1.1	3.1	.89

* Standard Deviation

most nearly approximates the actual teacher grouping. This
would suggest that the *Gates Test* score, less the constant, is
the best guide for placing children in instructional groups.

With the results of Tables V and VI in mind, an analysis
of Tables VII and VIII will substantially reinforce the signifi-

Table VI   The Mean Scores and Standard Deviations of the Several
Procedures When Examined on a Five Group Status

Reading groups	G	SD*	B	SD	I	SD	F	SD	M	SD	G−2	SD
1.5	3.7	2.2	2.4	1.4	1.0	0.45	2.5	1.6	1.4	0.98	1.7	.47
2.0	3.8	1.8	2.5	1.1	0.7	1.4	2.5	1.7	1.4	0.9	1.8	.43
2.5	4.6	2.2	3.4	1.1	1.9	1.0	3.8	1.6	2.3	1.1	2.6	.63
3.0	5.6	2.5	5.0	2.0	2.5	0.71	5.0	2.0	3.8	0.79	3.6	.57
4.0	6.0	2.0	4.4	0.89	3.6	0.89	5.6	1.8	4.1	0.81	4.0	.54

* Standard Deviation

cance of the previous conclusions. The mean scores on the
Gates Advanced Primary Reading Test, less the constant, appear to be approximating the teacher's groups more than any

Table VII   The Results of the t Test of the Significance of the
Difference Between the Mean Scores of the Several Procedures
on a Three Group Status

				Significance levels	
Reading groups	M	G	G−2	1%	5%
2.0	3.472	12.9	3.7	2.262	3.25
2.5	0.1117	12.44	1.32	2.179	3.055
3.0	0.367	7.926	0.5185	2.201	3.106

Table VIII   The Results of the t Test of the Significance of the Difference Between the Mean Scores of the Several Procedures on a Five Group Status

Reading groups	M	G	$G-2$	Significance levels 1%	5%
1.5	0.66	9.9	0.8571	2.776	4.604
2.0	2.46	11.8	1.333	2.447	3.707
2.5	0.577	13.1	0.625	2.131	2.947
3.0	3.0	17.0	3.6	12.706	63.657
4.0	0.25	7.26	0.148	2.776	4.604

of the other test scores. Although this appears to be the case, the Modified criterion on the *Informal Reading Inventory* also approximates the teacher's grouping but to a lesser degree. It is important to note that on the basis of three reading groups, the lowest reading group reflects a significant difference between the means. This difference might suggest that the teacher's grouping has overrated the students at that level.

SUMMARY

This investigation was initiated to establish if one of several common devices used for reading level group placement was better suited for the task than some of the others. The results of this investigation reveal that, generally speaking, any of the instruments studied could be used as a grade placement criterion. However, in terms of the statistical analysis, the *Gates Advanced Primary Reading Test* consistently appears to agree more nearly with the teacher placement than any of the other tests when the constant, 2.0, is subtracted from the test scores. In addition to it being a group, standardized test, the fact that it is easy to administer and score and requires no training, unquestionably makes it the superior device for reading group placement. This is a rather severely limited view for the reading teacher in that the *Gates Test* provides very little diagnostic information.

Although diagnostic information is not a consideration of this study, it is a consideration of the teacher. As such, it cannot be divorced from the implications of the results of this study. Consequently, it can be said that the Modified criterion of the *Informal Reading Inventory* is an acceptable reading group placement criterion and has the advantage of providing diagnostic information. The only disadvantage is that it takes some training to administer and interpret. The *Gates Test* then is the best one to use as an initial grouping device and the Modified criterion on the *Informal Reading Inventory* is the best to use as a teaching aid.

For Further Reading

Barrett, Thomas C. "Visual Discrimination Tasks as Predictors of First Grade Reading Achievement," *Reading Teacher* 18 (January, 1965) : 276–82.

Belden, Bernard R., and Lee, Wayne D. "Readability of Biology Textbooks and the Reading Ability of Biology Students," *School Science and Mathematics* 61 (December, 1961) : 689–93.

Burnett, Richard W. "The Diagnostic Proficiency of Teachers of Reading," *Reading Teacher* 16 (January, 1963) : 229–34.

McCracken, Robert A. "Standardized Reading Tests and Informal Reading Inventories," *Education* 82 (February, 1962) : 366–69.

McDonald, Arthur S. "Research for a Classroom: Reading Potential: Appraisal or Prediction," *Journal of Reading* 8 (October, 1964) : 115–19.

Pond, Frederick L. "A Simplified Method for Scoring an Inventory of Reading Experiences," *Journal of Educational Research* 45 (April, 1952) : 585–97.

Preston, Ralph C. "The Reading Status of Children Classified by Teachers as Retarded Readers," *Elementary English* 30 (April, 1953) : 225–27.

Purcell, John W. "Poor Reading Habits: Their Rank Order," *Reading Teacher* 16 (March, 1963) : 353–58.

Sipay, Edward R. "A Comparison of Standardized Reading Scores and Functional Reading Levels," *Reading Teacher* 17 (January, 1964) : 265–68.

Spaights, Ernest. "Accuracy of Self-Estimation of Junior High School Students," *Journal of Educational Research* 58 (May–June, 1965) : 416–19.

Section Four

PROCEDURES AND PROBLEMS IN MEASURING SPECIFIC READING SKILLS

Almost every standardized reading test published today includes subtests to measure "specific" reading skills. The value of these subtests has frequently been questioned. Most test publishers caution classroom teachers not to place too much faith in the diagnostic validity of the subtest scores. Lennon pointed out, in an earlier article in this book, that researchers have discovered that the usual list of specific reading skills cannot be measured as distinct factors. Other reading and measurement authorities say that we need to look at reading performance from new and different perspectives and recommend that new subtests of reading, which will have diagnostic and educational validity, be developed.

Until new measurement approaches and tests are proven to be useful, the reading-test consumer should be especially aware of the shortcomings of present standardized reading tests as measures of specific reading skills. Traxler discusses some of these limitations in Article 17 and indicates what he feels are the diagnostic values of such tests.

In Article 18, Kingston discusses the measurement of comprehension and suggests that reading comprehension is not a unitary skill but is dependent on the reader's purpose for reading, the subject matter of the material, and the reader's personality structure. A new approach to the measurement of reading comprehension, the cloze procedure, is described in Article 19, by Rankin, who maintains that the cloze procedure is not only more valid but also more reliable for measuring reading comprehension than other approaches are.

The problems of measuring the strength of students' reading vocabulary beyond merely a superficial level are discussed in Article 20, by Dolch and Leeds, and in Article 21, by Kruglov. Dolch and Leeds describe their study of present reading vocabulary tests and analyze the levels of vocabulary strength measured by the tests. Kruglov reports a study in which she developed a vocabulary test designed to measure qualitative levels of students' vocabularies.

The problems of measuring reading rate separate from or in conjunction with reading comprehension are the topic of the next two articles. In Article 22, Rankin presents a review of the research on reading rate and comprehension. These studies cast considerable doubt on the usually accepted belief that fast readers are good readers. Article 23, by Humphrey, indicates that two procedures for measuring reading rates produce very similar results. The first method was to allow examinees to read an entire selection and then compute the rate of reading by determining how long it had taken them to read; the second was to allow examinees to read for only a specified time and then determine their reading rate by how far they had read in the given time.

The final study in this section, Article 24 by Bracken, is a practical guide for evaluating students' reading ability in content areas. Bracken contends that not only can distinct reading abilities be measured in each subject area but that this evaluation must be conducted if effective instruction is to take place.

These guiding questions may prove helpful in examining the dilemmas in measuring specific reading skills:

1. What is the goal of the measurement of specific reading skills?
2. How should subtest scores of standardized reading tests be used?

3. What information is not revealed by the usual tests of reading rate, vocabulary, and comprehension?
4. Why do reading subtests usually correlate at the same level with measures of different reading skills as they do with measures of the same reading skills?
5. How can more effective reading instruction be planned if standardized reading tests have little or no diagnostic validity?

17

Values and Limitations
of Standardized Reading Tests

ARTHUR E. TRAXLER

I am going to reverse the key words in the title and consider the limitations first and the values second. This reversal does not mean that I believe the limitations are more important than the values, but there are certain limitations which are inherent in the reading process and which logically ought to be considered first of all.

LIMITATIONS

The *first kind of limitation* is to be found in the nature of the reading act, and this limitation can never be entirely resolved. If reading were wholly, or even mainly, a mechanical process, as is implied in some theoretical discussions and some methods for the teaching of reading, then measurement would be comparatively simple. An observable manifestation of the mechanics of reading is found in eye movements, which are measurable and, in fact, have been measured precisely for many years.

REPRINTED from *Evaluation of Reading*, Supplementary Educational Monograph No. 88, "Values and Limitations of Standardized Reading Tests" by Arthur E. Traxler by permission of the University of Chicago Press and the author. Copyright, 1958, The University of Chicago Press.

But learning to read is much more than learning the mechanical aspects, as every teacher knows from experience and as Gates,[1] Gray,[2] and other reading specialists have frequently emphasized. Reading is a complex, unified, continuous activity which does not naturally fall into subdivisions or measurable units. In this respect, reading differs from other basic skills, such as arithmetic and spelling. You can take a problem in multiplication or a set of such problems, or you can take a list of spelling words representing, let us say, the *i-e e-i* rule, and study pupil's achievement on these in isolation. But reading is a process which flows past as you try to appraise it. You can arrest the flow to examine some aspect, but then it ceases to be reading.

Moreover, reading which is at all mature is an associative thinking process deep within the recesses of the mind. There is no way for an observer to be sure at a given moment whether a subject reading silently is gleaning facts or gathering main ideas or evaluating the writer or gaining esthetic satisfaction or, in fact, whether he is really putting his mind to the printed page at all. Much can be inferred about the person's ability by having him read aloud. An oral reading test is undoubtedly one of the best ways of appraising the reading ability of a pupil, but, since it must be administered individually, this kind of measure requires too much time for extensive use with large numbers of pupils.

Since, except for a superficial estimate of speed, no aspect of silent reading can be measured without interrupting the process, we customarily resort to a kind of addendum to the reading process itself. We ask a series of questions when the reading is finished and hope that the answers to those will indicate the quality of the comprehension which took place while the reading was being done. This isn't as good as we would like it to be, but it is about the best we can do, and,

---

[1] Arthur I. Gates, "Character and Purposes of the Yearbook," *Reading in the Elementary School,* Forty-eighth Yearbook of the National Society for the Study of Education, Part II (Chicago: University of Chicago Press, 1949), p. 3.
[2] William S. Gray, "Essential Objectives of Instruction in Reading," *Report of the National Committee on Reading,* Twenty-fourth Yearbook of the National Society for the Study of Education, Part I. (Bloomington, Ill.: Public School Publishing Co., 1925), p. 16.

as will be indicated later, this rather clumsy procedure does yield valuable information about reading comprehension.

Since we cannot measure reading "all of a piece" while the act is taking place, we usually have recourse to some artificial and presumably logical analyses of the process and then build our tests upon the elements into which reading was analyzed. These analyses are likely to be somewhat different, depending upon the predilections of the persons doing the analysis. A survey of twenty-eight published reading tests showed that attempts were being made to measure forty-nine different aspects of reading ability, although some of these differed little except in the names assigned to them by the test authors.[3]

Factor analysis is of some help in identifying the fundamental areas of reading which ought to be measured. For instance, Davis[4] carried on a factor analysis of the Cooperative Reading Comprehension Test some years ago and reported that most of the variance was accounted for by two factors—word knowledge and reasoning in reading. However, the components of reading logically identified by reading specialists may differ considerably from those based on statistical analysis.

There is considerable agreement among those who have constructed reading tests based upon logical analysis of the reading process that three broad aspects of reading on which information is needed are speed, vocabulary, and comprehension. But if these are accepted as the main components toward which measurement should be directed, a *second kind of limitation* arises because of the complex nature of the subdivisions.

For instance, the measurement of rate of reading is not the simple procedure it may at first seem to be. There is not just one rate of reading for an individual; there are innumerable rates depending upon the nature of the material and the purposes of the reader. The speed at which a good reader

[3] Arthur E. Traxler, "Critical Survey of Tests for Identifying Difficulties in Interpreting What Is Read," in William S. Gray (ed.), *Promoting Growth Toward Maturity in Interpreting What Is Read*, Supplementary Educational Monographs No. 74 (Chicago: University of Chicago Press, 1951), p. 196.

[4] Frederick B. Davis, "Fundamental Factors of Comprehension in Reading," *Psychometrika*, IX (September 1944), 185–97.

covers an exciting novel may be several times as fast as his rate of reading a research article in a professional journal. The more mature the reader, the more his speed will vary. If a rate score of three hundred words a minute is obtained for a pupil on a reading test, one cannot say that this is his normal reading rate; one can say only that this was his rate on the material used in the test and under the kind of motivation which the test provided.

Most individuals, however, maintain somewhat similar *relative* reading speeds in different reading situations. So a pupil's standard score or percentile rating is likely to be fairly stable from one reading test to another, provided the test is long enough to yield reliable results. In some reading tests an attempt is made to obtain a speed score in just one minute of reading time. This is much too short an interval. Three minutes of reading time is the minimum for a reliable rate score, and at least five minutes of reading time would be preferable.[5]

Similarly, the measurement of reading vocabulary is complicated by a number of variables. There is not only a general reading vocabulary; there are also vocabularies of special fields. An individual's standing within a norm group will be affected to some extent by the relative weight given in the vocabulary test to the different special fields. If a major proportion of the test words happen to come from the fields of mathematics and science, pupils with special reading facility in the humanities and social studies will be handicapped, and vice versa. Nevertheless, a reading vocabulary test which is carefully and scientifically prepared is one of the most reliable and valid of all tests for use in placing an individual in a norm group.

The anomalous nature of part scores on reading tests is nowhere more evident than it is in the case of reading comprehension tests. The kinds of questions used and the manner of responding to the questions differ widely. In some comprehension tests the subject may refer back to the reading material while answering the questions, whereas in others he must recall what he has read. Some comprehension tests con-

[5] Arthur E. Traxler, "The Relationship between the Length and the Reliability of a Test of Rate of Reading," *Journal of Educational Research* XXXII (September 1938), 1–2.

sist largely of factual questions, others stress main ideas, and still others attempt to measure critical thinking, inferences, or appreciation stimulated by the reading passage.

When the comprehension score is broken down into part scores, the variety of the scores may be inferred from the names of some of the parts. These include, among others, paragraph comprehension, main ideas, fact material, directed reading level of comprehension, general significance of passage, use of references, relevant and irrelevant statements, true and false deductions, and ability to perceive relationships.

Yet research indicates that attempts by testmakers to differentiate among various aspects of comprehension have not usually been very successful. The intercorrelations of the subscores, when corrected for attenuation, tend to be so high that they suggest that almost the same thing is measured by the different subtests.[6] This seems to be something closely akin to what Davis called reasoning in reading, or something very similar to that broad area of general intelligence which is measured by paper-and-pencil group tests of mental ability.

This brings us to a *third limitation of reading tests*— the lack of clear differentiation between measurement of reading comprehension and measurement of intelligence. In a sense, the better and more searching the reading test is, the greater this limitation becomes. It was pointed out earlier that reading, particularly high-level reading, is actually a form of thinking. But thinking is the process through which intelligence is manifested. So, when we give a reading test that really probes ability to think about the reading material, are we measuring reading or intelligence? The answer is that scores on this kind of test represent a composite of both intelligence and ability to read. Hence, it is very difficult to predict how much the scores of individuals who are low on such a test may be improved by teaching. For some individuals the possibilities of improvement are considerable; for others the main determiner of low reading comprehension scores is low

---

[6] Arthur E. Traxler, "A Study of the Van Wagenen–Dvorak Diagnostic Examination of Silent Reading Abilities," *1940 Fall Testing Program in Independent School and Supplementary Studies*, Educational Records Bulletin No. 31 (New York: Educational Records Bureau, 1941), pp. 33–41.

verbal intelligence, and the prognosis for significant improvement is not favorable. Teachers need to recognize this failure of even the best reading tests to differentiate between reading comprehension and intelligence and to be prepared to accept the fact that not every pupil with a low reading score is capable of much improvement. But it is almost impossible to predict in advance which pupils with low reading scores are capable of improvement and which ones are not, unless scores are also available on such measures as an individual intelligence test and a listening comprehension test.

A *fourth limitation of reading tests* is the time-consuming nature of the measurement of reading, particularly reading comprehension. Vocabulary test items can be done quickly, but reading comprehension tests are not efficient because of the necessity of covering both reading passages and questions based on them. It is not unusual for a reading test to require the reading of a paragraph of two hundred words or so in order for the pupil to be able to answer four or five questions. Since many schools demand tests which can be administered within forty minutes, the number of comprehension questions used is likely to be too small for high reliability. If attempts are made to subdivide the comprehension test into parts measuring different aspects of comprehension, as is true of some reading tests, and if the comprehension test, along with a vocabulary test and a speed test, is squeezed into a forty-minute period, one may expect the subtest scores to be almost valueless for the study of individuals, although of some use in the study of groups.

This limitation of reading tests can readily be removed if schools will agree to devote a period of two or three hours to the measurement of reading instead of forty minutes or less.

VALUES

Notwithstanding the limitations of standardized reading tests, it would be next to impossible to plan and carry on a modern reading program without them. They have a number of positive values for instruction in reading in all schools. Some of these were referred to in connection with the discussion of limitations.

Perhaps the *most important value* of a reading test, or any other standardized test, is that it lends a certain amount of definiteness to our thinking about the achievement of a pupil or a group. Without reading tests it is possible to say in a vague or general way "Here is a pupil who appears to be a good reader; here is another who doesn't read well; and here is another who doesn't seem able to read at all." But we cannot be very confident about our classification when it is done simply on a subjective basis.

Reading tests enable us to speak about reading ability in quantitative terms with considerable confidence, provided we keep in mind that every test score contains an error of measurement and that we recognize the unimportance of small differences in score.

A reading test may be given to a seventh-grade class, and then it is possible to say, "That pupil reads about as well as the average ninth grader; this pupil is approximately at the fifth-grade level in reading ability; and here is a very retarded pupil whose reading is still on the level of grade two." Moreover, if the test yields part scores, we can make such further quantitative statements as "In comparison with the norms for his grade, John has a rate of reading percentile of 96; a vocabulary percentile of 52; but a comprehension percentile of only 15."

These kinds of information lend definiteness and direction to the planning of reading instruction for both groups and individuals. They provide a reasonably firm basis for developmental, corrective, and remedial programs even though teachers need to remind themselves occasionally that the basis is not quite so solid and dependable as the bald, bold figures suggest, because of the limitations of reading tests already mentioned.

A *second value* of reading tests is for the appraisal of growth of individuals and groups in a developmental reading program. Is the total reading program of the school well designed to bring about normal or better growth of pupils at all grade levels and levels of ability? If not, where do the weaknesses exist? Such questions as these cannot be answered simply through the use of observation and teacher judgment. But if different forms of tests yielding comparable scores are used annually, and if the results are carefully studied, a constant check can be kept on the reading program as a whole and on the rate of reading growth of individual pupils.

A *third value* of reading tests lies in diagnosis of the strengths and weaknesses of groups and individuals as a starting point for corrective or remedial work. However, it should be kept in mind that reading tests are not in themselves diagnostic. They yield worthwhile information for diagnosis only when someone attempts to relate the results to other kinds of information about the pupil.

Still another value of reading tests lies in the early identification of gifted pupils. Nearly all gifted pupils read well, particularly in the field of their greatest ability and interest. Not infrequently, one of the first indications of unusually high mental ability is the tendency of a young child to begin reading on his own a year or two before he reaches the age of school entrance. When he enters school, his reading ability may be beyond the usual reading test designed for the lower primary grades, and a more difficult test may be needed in order to measure his actual achievement. It is desirable to supplement the school's regular testing program with reading tests appropriate to the ability level of very superior children so that suitable activities may be planned for them. Too often attempts to identify the gifted are delayed until the junior or senior high school level. This is frequently too late, for by that time many potentially outstanding children will have fallen into habits of an easy mediocrity in reading, as well as in other school activities.

VALUES AND LIMITATIONS OF DIFFERENT KINDS OF READING TESTS

Now I should like to comment briefly on the values and limitations of several types of reading tests.

One kind is that which yields only one total score. Forty or fifty years ago, when the first objective tests appeared, a number of reading tests were one-score tests, but tests of this kind almost disappeared from the scene until 1957, when the Sequential Tests of Educational Progress (Educational Testing Service, 1957), or STEP, were published. At each level, the reading test of this series is a seventy-minute test yielding only one over-all score. The STEP Reading Test is a most carefully constructed test, but it is difficult to see how it will be of much value in a reading program if used alone.

However, there is also in the STEP series a Listening Comprehension Test. It is believed that a listening test is one of the best measures of potential reading ability, although more research evidence is needed on this point. In any event, the STEP Listening Test and the STEP Reading Test, when used together, should furnish some information having broad diagnostic value.

At the other extreme, there is the kind of reading test in which an attempt is made to obtain within a class period a large number of part scores for purposes of diagnosis. This type of test is well illustrated by the Iowa Silent Reading Tests (World) and the California Reading Tests (California Test Bureau). Such tests, in which the time limits for the parts are very brief, either will have a large speed component in all scores, or the number of questions in each part will be so small that the scores will be low in reliability, or both. The total scores on these tests are often highly reliable, but it is more appropriate to use the part scores on tests of this kind for the study of groups than for individual diagnosis.

A third kind of reading test is aimed at the measurement of three aspects of reading believed to be especially important, such as rate, vocabulary, and power of comprehension. Fairly reliable measures of these aspects may be obtained within a class period, although the reliability of the comprehension score tends to be somewhat low.

In the primary grades the measurement of three or more aspects of reading ability within the same class period presents difficulties because of the short attention span of young children. Gates met this problem by having his Primary Reading Tests (Bureau of Publications, Teachers College) printed separately—one each for word recognition, sentence reading, and paragraph reading. The Gates tests continue to be among the most satisfactory reading tests at this level.

The most logical way of meeting the needs for a quickly administered survey test and dependable diagnostic scores would seem to be through a coordinated battery in which the survey test would be given first, to be followed by diagnostic tests appropriate to the weaknesses indicated on an individual or small-group basis. Thus far, the only tests of this kind are the Diagnostic Reading Tests (Committee on Diagnostic Reading Tests, Inc.). The committee has also undertaken to provide teaching materials for use in overcoming the weaknesses revealed by the diagnosis.

As already suggested, reading tests furnish only a portion of the information needed in carrying on a school reading evaluation program. So far as is possible, these tests should be used in conjunction with individual tests of mental ability, listening ability, achievement tests in the content areas, measures of interests, and inventories of personal qualities. Standardized reading tests have a limitation, in addition to those mentioned earlier, in that they furnish no direct information about interests or personality. As all teachers know, the sources of reading difficulty are not always to be found in the learning area; they often originate in the pupil's home, in his social group, in health and physical handicaps, or in his general adjustment to the environment of the school.

Reading-test scores reach their greatest meaning and usefulness when they fall into place in a comprehensive individual cumulative record.

18

The Measurement
of Reading Comprehension

ALBERT J. KINGSTON, JR.

In a previous report the writer discussed some of the
weaknesses of the standardized reading test from the viewpoint of reliability, validity, and usability.[1] Last year in an
excellent paper, Stroud explored the background of measurement in reading improvement.[2] The purpose of the present
paper is to examine critically, the fundamental assumptions
and methods employed to measure one of the most important
factors of reading ability—reading comprehension.

Almost all reading tests of the survey type presume to
yield a comprehension score from which certain generalizations
may be made. The validity of such generalizations is open to
question. Does a comprehension score yield information concerning a student's ability to understand materials with identi-

---

[1] Kingston, A. J. Cautions Regarding the Standardized Reading Test.
The Fourth Yearbook of The Southwest Reading Conference, Fort
Worth, Texas: Christian University Press, 1955, pp. 11–16.

[2] Stroud, J. B. Background of Measurement in Reading Improvement.
The Eighth Yearbook of The National Reading Conference, Fort Worth,
Texas: Christian University Press, pp. 77–88.

REPRINTED with permission of Albert J. Kingston, Jr., and the National
Reading Conference, Inc. "The Measurement of Reading Comprehension,"
in *Research of Evaluation in College Reading:* Ninth Yearbook of the
National Reading Conference, Oscar S. Causey and Emery P. Bleismer,
eds. (Fort Worth, Texas: Texas Christian University Press, 1960), pp.
88–93.

cal content or his ability to handle concepts of similar abstraction or basically indicate his skill in understanding language written at identical difficulty levels or phrased in similar fashion? Practically all standardized reading tests key the answer to these important questions. Typically the survey type of reading test measures reading comprehension by presenting a student with various types of reading materials which are read under timed conditions. The selected passages may or may not consist of a variety of subject areas and may or may not consist of various levels of difficulty. It is a rare test author who justifies his selection of materials on theoretical grounds. Generally, the pupil's comprehension of what he has read is checked by items of the multiple-choice type and the typical scoring formula provides for a compilation of scores. Usually no effort is made to determine whether an individual has previous knowledge of the subject discussed, is interested in or motivated by the subject, or is wise to the ways of reading tests or not. The set of previous experiences of the reader are assumed as being constant. Perhaps one important reason for the usual scoring methods is that by compiling the comprehension items the writer increases the length of the test and hence probably increases the statistical reliability of the instrument.

Most reading specialists have expressed dissatisfaction with reading survey tests. The concept of reading rate in relation to comprehension seems to have caused more concern than the methods of determining comprehension itself. The concern of the reading specialist grows out of a recognition that any test must constitute a valid and representative sample of the behavior being judged. Specialists long have been aware that there is a tenuous relationship between the tested skills and achievements and the day-to-day reading habits and skills of many students. It may be that some of us expect or demand too much of reading tests. All educational measurement is relative in the sense that tests furnish a common basis on which we can compare the behavior of two or more persons. Perhaps we are looking for tests which will do more than they can do—furnish merely one basis for comparison. Significant, positive correlations indicate that performances on reading tests are related to such characteristics as perception, personal-social adjustment, mental ability, language capacity, and numerous other factors. The nature of these relationships is interesting to speculate about. Are such relationships obtained because measures of reading are weighted with some unknown factor or are we dealing with a global factor which is an underlying component of personality? One reason why reading test authors have been able to ignore such questions is that the characteristics which correlate with reading test performance also function to assist the college student adjust to academic study, and also assist the adult worker to perform more successfully on the job. Other things being equal, the students and adult employees who are perceptive, best adjusted, brightest, and most verbal will tend to perform more satisfactorily in school or at work. The errors in reading measurement caused by a lack of refinement and theoretical basis tend to be constant and in the direction of apparent validity. Despite the recognition that most of the commonly employed reading tests do have some claims for validity, the concern of reading specialists for improved measures of reading comprehension is encouraging.

Measurement is dependent, in part, upon the careful delineation of the behavior to be measured. One of the problems in appraising reading ability is that we are still uncertain about its nature. We describe it as a complex rather than a simple skill, but then simply list the component parts. We ignore the process of integration. Measures of reading tend to have little or no relationship to either current personality theory or to current learning theory. The failure of test constructors to provide a theoretical framework for measuring reading comprehension may result from the failure of reading specialists to demand such developments. Test constructors tend to develop measures which meet the needs and demands of their users. As reading specialists, I feel that we must share the responsibility for the direction reading appraisal has taken. One example should be sufficient to establish this contention. The concept of reading rate as an independent factor in reading achievement is both spurious and illogical. Taken by itself reading rate is meaningless. The common belief that a person has merely one reading rate is one we strive to overcome in our reading improvement programs. We try to teach our students to adjust their reading rate to suit their needs and the nature of the material being read. Yet, we are content with an instrument which yields a single score based upon a limited reading selection. It is unlikely that a reading survey test would sell, however, if it failed to yield such a score. A number of other practical aspects of testing such as ease of administration and scoring, facility in interpretation can be cited which have resulted in limitations in test design and scope.

If the measurement of reading comprehension is to be improved, a somewhat different basis for appraisal must be established. Reading essentially is a form of communication in which a reader interacts with an author. As in all types of communication, the person receiving the message must attend to, take-in, respond to, and perhaps evaluate that which is communicated. Effective communication, therefore, depends upon such factors as the ability and willingness of the receiver to relate to the person communicating and his possession of a similar background so that he can utilize the knowledge, symbols, or concepts being transmitted in a manner like that of the communicator. He also must have had sufficient learnings and experience so that he is able to accept or reject the concepts and generalizations which the communicator makes. When the person receiving the message fails to respond because of different conceptualization of the verbal symbols, misinterpretation of language, or because of limitations in cognitive ability which prevent understanding, we conclude that there is no communication. In the case of communication in reading we say that the reader fails to comprehend. Reading comprehension, therefore, results from a constellation of many factors and the reading comprehension score actually reflects the total behavioral response of the organism to a complex process. It seems likely that the poor comprehension scores of many college students reflect intellectual and personality components as measured by global behavior to a greater degree than they reflect weak reading mechanics or appraise reading skills. Such a conclusion would account for the success of counseling-centered programs, for they function to alter the adjustive behavior of their clients, with a view to helping them to relate to other persons or become more flexible in their perceptions of the world.

If we can consider measures of reading comprehension as actually being measures of a student's ability to communicate, we are still faced with a problem of defining and refining that which is transmitted. If we ask an individual to look in the phonebook and find the telephone number for Mary Jones who lives on Locust Street—and if the student successfully accomplishes the task, he has demonstrated comprehension. When the new bride opens a cookbook and successfully follows the directions for making chocolate cake, she also demonstrates comprehension. The student of statistics who uses his textbook to organize and solve a probability problem also is comprehending. Each has communicated with a written source and satisfied a need. Are all types of behavior identical? Can success in each be predicted equally well from a single reading comprehension score? Obviously, the answer is no. Many who have examined the literature on college and adult reading programs are struck by the fact that the bulk of reports which describe various types of programs indicate that students made substantial gains in rate while little or no gains in comprehension were noted. A favorite phrase employed is "without significant loss of comprehension." Most of us have noted that we can alter the reading rate of students by providing them with different motivations. Are our difficulties in improving comprehension due to the fact that it is more fundamental to total personality organization, and hence, more difficult to alter or change? Or is reading comprehension so complicated by non-measurable factors that our tests lack precision for appraising changes? Perhaps our basic need is to re-define what we mean by comprehension skills in a different manner.

If we regard reading comprehension as a measure of the degree to which a communicator and a communicant are *en rapport,* a mere quantitative enumeration of the number of concepts acquired and the speed with which such stimuli are acquired might be considered a basis for measurement. Comprehension scores based upon measures obtained in this fashion have the advantage of being developed within a single theoretical framework. Generally, however, we feel that the mere recognition of stimuli encountered in a reading selection do not measure the higher mental processes we desire to evaluate. More often, we seek to evaluate the associative recall of the reader and some of our comprehension items are designed to measure the ideas elicited or indirectly related to the materials read. It is difficult to decide whether such measures are measures of reading comprehension or measures of cognition. It seems reasonable to assume that if we could develop instruments which would measure the speed with which a reader associates the concepts presented in a reading selection without involving other mental processes, we might obtain greater precision in testing. Such a test might be expected to have a somewhat lower correlation with the usual global type of intelligence test.

One of the real difficulties we face in measuring reading comprehension, however, is due to our failure to recognize that the reading process is communication that presumably implies some learning on the part of the reader. Implicit in our reading tests and in our assumptions concerning the reading process is the belief that through the communicative process certain changes occur in the behavior of the reader. Note how closely this belief resembles Hilgard's definition of learning. "Learning is the process by which an activity originates or is changed through reacting to an encountered situation, provided that the characteristics of the change in activity cannot be explained on the basis of native response tendencies, maturation, or temporary states of the organism" (e.g., fatigue, drugs, etc.).[3]

If we consider the reading act as a communicative process from which certain behavioral changes occur in the reader, we are dealing with a description of a learning situation. It may be that some of our confusion concerning the measurement of reading comprehension stems from our failure to relate its measurement to contemporary learning theory. Most of our measures have little or no theoretical basis but rather reflect both eclecticism and empiricism in design and content. Any item which yields a statistical coefficient which is reliable or valid is utilized. At present, we make no effort to determine what previous knowledge the reader brings to the situation. We ignore his personality components although we give lip

[3] Hilgard, E. R. *Theories of Learning*, New York City: Appleton-Century, 1956, p. 3.

service to his set and motivations. It seems to me that measures of reading comprehension developed within the theoretical framework of a behavioristic learning theory might have merit. Skinner's conditioning theory has the merit of being descriptive. His concept of respondents as responses elicited by known stimuli and his description of emitted responses or operants as related to prior stimuli might be employed as a basis for discriminating responses elicited by the reading process and those which are brought to the situation as a result of previous learning. A somewhat different approach might utilize the cloze procedure. A reading measure which combines the cloze test with more conventional passages might serve to furnish a basis for comparing the interaction of reader and writer with the degree of intake of the reader.

It is suggested that the concept of reading comprehension should be subject to careful re-examination and review. We cannot determine at present whether the positive correlations obtained between measures of comprehension and personality and intelligence are due to genuine relationships or impurities of measurement in each area. It is possible that a more behavioristic or descriptive definition of reading comprehension may be of assistance. Certainly, a closer rapprochement with current learning theory is desirable. Our empirically designed and developed reading tests may have outlived their usefulness. At best, such measures sacrifice many measurement techniques which might be experimented with for reasons of practicality or usability. It seems likely, however, that a number of roads for research are available for the research worker.

19

The Cloze Procedure—
Its Validity and Utility

EARL F. RANKIN, JR.

The cloze procedure is a recently developed technique for the construction of tests to measure the effectiveness of communication. This technique was introduced in 1953 by Wilson Taylor, who was at that time a graduate student at the University of Illinois. Although a few articles and papers on the cloze procedure have been published during the past five years, it is still relatively unknown among specialists in the field of reading. Indeed, it is little known in the general areas of psychology and education. The little use which has thus far been made of the cloze procedure in these professional areas is due, in part, to the inevitable "social lag" existing between publication of a new idea and the diffusion of this information among members of a given social group. Communication about the cloze procedure to specialists in reading has not been facilitated by the fact that written accounts of the technique have, for the most part, been limited to three unpublished doctoral dissertations, an armed forces technical memorandum, and several publications in the field of journalism. This is unfortunate, for the cloze procedure has tremendous potentiali-

REPRINTED with permission of Earl F. Rankin, Jr., and the National Reading Conference, Inc. "The Cloze Procedure—Its Validity and Utility," in *Starting and Improving College Reading Programs:* Eighth Yearbook of the National Reading Conference, Oscar S. Causey and William Eller, eds. (Fort Worth, Texas: Texas Christian University Press, 1959), pp. 131–44.

ties for practical use in the field of reading. It can be adapted
to the study of any communication component (i.e., writers,
messages, or readers), and cloze tests can easily be constructed
and scored by personnel who are neither experts on the subject matter of the test nor in the intricacies of test construction. (This last statement should not be construed as a reflection upon the degree of "expertness" of professionals in
the field of reading.) Thus far, the potentialities of the cloze
procedure as a research tool or as a technique for use in reading clinics or classrooms have scarcely begun to be realized.

In presenting this paper, it is not my intention to provide answers to many specific methodological questions which
would enable one to make effective use of the technique in
test construction. Instead, I shall present a summary of evidence concerning the empirical validity of the procedure as a
technique for measuring readability, intelligence, pre-reading
knowledge, and several components of reading comprehension.
In addition, I shall offer several suggestions concerning the
usefulness of the technique. Theoretical problems will be considered only in so far as they affect validity or utility. But
before attending to these matters, let me present a brief description of this technique which, I assume, is new to most
of you.

RATIONALE OF THE CLOZE PROCEDURE

The word "cloze" was coined by Taylor from the *Gestalt* concept of "clozure," a tendency for an organism to form a complete whole by filling in gaps in a structure. In constructing a
cloze test, a message is mutilated by deleting certain words
and substituting underlined blank spaces of constant length. A
person taking the test is instructed to guess the precise word
which was deleted from each space. If, for example, a person
taking the test finds the statement, "The professor assigned
a _____ of readings to his students," he may form a complete structure by writing the word "book" in the blank space.
Provided that the original message contained the word "book,"
the subject will receive credit for the correct answer only if

the exact word "book" is filled in. At this point you are no doubt thinking, "A structured whole could be formed by filling in the word 'selection' or 'group,' etc. Why does the respondent have to fill in the precise word that was deleted?" Before answering this question we must first consider the rationale underlying the use of the cloze procedure.

A "cloze unit," as defined by Taylor[1] is "any single occurrence of a successful attempt to reproduce accurately a part deleted from a 'message' (any language product) by deciding, from the context that remains, what the missing part should be." To the extent that the reader and the writer have similar backgrounds of experience, interests, language habits, etc., the reader should be able to make accurate predictions of words which have been deleted. In the words of Wilson and Carroll,[2]

> The underlying logic of the method is as follows: . . . If the encoder producing a message and the decoder receiving it happen to have highly similar semantic and grammatical habit systems, the decoder ought to be able to predict or anticipate what the encoder will produce at each moment with considerable accuracy. In other words, if both members of the communication act share common associations and common constructive tendencies, they should be able to anticipate each other's verbalizations.

Thus, the cloze procedure is an objective measure of language correspondence between reader and writer.

It may be inferred, however, that the ability to make correct word predictions of the precise words deleted in a cloze test is indicative of the respondent's grasp of "meaning" contained in the message. The ability to predict the precise word used by the writer is more indicative of the reader's understanding of the writer's total meaning (with all its se-

---

[1] Taylor, W. L., "Cloze Procedure": A New Tool for Measuring Readability, *Journalism Quarterly*, 1953, 30, 415–433.
[2] Wilson, K., and Carroll, J. B., Applications of Entropy Measures to Problems of Sequential Structure, Ch. 5, Psycholinguistics: A Survey of Theory and Research Problems, *Supplement to the Journal of Abnormal and Social Psychology*, 1954, 49, 103–112.

mantic and stylistic connotations) than the prediction of a synonym with similar, but never quite the same, connotations or the prediction of another word which merely produces a plausible sentence. Empirical evidence related to this point will be presented in a later section of this paper.

Since it is possible to study the correspondence in the language habits of the reader and the writer as a function of writer, message, or reader experimental variables, the cloze procedure can be used to study the communication process from several viewpoints. Thus far it has been used to study reliability[3,4,5,6] and information[7] (or lack of redundancy) of messages, knowledge,[8,9] comprehension,[10,11,12] and intelligence[13,14] of readers. It has not, thus far, been used to study writers as such.

[3] Sukeyori, Shiba, A Study of the Measurement of Readability; Application of the Cloze Procedure to the Japanese Language, *Japanese Journal of Psychology*, 1957, 28, 67–73.
[4] Taylor, W. L., "Cloze Procedure": A New Tool for Measuring Readability, *Journalism Quarterly*, 1953, 30, 415–433.
[5] ————. KM readers lend hand to science; "cloze" method works in written Korean and may serve as a tool for Korean language reform, *Korean Messenger*, 1954, 3, 4–5.
[6] ————, Language Rules, Usage, and Readability, *Technical Writing Review*, 1954, 1, 5–6.
[7] ————. Application of "cloze" and entropy measures to the study of contextual constraint in samples of continuous prose. Unpublished Ph.D. dissertation, University of Illinois, 1954.
[8] Rankin, Jr., E. F., An Evaluation of the Cloze Procedure as a Technique for Measuring Reading Comprehension, Unpublished Ph.D. dissertation, University of Michigan, 1957.
[9] Smith, D. E. P., Wood, R. L., and Carrigan, P., Manual for the SA-S Senior and Junior Scales, Bureau of Psychological Services, Ann Arbor: University of Michigan, 1957, 1–38.
[10] Jenkinson, M. E., Selected Processes and Difficulties in Reading Comprehension. Unpublished Ph.D. dissertation, University of Chicago, 1957.
[11] Rankin, Jr., E. F., An Evaluation of the Cloze Procedure as a Technique for Measuring Reading Comprehension, Unpublished Ph.D. dissertation, University of Michigan, 1957.
[12] ————. The Cloze Procedure: How it Predicts Comprehension and Intelligence of Military Personnel, *Technical Memorandum No. 13 to the United States Air Force*, Human Resources Research Institute, University of Illinois, Division of Communications, 1953, 1–22.
[13] Jenkinson, M. E., Selected Processes and Difficulties in Reading Comprehension, Unpublished Ph.D. dissertation, University of Chicago, 1957.
[14] ————. The Cloze Procedure: How it Predicts, *Technical Memorandum No. 13*, University of Ill., 1953, 1–22.

COMPARISON WITH SIMILAR TECHNIQUES

In constructing a cloze test, the words to be deleted are selected by a mechanical procedure such as leaving out every 5th or 10th word or by selecting words through use of a table of random numbers. Words may be deleted throughout the length of the entire article or deletions may be restricted to samples of lines from the total passage, provided that the line samples are chosen by some random or "every nth" procedure. According to the purposes of the test constructor, word deletions may be made without reference to the type of word selected or may be restricted to certain grammatical forms such as nouns and verbs. The only restriction is that the method used be mechanical and objective. The test is scored simply by counting the number of blanks correctly filled in.

In several respects, this technique is not unlike other techniques which have been in use for some time. One of the earliest attempts to construct an intelligence test was the Ebbinghaus Completion Test devised in 1897, in which a person's ability to fill in blanks in sentences was used as the criterion of intelligence. Teachers have long used incomplete sentences (for example, "France is on the continent of _____") to measure classroom achievement. Vocabulary context tests are commonly used to measure the ability to predict the meaning of an unknown word from a grasp of its contextual clues. The cloze procedure, however, should not be confused with these or similar techniques.

In sentence completion tests the words omitted are apt to be restricted to the ends of sentences and unrelated to other sentences. Furthermore, the words to be omitted are determined by the test constructor in terms of their specific meanings and the purpose of the test. In contrast, cloze units may occur at any point in a continuous message, are chosen mechanically, and are interrelated so that success or failure in predicting one word may influence subsequent success or failure in predicting other words.

Unlike vocabulary context tests in which the focus is upon the person's ability to guess the meaning of a word located in a sentence by using contextual clues immediately surrounding the word, the contextual clues in a cloze test may be far removed from a particular cloze unit. In addition, the cloze test presents no word structure clues, as does the vocabulary context.

VALIDITY

The Measurement of Readability

The measurement of the structural difficulty of a message is of considerable importance both to the practitioner and the researcher in the field of reading. Several formulae have been devised to measure readability. Perhaps the most commonly used techniques are the Flesch and Dale-Chall formulas. Both techniques are characterized by the counting of elements in a message. The Flesch technique counts syllables per word and the number of words in a sentence, and the Dale-Chall device counts the words per sentence and the number of words not found on a list of commonly used words. Both approaches are based upon the simple notion that messages with polysyllabic or unusual words and long sentences are more difficult to read than articles with short or common words arranged in short sentences. Both readability formulae can be fooled if a message contains short words which are highly abstract or unusual and/or short sentences written in a highly atypical style. In addition, neither formula is able to measure the reading difficulty of a message relative to a particular group of readers with particular backgrounds of experience or interests.

Although only a few studies have utilized the cloze procedure as a measure of readability it appears to be a valid measure which is not subject to the previously mentioned limitations of the Flesch and Dale-Chall formulae. It is based upon the assumption that the interaction of all semantical, grammatical, and stylistic characteristics of a message will affect the degree of redundancy (that is, the predictability) of a message. A highly redundant article should be easy to read because it contains many common words arranged in commonly used patterns or cliches so that the reader is, in large degree, aware of "what is coming next" at any point in the article. A cloze test may be considered as a sample of message redundancy, because it samples the reader's ability to predict "what word comes next" at randomly chosen points in the article. That it is a good measure of message redundancy is indicated by the correlation of −.87 which Taylor[15] obtained between cloze scores and a measure of "information" in a sample of continuous prose.

When both the Flesch and Dale-Chall readability formulae and the cloze procedure were applied to samples from the writings of James Boswell, Julian Huxley, and Henry James, Taylor[16] found the readability of the three passages to be rank ordered similarly by each technique. However, the superiority of the cloze procedure was demonstrated when articles were selected which could be reasonably evaluated by the cloze procedure and not by the readability formulae. Such materials consisted of an obviously difficult passage by Gertrude Stein with short common words and short sentences (rated easy by both formulae) and a difficult passage by James Joyce with short words and sentences but containing words not found in dictionaries (rated easy by the Flesch formula). Both of these passages were ranked as the most difficult by the cloze procedure. Within the limitations of this study based upon small samples of both materials and subjects, the cloze procedure appears to be a highly valid measure of readability. Other studies have indicated that it can also be applied to the measurement of readability of the Korean and Japanese languages.[17,18]

The Measurement of Intelligence

When cloze tests are constructed by deleting words without consideration of the type of word being deleted (hereafter to

[15] ————. Application of "cloze" and entropy measures to the study of contextual constraint in samples of continuous prose. Unpublished Ph.D. dissertation, University of Illinois, 1954.

[16] Taylor, W. L., "Cloze Procedure": A New Tool for Measuring Readability, *Journalism Quarterly*, 1953, 30, 415–433.

[17] Sukeyori, Shiba, A Study of the Measurement of Readability; Application of the Cloze Procedure to the Japanese Language, *Japanese Journal of Psychology*, 1957, 28, 67–73.

[18] ———— KM readers lend hand to science; "cloze" method works in written Korean and may serve as a tool for Korean language reform, *Korean Messenger*, 1954, 3, 4–5.

be referred to as the "any word" deletion system), a definite relationship is found between cloze test results and intelligence tests. Taylor[19] obtained correlations of approximately .73 between a cloze test based upon a technical article on the Air Force supply system and the Air Forces Qualification Test. Sub-test correlations ranged from .82 to .85 for Word-knowledge and from .70 to .76 for Arithmetical reasoning. In a study using high school students and literary type materials, Jenkinson[20] obtained a correlation of .69 between cloze scores and intelligence quotients. These obtained correlations compare favorably with the correlation between standardized reading tests and intelligence test results.

It should be noted that these results were obtained only when all types of words were deleted. Taylor[21] obtained lower correlations (.46–.59) with intelligence when he deleted only nouns, verbs, and adverbs, all of which were found to be the most difficult words to guess. The guessing of these difficult words, however, proved to be more closely related to knowledge of the content of the article than did the prediction of words without restriction as to type. This is important for it suggests the possibility of reducing the influence of intelligence upon the measurement of comprehension through the selection of types of words to be deleted.

The Measurement of Pre-reading Knowledge

To measure pre-reading knowledge of the content of an article, cloze tests may be administered prior to subjects reading the article upon which the cloze test is based. The validity criterion in such studies is a second test based upon the content of the same article as the cloze test. Using an "any word" deletion system, Taylor[22] obtained a correlation of .70 between a cloze

[19] ———. The Cloze Procedure: How it Predicts, *Tech. Memorandum No. 13*, University of Ill., 1953, 1–22.

[20] Jenkinson, M. E., Selected Processes and Difficulties in Reading Comprehension, Unpublished Ph.D. dissertation, University of Chicago, 1957.

[21] ———. The Cloze Procedure: How it Predicts Comprehension and Intelligence of Military Personnel, *Technical Memorandum No. 13 to the United States Air Force*, Human Resources Research Institute, University of Illinois, Division of Communications, 1953, 1–22.

[22] ———. The Cloze Procedure: How it Predicts, *Technical Memorandum No. 13 to the USAF.*, 1953, 1–22.

test based on the Air Force technical material and an objective test of the material. However, when he constructed a test deleting only nouns, verbs, and adverbs, his correlation was increased to .92. Rankin,[23] using a noun-verb deletion system, found a correlation of .59 between a cloze test based upon "science" material and an objective test covering the same article as the cloze test. Due to low test readability, this .59 correlation is an underestimation of the test's validity. When corrected for attenuation the "real" correlation was .86.[24]

It is quite possible for a test to be valid for a total group even though its validity may vary as a function of sub-group characteristics. A number of studies carried out by Smith and his colleagues at the University of Michigan[25,26] have pointed to a relationship between personality factors and reading comprehension. Smith et al. found the personality dimension "permeability," as measured by the SA-S Senior Scales, to be related both to degree of comprehension and to improvement in comprehension. Permeable individuals tend to be relatively flexible, disorganized, and extroverted, whereas impermeable personalities are relatively rigid, organized, and introverted. Rankin[27,28] hypothesized that individuals with above average level of permeability would display less consistency of test responses than impermeable individuals, both within a given test and between different tests. Thus, both test reliability and validity would vary as a function of permeability. These hypotheses were confirmed for the pre-reading cloze test. As a

[23] Rankin, Jr., E. F., An Evaluation of the Cloze Procedure, University of Michigan, 1957.

[24] Due to the low test reliability of the "noun-verb" deletion test forms used in Rankin's study, all obtained correlations are serious underestimations of relationships. Therefore, all subsequent references to these results will be given as attenuated correlations unless otherwise indicated.

[25] Smith, D. E. P., Wood, R. L., Downer, J. W., and Raygor, A. L., Reading Improvement as a Function of Student Personality and Teaching Method, *Journal of Educational Psychology*, 1956, 47, 47–59.

[26] Smith, D. E. P., Wood, R. L., and Carrigan, P., Manual for the SA-S Senior and Junior Scales, Bureau of Psychological Services, Ann Arbor: University of Michigan, 1957, 1–38.

[27] Rankin, Jr., E. F., An Evaluation of the Cloze Procedure, University of Michigan, 1957.

[28] ———. Cloze Test Validity as a Function of Reader Personality, University of Cincinnati, 1958. (Mimeographed)

measure of pre-reading knowledge, the test proved to be relatively unreliable (split-half reliability coefficient = .57) for permeable subjects and more reliable (split-half reliability coefficient = .73) for impermeable subjects. Also, the validity coefficient (uncorrected for attenuation) was only .38 for permeable subjects as compared to .71 for impermeable subjects (p«. 002 for the difference between coefficients).

It is interesting to note that when the cloze test was administered after reading the article upon which it was based, no differences in reliability and validity were found between permeable and impermeable personalities. This finding may be interpreted in terms of the need of permeable readers for structure in predicting the missing words in a cloze test. Permeable people are characterized by a relative lack of ability to organize ideas as compared to the less imaginative but more organized impermeable individuals. Before reading an article upon which a cloze test is based, the structure of the remaining context of a pre-reading cloze test is much less clear to the reader than it is after reading the article. Thus, the relatively disorganized person is at a disadvantage on the pre-reading cloze test and the highly organized person is able to capitalize on his major asset. After reading the article, the structure of the remaining context is not so nebulous, and the difference between validity coefficients for the two types of personality disappears.

Validity coefficients for total groups on pre-reading cloze tests are reasonably high. However, the pre-reading cloze test is not recommended for the study of individuals unless their level of permeability has been ascertained.

The Measurement of Reading Comprehension

The validity of cloze tests to measure reading comprehension will be considered from the standpoint of general and specific comprehension, the comprehension of facts versus relationships, and comprehension as process versus product.

General Versus Specific Comprehension   The cloze procedure can be used to construct tests for the purpose of measuring either general reading comprehension as measured by standardized reading tests or the specific comprehension of a particular article.

Two studies have been carried out on the measurement of general reading comprehension. Jenkinson[29] correlated cloze scores with results of the "vocabulary" and "level of comprehension" sub-tests of the *Cooperative English Test, C-2* and obtained correlations of .78 and .73, respectively. Rankin,[30] using the *Diagnostic Reading Test, Survey Section* as a criterion of general reading skill, obtained the following correlations (uncorrected for attenuation) with cloze scores: Story Comprehension .29, Vocabulary .68, and Paragraph Comprehension .60. All of the previously mentioned results, based upon the "any word" deletion system, show a substantial relationship between cloze test scores and results of standardized reading tests.

Even so, the cloze procedure produces tests which tend to measure specific comprehension of an article better than general comprehension. The highest correlation in Jenkinson's[31] study was .82 between cloze test results and objective questions based upon the same material as were the cloze tests. Rankin,[32] using a noun-verb deletion system obtained correlations ranging from .45 to .65 between the cloze test and the *Diagnostic Reading Test, Survey Section* sub-tests, but found a significantly stronger relationship ($r = .78$) between the cloze test and an objective test covering the same article.

Comprehension of Facts Versus Relationships   The type of comprehension measured by a cloze test is a function of the type of words selected for deletion. For example, if a statement reads, "The _____ was given the book," the structure of the sentence is quite clear even in the absence of the noun "professor." This being the case, filling in the correct word should reflect, primarily, the respondent's knowledge of

[29] Jenkinson, M. E., Selected Processes and Difficulties in Reading Comprehension, Unpublished Ph.D. dissertation, University of Chicago, 1957.
[30] Rankin, Jr., E. F., An Evaluation of the Cloze Procedure, University of Michigan, 1957.
[31] Jenkinson, M. E., Selected Processes and Difficulties, University of Chicago, 1957.
[32] Rankin, Jr., E. F., An Evaluation of the Cloze Procedure, University of Michigan, 1957.

the name of the agent receiving the book. On the other hand,
if the statement read, "The professor _____ given the book,"
the absence of the word "was" would remove the necessary
clue for the respondent's knowledge of the structural relation
between "professor" and "book" (since the insertion of "has"
would change the relationship). In this latter case, guessing the
correct word should reveal, primarily, the respondent's grasp
of relations between words or ideas in the sentence. These examples illustrate two aspects of meaning which may be
"tapped" by a cloze test. The first type of meaning refers to
the meaning of individual words as they might be defined in
a dictionary. Fries[33] calls this "lexical meaning" and differ-
entiates it from "structural meaning" which is signaled by a
system of morphological and syntactical clues apart from
words as vocabulary units. Although time does not permit a
thorough consideration of this point, it can be shown that if
one deletes nouns and verbs from a sentence, he will reduce
the total amount of lexical meaning in the sentence more than
the total amount of structural meaning. Therefore, a cloze
test from which only nouns and verbs have been deleted should
measure, primarily, "lexical comprehension" (that is, the comprehension of substantive content or relatively independent
ideas). Structural meaning, according to Fries, is signaled by
(a) individual "function words" which include such words as
verb auxiliaries, articles, prepositions, conjunctions, possessive
and relative pronouns, etc.; (2) syntactical or word order
clues; and (3) morphological clues such as verbal inflections.
Since a random (or "every nth") word deletion should sample
all of these clues to structural meaning and still leave many
nouns and verbs, which occur in great abundance, in the remaining context to signal lexical meaning, an "any word"
deletion form should reduce the total amount of structural
meaning more than the total amount of lexical meaning. Therefore, a cloze test so constructed should measure, primarily,
structural comprehension (that is, the comprehension of interrelationships between ideas).

To test the hypothesis, that a "noun-verb" form of the

---

[33] Fries, C. C., *The Structure of English*, New York: Harcourt, Brace &
World, 1952.

cloze test will measure lexical better than structural comprehensions and that an "any word" test will measure "structural" better than "lexical" comprehension, Rankin[34] used the Story Comprehension sub-test of the *Diagnostic Reading Test, Survey Section* as the criterion of "lexical comprehension" because the test questions are primarily factual. He used the Vocabulary and Paragraph Comprehension sub-tests as criteria of "structural comprehension" because the Vocabulary test measures ability to grasp abstract symbols embedded within a verbal context and the Paragraph Comprehension questions consist of such items as identifying the main idea, drawing inferences, etc. Results confirmed the hypotheses. The noun-verb test correlated .57 with Story Comprehension as contrasted with .42 and .39 with the Vocabulary and Paragraph Comprehension sub-tests ($p \ll .05$ for both comparisons). The "any word" form also correlated highly with intelligence. It may be inferred that intelligence is more closely related to structural comprehension than it is to lexical comprehension. Both of these two components of meaning are closely interrelated, and yet the cloze procedure may be used to emphasize the measurement of one or the other aspect of total meaning, depending upon the purposes of the test constructor.

Comprehension as Product Versus Process   The usual method of measuring reading comprehension is to measure the end product of the reading process by asking questions concerning the material after the reader has completed reading a passage. A cloze test may be used to measure comprehension as product by administering the cloze test based on a total passage (or some portion thereof) immediately after the reader has completed the passage. Taylor[35] reports a correlation of .80 between cloze test results and an immediate recall test, and, as was previously reported, Rankin[36] found a correlation of .78 in a similar comparison. Apparently cloze

---

[34] Rankin, Jr., E. F., An Evaluation of the Cloze Procedure, University of Michigan, 1957.
[35] ———. The Cloze Procedure: How it Predicts, University of Illinois, Division of Communications, 1953, 1–22.
[36] Rankin, Jr., E. F., An Evaluation of the Cloze Procedure, University of Michigan, 1957.

tests are valid measures of comprehension defined as post-reading comprehension.

Perhaps the greatest potential of this technique lies in its use for measuring reading comprehension as an on-going process. If two people make the same score on a test administered after reading an article, and one person knew more about the subject to begin with, the amount of learning is quite unequal between the two readers. If one wants to measure the amount learned through reading a passage, it is relatively easy to construct two cloze tests based upon samples of an article and to administer one test before and the other after reading the passage. Both Taylor[37] and Rankin[38] have obtained "gain" scores between pre- and post-reading cloze tests significant at the .001 level. Such measures do not confuse "post-reading knowledge" with reading as a learning process. Learning-gain scores serve to reduce the advantage held by individuals with an initially high level of information but who may or may not be superior readers. Unfortunately, the influence of personality upon the pre-cloze test performance limits the usefulness of this comparison. Also it is important to remember that unless the effects of regression upon gain scores is measured, the gain score may be the largest for those individuals with the lowest initial scores.

Another use of the cloze procedure to study reading as a process was made by Jenkinson[39] who selected high school students for individual interviews who had previously made very high and very low cloze test scores. During the interview, each subject took another cloze test and, while taking the test, verbalized his reasons for the insertion of words. The introspective and retrospective verbalization of these two groups were analyzed. The high-scoring students demonstrated significantly greater superiority in such characteristics as recognizing syntactical clues, sensitivity to style, fusion of separate meanings into ideas, recognition of implied mean-

---

[37] ————. The Cloze Procedure: How it Predicts, University of Illinois, Division of Communications, 1953, 1–22.
[38] Rankin, Jr., E. F., An Evaluation of the Cloze Procedure, University of Michigan, 1957.
[39] Jenkinson, M. E., Selected Processes and Difficulties in Reading Comprehension, University of Chicago, 1957.

ings, verbal flexibility, knowledge of word meanings and language structure. It is doubtful that the "catichistic method" (to use Jenkin's apt phrase) which equates "comprehension" with the ability to answer questions after reading could yield such insightful findings of the underlying factors involved in the process of reading.

UTILITY

The striking utility of the cloze procedure lies in the ease with which it can be used in test construction. This fact can best be appreciated if one compares the time and effort expended in writing a set of objective questions which have suitable reliability with the corresponding time and effort involved in simply deleting, say every 5th word in an article or some portion of the article. The need for careful selection of questions for an objective test and the problems involved in writing these questions demand considerable skill and training, whereas, different cloze tests can be easily constructed in quantity by clerical personnel.

Even though responses to cloze tests are written-in by persons taking them, they can be easily scored with a hand scoring key. Such scoring is very simple because it is strictly objective. The exact word that was deleted must be filled in. Taylor[40] has shown that the more laborious procedure of giving credit for synonyms does not yield a more discriminating measure of readability, and Rankin[41] found that test reliability and validity was not improved by synonym scoring.

Another feature of this technique which contributes to its general utility is that it can be used to construct equivalent test forms drawn from the same or similar materials. It is possible to construct multiple test forms with similar means and variances and high intercorrelations.[42]

[40] Taylor, W. L., "Cloze Procedure": *Journalism Quarterly*, 1953, 30, 415–433.
[41] Rankin, Jr., E. F., An Evaluation of the Cloze Procedure, University of Michigan, 1957.
[42] Rankin, Jr., E. F., An Evaluation of the Cloze Procedure, University of Michigan, 1957.

An apparent limitation upon the usefulness of this device is the influence of personality factors upon test performance. As was previously mentioned, reliability and validity of cloze tests administered before reading an article are low, for individuals with above average anxiety performed more poorly than other subjects on one out of four equivalent test forms[43]. If it turns out that cloze test results are peculiarly susceptible to influence by extraneous personality factors, this would certainly limit the usefulness of the technique. However, not a great deal is known about the interrelationships between personality factors and test performance on other types of tests. Subsequent research may indicate that test reliability and validity vary, in general, as a function of certain personality dimensions.

From the standpoint of the classroom teacher, the cloze procedure has many potential uses. The teacher could readily determine the readability of textbook material relative to the type of students in a given class. Both general comprehension skills and specific comprehension relative to particular subject matter material could be determined. Discrepancies between these two types of comprehension might provide suggestions for individualizing teaching techniques. The use of the pre-reading test as a test of information about a given subject could be used to assess readiness for the class as a whole, but not individual differences in readiness.

The remedial reading specialist will find many uses for this technique. The use of introspective reports combined with the cloze test (as used by Jenkinson[44]) appears to have considerable diagnostic value. By varying the type of words to be deleted, the reduction of the influence of intelligence upon reading test results might permit the evaluation of improvement over time which is masked by the relative constancy of intelligence. The use of several test forms from the same article should permit a more continuous assessment of progress for the class as a whole than can be attained through the usual before-after comparison. It seems quite likely that "cloze ex-

---

[43] *Ibid.*
[44] Jenkinson, M. E., Selected Processes and Difficulties in Reading Comprehension, University of Chicago, 1957.

ercises" might be of value in improving the use of context clues or vocabulary.

For the researcher, this technique will permit the study of the underlying process involved in reading. The use of "pre-post reading" gain scores may permit the study of reading as a learning process rather than a final product. The study of the interrelationships between "lexical" and "structural" comprehension might prove to be of practical as well as theoretical value.

Although the cloze procedure appears to be a valid and useful measure of readibility, intelligence, knowledge, and reading comprehension, only a few studies have been carried out to assess the validity and usefulness of the technique under varying conditions. Many problems need to be investigated such as its applicability to different types of materials and at various age levels and the size of the word deletion sample necessary to measure the readability or comprehension of a total article. It is only through a combination of theory building, research, and practical usage that the potentialities of the cloze procedure can be fully realized.

20

Vocabulary Tests
and Depth of Meaning

E. W. DOLCH AND DON LEEDS

How well do our existing vocabulary tests measure children's knowledge of word meaning? That was the question which started a study which has led to interesting results and conclusions, and that has raised still more questions about the measuring of children's word knowledge.

The first approach was to compare existing vocabulary tests. Five tests were studied, three by authorities in the field of reading, and two which are in nationally used batteries of achievement tests. The tests were the Thorndike, Gates, Durrell-Sullivan, Stanford, and Metropolitan. The words used in these tests were listed by parts of speech and close agreement was found as to the percentages of each of the parts of speech included.

A sampling was then made of a widely-used school dictionary, a sampling that equalled the total number of words used on all the vocabulary tests studied. A school dictionary was used instead of the large unabridged dictionary because, after all, vocabulary tests are intended for school and there should be some relation therefore between vocabulary tests and

REPRINTED from *The Journal of Educational Research*, vol. 40 (November 1953), pp. 181–89, "Vocabulary Tests and Depth of Meaning" by E. W. Dolch and Don Leeds. Reprinted with the permission of the *Journal of Educational Research* and the authors.

a dictionary used by children. The words of the sampling were then listed by parts of speech using as the part of speech for each word the one given first by the dictionary, and the percentages compared with the percentages of the total of the vocabulary test list. Results appear on Table 1.

Table 1   Comparison of Percentages of Parts of Speech on Dictionary Sampling and Vocabulary Test List

	N	*V*	*Adj.*	*Adv.*	*Prep.*	*Interj.*
Dictionary	58.83	15.08	21.98	3.87	.21	—
Vocabulary Tests	45.64	29.52	21.72	3.03	.002	.001

Different-sized dictionaries, made according to different policies, might have given different results.

The table shows not too great a difference between the vocabulary test list and the dictionary sampling. The greater weight given by the tests to verbs might have been caused by the fact that very often a word may be used both as a noun and as a verb, and the tests might have given preference at times to the verb meaning because it was easier to make a test item for it. For instance on one vocabulary test appeared the words *feast* and *annex*. At first glance these would seem to be nouns but it would be hard to make a short definition of them as nouns. Instead the test defined them as verbs and used as synonyms the verbs "to eat" and "to add." At any rate, the vocabulary tests agree rather well with a sampling of a single dictionary.

But the dictionary gives many meanings of words, and not just one meaning as given by a vocabulary test. How were the tests related to the dictionary on this point? Each one of the 770 words contained in all the vocabulary tests was looked up in the dictionary. It was found that, in general, the vocabulary tests used as the "right" answer, the first definition given in the dictionary. This particular dictionary follows the practice of giving first what the makers considered to be the "most common meaning" of the word, in contrast with some dictionaries which give first the original or historically first meaning of the word. Our conclusion must be, therefore, that in general the standard vocabulary tests are measuring a sampling of the school dictionary, especially the most common meaning of each word tested.

What about the further meanings given by the dictionary? Apparently the standard vocabulary test can help us very little with them. These further meanings are of at least three kinds.

1. *Same spellings from different roots.* In the dictionary we find many cases where the same spellings come from different roots and therefore have quite different meanings. For instance, there are three different words all spelled "box." One word means a container, the second word means to strike with the open hand, and the third word means a small tree used in gardens. The dictionary shows these as separate entries, with small serial numbers beside them. Of the dictionary sampling we took, 6.2% of the words had other words of this type, with the same spelling but with different meaning. Naturally, these "same spelling" words cannot be fully tested by the usual vocabulary test. The school considers them in the language course under the study of homonyms.

2. *Derived meanings.* Many words in the dictionary have, in addition to the most common meaning, other meanings which are derived from it through analogy or through application to various special fields of use. In the case of one of the words spelled "box," one meaning is "the amount of box can hold," as "he can eat a whole box of candy." This meaning is derived from the size of the box or container. The meaning "to box an article for shipment" comes from the action connected with the idea of a box. The meanings "a driver's seat on a coach, a theatre box, a sentry box" are derived from a similarity to the form of a box. There are endless methods of deriving meanings from the fundamental or basic or first meaning. Vocabulary tests have so far not entered this field of derived meanings.

3. *Figurative meanings.* There are endless figurative meanings also for most words. We often say, "I was certainly in a box" when we really mean "predicament" but use the figure of "box" instead. Some of these meanings are given in the dictionary and some are not. The larger the dictionary, the more of them are given. But no dictionary can include all the possible figurative meanings that writers may think of for

words. Naturally, the vocabulary test does not include figurative meanings.

To summarize, we found that the vocabulary tests almost universally used only the first or most common definition of a word, *leaving out,* (1) homonyms, (2) derived meanings, and (3) figurative meanings.

But did the standard vocabulary tests actually measure this first or most common meaning? The next step in the study was to try to answer this question.

DEPTH OR DEGREE OF MEANING

The homonyms, derived meanings, and figurative meanings just mentioned may be thought of as degrees of meaning beyond the most common meaning. But the most common meaning has also degrees of meaning, or different depths of meaning. Our question is, how well do vocabulary tests measure depth in the case of this most common meaning? To try to answer this question, an intensive study was made of the way one of the vocabulary tests tried to test word meaning. This test was chosen because of its wide use and general excellence.

This test used two devices to measure word meaning: (1) synonyms and (2) the classification or part-whole method. Let us look first at the classification method as it was used with nouns. The meaning of 18 nouns was measured as follows:

Meaning of Nouns by the Classification Method

Test word	Tested by marking the class	Test word	Tested by marking the class
red	color	murderer	killer
rabbit	animal	dome	roof
mother	woman	portal	door
cow	animal	mane	hair
orange	fruit	pew	seat
shower	rain	dahlia	flower
pole	stick	desertion	leaving a position
lane	path	spinster	woman
colonel	officer	insignia	badge

(Two nouns were tested by this method in reverse. That is, the words were *vehicle* and *projectile,* which are classes of things, and they were tested by marking one thing in each class, i.e. carriage and bullet.)

In the case of these nouns, for one to know the class to which each belongs may be a first degree or minimum meaning. It would help in reading, especially if the context aided. But one who knew only this first degree of meaning would have a very vague idea of the word and could not use it very well in either speaking or thinking. Suppose all one knows about an orange is that it is "some kind of a fruit" or all the meaning one has for colonel is "some kind of officer." He could not think intelligently about either. So this method of testing the minimum meaning is useful to some degree for reading but not for other language use.

DEPTH OF MEANING BY THE SYNONYM METHOD

By far the commonest method of testing word meaning on this standard test was by synonyms. In fact synonyms were used 76% of the time in the entire test. The problem of testing meaning by synonyms is well known in the definition of synonyms given in the *New International Dictionary* as follows: "Synonyms are words which express what is essentially the same idea but which (commonly) differ from one another, (1) in some shade of meaning, (2) in emphasis or (esp.), (3) in their connotations." The synonyms given by the test for 14 nouns are on the next page.

Does the checking of a synonym tell that one knows the meaning of a word? First, we have to assume that the testee knows the meaning of the synonym and has not just heard the two words together so that he merely associates them in some way. If the testee does know the meaning of the synonym, he at least knows the degree or depth of meaning carried by that synonym. To know what that meaning is would require still further testing. If the meaning the testee has for the synonym is slight the meaning of the word is just as slight.

Second, does the testee know the difference between the

Meaning of Nouns by the Synonym Method

Test word	*Synonym given as the meaning*
disaster	ruin
gap	opening
splendor	glory
bravery	courage
strife	fighting
comment	remark
flaw	fault
malady	sickness
symptom	sign
avalanche	landslide
carousal	revel
lethargy	apathy
animation	liveliness
buoyancy	lightness

meaning of the synonym and the meaning of the test word? The vocabulary test obviously cannot answer that question.

For the other parts of speech on the test, the method was in all cases synonyms. As the problems with them are the same as with the problem of synonyms of nouns we shall not present the results here because of lack of space.

TESTING OF FURTHER DEPTH OF MEANING

Having seen that vocabulary tests attempt to test merely the commonest meaning of a word, and test that either by giving a classification or a synonym, we were interested to know if students who had gone through our school system knew more than just this minimum meaning or synonym meaning of these words. Could we test further meaning of the words?

To attempt to test "further depth of meaning" we constructed a test based upon the standard vocabulary test just referred to. Our Depth of Meaning test *gave* the testee, in each instance, the information that the standard test required and then asked for more meaning.

For instance the following items are typical:

Classification Method

Standard test	Depth of meaning test
A cow is	A cow is an animal that
animal	a. is found in zoos
shy	b. is used for racing
red	c. gives milk
fish	d. does not have calves
coat	
A colonel is	A colonel is an officer who commands
officer	a. a battleship
medicine	b. a police department
harness	c. a regiment of soldiers
poetry	d. a company of soldiers
disease	

Synonym Method

Disaster is	A disaster is ruin that happens
find	a. suddenly
shot	b. within a year's time
ruin	c. to all people
fence	d. gradually
object	
Lethargy is	Lethargy means apathy but refers more to
apathy	a. the body than the feelings
wild animal	b. men than to women
debt	c. sleep than to waking
liveliness	d. the soul than to the body

As will be noted from the examples, the Depth of Meaning Test in each case admitted possession of the knowledge asked for by the Standard vocabulary test, and then asked for some difference from others in the same classification. In the case of synonyms, it asked for the difference between the synonyms. The difference required as correct was that given in the *New International Dictionary,* both in the definitions of the two words and in the paragraphs explaining the differences between synonyms.

The Depth of Meaning Test was given to groups of college freshmen, college seniors and teachers in service. Since this study is merely exploratory, it will be sufficient to give the general results and we will do this only for the nouns, since the verbs and adjectives gave about the same result.

RESULTS OF DEPTH OF MEANING TEST

For most of the nouns which the standard test measured by classification, the adults had learned also the further meaning required by the depth of meaning test. On some of the words, however, they definitely had not. In this group, the percentage of adults knowing the further meaning required were:

shower	57%
lane	63%
colonel	70%
portal	47%
dahlia	27%

In the case of shower, many adults thought the word meant a light rain, whereas the dictionary very definitely says it means a short rain, whether light or heavy. For lane, we required the country meaning but many adults knew only the traffic lane meaning. For portal, the adults were very vague as to how it differed from door. And they just did not know what a dahlia was like.

In the case of the synonyms it seemed definitely hard for the adults to differentiate between them. Of the ones we have listed, four were easy: disaster, symptom, avalanche, and buoyancy. But about one out of four adults could not distinguish between the synonyms for gap, splendor, bravery, comment, and flaw. And about half were wrong when trying to distinguish between synonyms for strife, malady, carousal, lethargy, and animation.

The same situation held true with the synonyms given by the standard test for verbs and adjectives. Space does not permit samples.

WHAT SHOULD WE EXPECT OF A VOCABULARY TEST

First of all, we must admit that existing vocabulary tests were not trying to measure scientifically a certain degree of meaning. They were just trying roughly to compare a child with other children of his own age with regard to the general field of vocabulary. We therefore are not criticising the vocabulary tests for doing something they did not try to do.

Having made this admission, we need to go on and to say that existing vocabulary tests certainly do not do a scientific job of measuring vocabulary. They ignore all but the most common meaning of a word, and then in cases of classification they test very little of that most common meaning, and when they use synonyms they test a very indefinite amount of knowledge.

It is to be hoped that in the future there will be an attempt made to measure scientifically what meaning children and adults have for words. Since words are the symbols with which we communicate with one another, it is important to know just what meaning or meanings words have for different people. Since words in reading are the symbols by which we try to get the thought a writer tried to put into a book, it is important that we have the right meaning and adequate meaning.

In this future scientific study, the first consideration will be that a word does not just have a "meaning." That naive assumption is all too prevalent even among educators. Instead, a word frequently has many meanings, and each of these meanings may be known in varying degrees by different people, or by the same person in the course of his life.

For each person, therefore, meaning is a growth, and it should be important for the school to know where any certain child is in that process of growth. How otherwise can the school wisely and efficiently help in the growth of meaning? Tests should tell us not merely that a child "knows something about" a certain word, but also how much he knows about it. Only then do we know what more he should know and how we can help him develop that added meaning.

21

Qualitative Differences in the Vocabulary Choices of Children as Revealed in a Multiple-Choice Test

LORRAINE P. KRUGLOV

The fact that individual vocabularies differ in quality, as well as in range, has only recently been considered in evaluating a person's level of intellectual functioning, although psychologists have been aware of qualitative differences in vocabulary responses for almost half a century. Traditionally, vocabulary differences have been considered in terms of range—how many words one can define—while the dimension of the quality of these word definitions has been largely ignored.

Feifel and Lorge,[1] in a review of the literature, indicated that Chambers in 1904, Binet and Simon in 1916, Terman in 1916, Piaget in 1926, and others at more recent dates noted that vocabulary changes not only in range but also in quality with age. Terman recognized that children's definitions varied in quality, some children giving definitions in terms of use and appearance, others in terms of synonyms. He felt that these qualitative differences indicated the maturity of apperceptive processes; nevertheless, the scoring system of the Terman Re-

[1] Herman Feifel and Irving Lorge, "Qualitative differences in the vocabulary responses of children." *J. of Educ. Psych.*, 1950, 41, 1–18.

REPRINTED from *The Journal of Educational Research*, vol. 44 (April 1953), pp. 229–43, "Qualitative Differences in the Vocabulary Choices of Children as Revealed in a Multiple-Choice Test" by Lorraine P. Kruglov. Reprinted with permission of Abrahams Magazine Service, Inc.

vision of the Binet-Simon Scale failed to consider these qualitative differences.

In a recent study Feifel and Lorge[2] described the types of definitions characteristic of different age levels (six to fourteen) with a view toward pointing up characteristic differences in thinking for these age levels. They classified responses to the forty-five item vocabulary subtest of the Form L Stanford-Binet Test into five categories as follows: (1) Synonym, (2) Use, Description, and Use and Description, (3) Explanation, (4) Demonstration, Repetition, Illustration and Inferior Explanation, and (5) Error. The mean number of responses within each category was compared among age groups. The main findings were:

1. Older children significantly more often employ the synonym type of definition than do younger children.

2. Children six to nine significantly more often give use and description types of responses than do older children.

3. Children six to nine significantly less frequently employ explanation types of responses than do older children.

4. Demonstration, illustration, inferior explanation and repetition types of responses increase from six to ten and decrease thereafter.

In general the younger children, aged six to nine, tend to perceive words as concrete ideas—in terms of use, description, demonstration—and do not generalize; the older children, aged ten to fourteen, tend to emphasize the abstract or 'class' feature of word meanings in their use of the synonym and explanation type responses. These qualitative differences in vocabulary, reflecting the conceptual level or mode of thinking of the child are a decided refinement on the 'range of vocabulary' which has been considered a major index of intellectual functioning to date.

Feifel and Lorge demonstrated these qualitative differences through an analysis of responses to a recall type test containing items like "What does *orange* mean?" The question arose as to whether such qualitative differences would be revealed on a recognition type test where all the choices for each item were correct but of different conceptual levels. Studies

[2] Herman Feifel and Irving Lorge, "Qualitative differences in the vocabulary responses of children." *J. of Educ. Psych.*, 1950, 41, 1–18.

have shown that a person's recognition vocabulary exceeds his recall vocabulary as far as vocabulary range is concerned. In the same way a child may recognize a definition at a more 'mature' level and choose it as the best definition of a word, even though he does not himself define the word at that level. The six-year-old might define an 'orange' as "you eat it" but he might recognize that it is "a fruit." Thus the six-year-old's recognition vocabulary might be qualitatively the same as the ten-year-old's.

If, however, the child's choices of responses are a reflection of his conceptual level, he might not recognize the more 'mature' definition as such, but might choose as the best meaning of a word a definition characteristic of his own conceptual level.

In addition to the theoretical issue, there are practical advantages to using a multiple-choice test. A major drawback in the estimation of a child's conceptual level from an analysis such as Feifel and Lorge made is the need for trained scorers and the time-consuming nature of such scoring. Using a recognition type, multiple-choice test would eliminate the need for personnel trained in qualitative scoring; in fact, such a test could be machine scored.

The present study is an attempt to find out whether the qualitative differences in vocabulary response, characteristic of the different age levels, as found by Feifel and Lorge in analyzing responses to a recall type vocabulary test, would also be demonstrated in a recognition type vocabulary test. Does the child's recognition vocabulary differ qualitatively from his recall vocabulary? Does he recognize more 'mature' definitions (i.e. those at higher developmental levels), as better than definitions characteristic of his own developmental level when both types of definition are presented to him?

A multiple-choice vocabulary test was constructed in which three or four of the five choices were correct according to the traditional scoring system for the Stanford-Binet, but of different qualitative levels according to the Feifel-Lorge study. Children, at different age levels, were asked to choose the 'best' meaning for each word. Responses at different age levels were analyzed to see whether qualitative differences hold up when a recognition type test is used.

CONSTRUCTION OF THE TEST

A number of problems arose in the course of constructing the multiple-choice vocabulary test. First of all, all words do not lend themselves to Feifel's four-fold classification system. Feifel, himself, noted that not all words permit a full range of qualitative differences to appear in the verbatim responses.[3] This is especially so for words that are not nouns and for the more difficult nouns. In addition, in a paper-and-pencil test, demonstration type responses had to be omitted. For these reasons the kind of words to be included in the multiple-choice test was limited.

The question of the form of the choices raised a second problem. Test construction theory recommends that all the choices be parallel in form, but because of the nature of this test, it was believed that the choices should parallel the verbatim responses given in the recall situation rather than parallel each other.

A third, and the most important, problem concerned the 'difficulty' or the familiarity of the words in the test to the subjects. To satisfy the requirements of a good vocabulary test, none of the five choices should be more difficult than the stem word. Moreover, for this particular test, those responses considered to represent a higher conceptual level, i.e., synonym and explanation, were to be no more difficult in terms of vocabulary range than responses representing the lower conceptual levels, i.e., use and description, and repetition-illustration-inferior explanation, or than the error responses. The *Thorndike-Lorge Teachers Word Book of 30,000 Words*[4] was used to obtain the frequency of occurrence in written English of each of the words used in the test. Where a response consisted of two or more words, the lowest frequency of occurrence of any word in the response was taken as the frequency of occurrence of the entire response.

[3] Herman Feifel. "Qualitative differences in the vocabulary responses of normals and abnormals." *Genetic Psych. Monographs*, 1949, 39, p. 67.
[4] Edward L. Thorndike and Irving Lorge. *The Teachers Word Book of 30,000 Words*. New York: Bureau of Publications, Teachers College, Columbia University, 1944.

One limitation of the use of the Thorndike word frequencies is that these frequencies are based upon occurrence in written English, while the test choices are based upon spoken English, and the two are not strictly paralled in frequency. Although frequency of occurrence is not the only, and may not even be the best index of word difficulty, it was felt that setting as criteria the requirements that the stem be no more frequent in occurrence than the five choices, and that the choices indicative of higher conceptual levels be no more frequent in occurrence than choices indicative of the lower conceptual levels would tend to equate at least one component of word difficulty.

The concern with frequency of occurrence was necessary to ensure that any qualitative differences found for the different age levels were not a function of the vocabulary range of that age level, but rather a function of the thinking processes of children of that age. If, for example, the synonyms and explanations were out of the vocabulary range of a particular age group while the descriptions and uses, and repetition-illustration-inferior explanations were within the vocabulary range of that age, vocabulary range (or frequency of occurrence) rather than mode of thinking might be the crucial factor in choosing the best meaning for a word.

A ten item vocabulary test was constructed using as stem words items 1, 2, 4, 6, 7, 10, 12, 14, 17, and 23 of the Stanford-Binet Form L vocabulary test. The five choices for each item were chosen from verbatim responses made by children to the recall type item. The test is presented in Figure 1.

Altogether there were fifty choices in the ten word vocabulary test. These choices are classified in Table 1.

Table 1   Classification of Choices in Vocabulary Test by Type of Response

Type of response	Number	Per cent
Synonym	10	20
Explanation	3	6
Use and Description	14	28
Repetition, Illustration, Inferior Explanation	9	18
Errors	14	28
	50	100

Figure 1

Name ———————————————— Age ———— Grade ——————

Below you will see a word in capitals. Five people were asked what
the word means. The five choices after the word are what the five
people said. You are to decide which of the answers is best. Sometimes more than one choice will tell correctly what the word means,
but you should choose only the one that you think is best. Write its
letter at the end of the line. The example shows how to do it.

DOG   A. you drink it
           B. it's a small animal
           C. something wooden
           D. a small house
           E. it means a pet dog   .   .   .   .   .   .   <u>B</u>

The best answer for DOG is a small animal, so the letter B
was put in the space at the end of the line. Do the others in the
same way. Go ahead and do the rest.

1. ORANGE   A. it's a fruit
                     B. you eat it
                     C. it's round and yellow
                     D. orange-like in orange juice
                     E. a kind of monkey   .   .   .   ——

2. ENVELOPE   A. it's a letter envelope
                     B. a wild animal
                     C. a container for a letter
                     D. white folded paper
                     E. something to mail things in   ——

3. PUDDLE   A. muddy water
                     B. like a small pool
                     C. you step in it and get wet
                     D. it's a riddle
                     E. it's a puddle that rain makes   ——

4. GOWN   A. you wear it
                     B. something like an elf
                     C. silk material
                     D. an evening gown for a ball
                     E. a lady's dress   .   .   .   .   ——

5. EYELASH   A. it's a hair on the eyelid
                     B. it protects your eye
                     C. an eye disease
                     D. a horse whip
                     E. you blink with it   .   .   .   ——

6. MUZZLE
   A. black leather
   B. something to keep an animal from biting
   C. like a leash
   D. covering for an animal's mouth
   E. it's a fight—a quarrel . . _____

7. LECTURE
   A. it's a game
   B. a long composition
   C. when a man talks
   D. it's a speech
   E. a stage platform . . . _____

8. SKILL
   A. performance
   B. something to cook with
   C. what you do very well
   D. acrobatic skill
   E. an ability . . . . . . _____

9. PECULIARITY
   A. a queer person
   B. when something odd occurs
   C. unusualness
   D. falsehood
   E. it happens very rarely . . _____

10. STAVE
   A. an oven
   B. it's like a staff
   C. you lean on it when walking
   D. it's wooden
   E. something you carry . . . _____

Twenty-six per cent of the choices were characteristic of Feifel's higher conceptual levels or more abstract approach —synonyms and explanations, forty-six per cent were characteristic of the lower conceptual levels or concrete approach —use and description, and repetition, illustration, and inferior explanation, and twenty-eight per cent were errors.

Eight of the fifty choices were more 'difficult,' in the sense of being less frequent in occurrence in written English than the stem word. In an ideal test none of the choices would have been less frequent in occurrence than the stem.

There were thirty-seven choices classified as use and description, repetition-illustration-or-inferior explanation, or error. The criterion set was that none of these choices characteristic of the lower conceptual levels be less 'difficult' than the synonym or explanation type response to the item. In the test there were fourteen of these thirty-seven choices which were less 'difficult,' i.e., more frequent in occurrence in written English, than the corresponding synonym or explanation type response. The other twenty-three choices characteristic of the lower conceptual levels were no less 'difficult,' i.e., no more frequent, than the synonym or explanation type responses.

PROCEDURE

The multiple-choice vocabulary test was given to a class at the third, fifth, seventh and eighth grade levels in a Brooklyn public school. Because the test requires that the pupils read the items, the lower end of the age range was necessarily limited.

The following directions were given to the class teachers who administered the tests to their own classes:

> Many people believe that children of different age groups define the same words in different ways. This test has been designed to study this theory. More than one answer is correct for each question on this test, but the children are to choose that answer which they consider best. It is to be emphasized that there is no 'right' answer.
>
> The teacher should read the directions with the younger groups. Stress the fact that the children should choose only one answer for each question. After reading the directions, allow five minutes to take the test. Collect all papers at the end of five minutes.

In addition to the public school sample the test was administered to a number of college graduates in order to compare their results with the responses of the children and with the responses typical of the higher conceptual levels, as found by Feifel and Lorge.

The total sample to which the test was administered is described in Table 2.

The per cent of each type of response chosen by subjects at each grade or age level was obtained—based upon the

Table 2   Sample Tested by Grade Level and Median Age

Grade level	Number	Median age
3	37	8
5	38	10
7	29	12
8	30	13
College graduate	15	21+

total number of responses, including omits and errors. Because it was believed that this method of computing per cents might penalize the younger groups for whom the error and omit scores were rather high, the per cents were recomputed based upon the total number of 'correct' responses for each grade, where a response was considered correct if it would have been correct on the Stanford-Binet Form L vocabulary test.

The hypotheses to be tested, based upon the Feifel-Lorge findings[5] were that the per cent of synonym and explanation type responses would increase from grade to grade, that the per cent of use and description response would decrease from grade to grade, and that the per cent of repetition, illustration, and inferior explanation type responses would increase to age ten (grade five) and decrease thereafter. Significances of differences between per cents were determined by the critical ratio technique, using a one-tailed test.

RESULTS

The number and per cent of times each type of response was chosen by each grade are presented in Table 3. In the test itself, twenty per cent of all choices are synonyms. Grade three chooses synonyms as twenty per cent of all their responses. There is an increase in the per cent of synonyms chosen from grade three to grades five, seven, eight and college graduates, with a slight reversal between grades five and seven. Grade seven appears to be somewhat out of line with the other grades,

[5] Herman Feifel and Irving Lorge. "Qualitative differences in the vocabulary responses of children." *J. of Educ. Psych.*, 1950, 41, 1–18.

suggesting that the students of this grade may not be equal in ability to the other students in the sample.

The per cent of use and description responses remains about the same for all grades except the college graduates who

Table 3   Number and Per Cent of Times Each Response Type Was Chosen by Each Grade

Grade	Synonym N	Per cent	Use- Desc. N	Per cent	Rep.- Ill. N	Per cent	Expla- nation N	Per cent	Error N	Per cent	Omit N	Per cent	Total N	Per cent
3	73	20	75	20	55	15	11	3	48	13	108	29	370	100
5	154	41	89	23	87	23	25	7	18	5	7	2	380	101
7	114	39	74	25	57	20	23	8	15	5	7	2	290	99
8	159	53	71	24	28	9	25	8	14	5	3	1	300	100
College	113	75	27	18	4	3	5	3	1	1	0	0	150	100
Test	10	20	14	28	9	18	3	6	14	28			50	100

show a slight decrease in choice of this type of response. None of the grades choose as many use and description type responses as are represented in the test itself.

The per cent of repetition-illustration-inferior explanation type responses increases from grade three to five, and decreases, thereafter. The per cent of explanation type responses increases to grade seven, stays the same at grade eight, and drops for the college graduates. The per cent of error responses is never as high as the per cent of error choices in the test, and from grade five upward the per cent of errors never exceeds five per cent of the total number of responses. Finally, except for grade three, the number of omits is negligible.

The per cents of each type of response chosen by the different grades were compared by means of the critical ratio technique—the significance of the difference between two per cents. The results, summarized in Table 4, indicate:

1. The per cent of synonym type responses increases with grade or age, the difference becoming statistically significant between grade three and the higher grades, and between grades three through seven and the college graduates.

Table 4   Critical Ratios of Per Cent of Each Response Type Chosen by Each Grade

	Grade			
	5	*7*	*8*	*College*
Grade 3				
Synonyms	2.10*	1.73*	3.00**	4.23**
Use and Description	.33	.50	.40	.17
Explanation	.80	.83	.83	.00
Rep.-Ill.-Inf. Exp.	.89	.56	.75	1.71*
Error	1.33	1.14	1.14	2.00*
Grade 5				
Synonyms		.17	1.00	2.43**
Use and Description		.18	.10	.42
Explanation		.17	.17	.67
Rep.-Ill.-Inf. Exp.		.30	1.56	2.50**
Error		.00	.00	1.00
Grade 7				
Synonyms			1.08	2.61**
Use and Description			.09	.54
Explanation			.00	.71
Rep.-Ill.-Inf. Exp.			1.22	1.89**
Error			.00	.80
Grade 8				
Synonyms				1.57
Use and Description				.46
Explanation				.71
Rep.-Ill.-Inf. Exp.				.86
Error				.80

* Significant at .05 level (t = 1.65 for one-tailed test).
** Significant at .01 level (t = 2.33 for one-tailed test).

2. The per cents of repetition-illustration-inferior explanation responses differ significantly between grade five and college graduates indicating that such responses reach a peak at grade five or age ten which corresponds to the peak found by Feifel and Lorge at age ten.

3. The per cents of use and description responses and of explanation responses do not differ significantly between any of the grade levels tested.

Because the method used above by comparing the per cent of each type of response per total number of responses would tend to give an unfair advantage to the older children who knew more word meanings, the per cents were recomputed on the basis of the total number of 'correct' responses. The question was then raised, "Among the correct responses do the older children choose qualitatively different responses than the younger children?" Computing per cents on the basis of total number of correct responses are there significant differences in the per cents of synonyms, use and description responses, explanations, and repetition-illustration-inferior explanation responses for the different grades or age groups? These revised per cents are presented in Table 5.

Table 5   Number and Per Cent* of Correct Responses of Each Qualitative Response Type Chosen by Each Grade

Grade	Total N	Correct N	Correct Per cent	Syno-nyms N	Syno-nyms Per cent*	Use-Desc. N	Use-Desc. Per cent*	Rep.-Ill. N	Rep.-Ill. Per cent*	Expla-nation N	Expla-nation Per cent*
3	370	214	58	73	34	75	34	55	26	11	5
5	380	355	94	154	44	89	24	87	24	25	7
7	290	265	93	114	42	74	27	57	21	23	9
8	300	283	94	159	56	71	26	28	10	25	9
College	150	149	99	113	76	27	18	4	3	5	3
Test	50	36	72	10	28	14	39	9	25	3	8

* Per cents based upon total number of correct responses.

All grades, except the third, choose about the same per cent of correct responses. For grades five through college graduates the per cents correct range from ninety-three to ninety-nine, with grade seven again appearing out of line with the other grades.

The per cent of synonyms increases from thirty-four in grade three to seventy-six for college graduates. The per cent of use and description responses decreases after grade three, remains relatively constant for grades five, seven, and eight, and drops again for the college graduates. The per cent of explanations increases from grade three to seven and decreases after grade eight. The per cent of repetition-illustration-inferior explanation decreases from grade to grade.

The revised per cents of each type of response chosen by the different grades were compared by means of the critical ratio technique. These data are presented in Table 6.

Table 6   Critical Ratios of Per Cent of Correct Responses of Each Qualitative Response Type Chosen by Each Grade

	Grade			
	5	*7*	*8*	*College*
Grade 3				
Synonyms	.91	.67	1.83*	3.00**
Use and Description	1.00	.67	.73	1.23
Explanation	.40	.67	.67	.33
Rep.-Ill.-Inf. Exp.	.20	.50	1.78*	2.87**
Grade 5				
Synonyms		.17	1.00	2.29*
Use and Description		.27	.18	.50
Explanation		.29	.29	.67
Rep.-Ill.-Inf. Exp.		.30	1.56	2.62**
Grade 7				
Synonyms			1.77*	2.43**
Use and Description			.09	.70
Explanation			.00	.86
Rep.-Ill.-Inf. Exp.			1.22	2.00*
Grade 8				
Synonyms				1.43
Use and Description				.62
Explanation				.86
Rep.-Ill.-Inf. Exp.				1.00

* Significant at .05 level (t = 1.65 for one-tailed test).
** Significant at .01 level (t = 2.33 for one-tailed test).

In general the findings were:

1. There is an increase in the choice of synonyms as correct responses from grade three through college graduates, the difference in the per cents of synonyms being significant between grades three–seven and college graduates.

2. There is a significant decrease in the per cent of repetition-illustration-inferior explanation type responses between grades three–seven and college graduates.

3. There are no significant differences between the per cents of use and description type responses and the per cents of explanation type responses chosen by the students in the different grades.

It seems appropriate at this point to compare the results of Feifel and Lorge's study[6] on the qualitative differences in vocabulary responses of children as revealed in a recall-type test with the results of this study on the qualitative differences in vocabulary choices of children as revealed in a multiple-choice recognition type test. Responses on both tests were classified into five categories: synonyms, use and description, explanations, repetition-illustration- and inferior explanations, and error. Feifel and Lorge compared the mean number in each response category for each age group from six to fourteen. In the present study the per cent in each response category per total number of responses and per total number of correct responses was compared for children in grades three, five, seven, and eight and for college graduates.

The results of the multiple-choice, recognition type test agree with those of the recall type test for the synonym, use and description, and repetition-illustration-inferior explanation type responses when the analysis is similar for the two tests—based upon the total number of responses. When the analysis is based only upon the number of 'correct' responses, the results agree for the synonym and the use and description categories. The results from the recognition test do not always reach the level of statistical significance reached by the recall test, due most probably to the smaller sample size and the limited length and difficulty range of the multiple-choice test. They do, however, indicate that recognition vocabularies, just as recall vocabularies, differ in quality as well as in range from one age or grade level to the next. The fact that the trends are similar for the two types of tests suggests that a longer revision of the multiple-choice test may yield as valuable information as the recall test with a considerable saving of time.

[6] Herman Feifel and Irving Lorge. "Qualitative differences in the vocabulary responses of children." *J. of Educ. Psych.*, 1950, 41, 1–18.

The most significant finding is the fact that even though a definition of a higher conceptual level is presented to the young child he tends to choose the response characteristic of the lower conceptual level—his own conceptual level. The younger child will tend to choose the use and description and the repetition-illustration-inferior explanation type definitions even when more abstract definitions in the form of synonyms are presented to him and are within his vocabulary range. He thus responds to the test in terms of his own conceptual level. Certainly further research along these lines will contribute to better understanding of the development of thought processes over the age span.

SUMMARY AND CONCLUSIONS

1. A ten item multiple-choice vocabulary test in which three or four choices were correct but of different qualitative levels was administered to a public school class at the third, fifth, seventh and eighth grade levels, and a group of college graduates.

2. Definite trends, and in some instances significant differences, were found between the younger children and the adolescents and young adults for synonym, use and description, and repetition-illustration-inferior explanation type responses.

3. Among the 'correct' responses the younger children tend to choose more use and description and more repetition-illustration-inferior explanation type responses than the adolescents and young adults. The older groups tend to choose more synonyms than the younger groups.

4. There are, therefore, qualitative differences in the choices of the 'best' response to vocabulary items—the younger children tending to choose more concrete definitions and the older groups more abstract definitions.

5. These findings closely parallel those obtained by Feifel and Lorge[7] who studied qualitative differences in vocabulary responses to a recall type test.

[7] Herman Feifel and Irving Lorge. "Qualitative differences in the vocabulary responses of children." *J. of Educ. Psych.*, 1950, 41, 1–18.

6. The results of this study suggest that a multiple-choice test of the type used in this study might be used to obtain better understanding of the mode of thinking and the level of intellectual functioning of the child. More intensive research in this area is certainly warranted.

22

The Relationship Between
Reading Rate and Comprehension

EARL F. RANKIN, JR.

Many varied opinions are held concerning the relationship between reading speed and comprehension. Some people maintain that in order to comprehend, one should read slowly with careful attention to each word. On the other hand, some authorities have stated that a fast rate of speed and good comprehension go together. Still others claim that reading speed and comprehension are not related because knowing one does not allow the prediction of the other. Surprisingly, some support can be found in the literature for each of these viewpoints. However, as we shall see, each viewpoint represents a simplification of a complex problem. Let us take a look at the research literature and see if we cannot gain some insight into the nature of this relationship.

There is widespread disagreement in the literature concerning the relationship between rate and comprehension. Blommers and Lindquist[1] reported finding correlations ranging

[1] Blommers, P., and I. F. Lindquist, "Rate of Comprehension in Reading: Its Measurement and Its Relation to Comprehension," *Journal of Educational Psychology*, 35: 449–473, November, 1944.

REPRINTED with permission of Earl F. Rankin, Jr., and the National Reading Conference, Inc. "The Relationship Between Reading Rate and Comprehension," in *Problems, Programs and Projects in College-Adult Reading:* Eleventh Yearbook of the National Reading Conference, Emery P. Bliesmer and Ralph C. Staiger, eds. (Milwaukee, Wisconsin: The National Reading Conference, Inc., 1962), pp. 1–5.

from −.47 to .92 presented in the research literature on the problem. In an often-cited early study Judd [2] concluded that "high rate and good quality are commonly related and that low rate and poor quality are commonly related." Gates[3] obtained a correlation of .84 between a composite rate score and a composite comprehension score based upon five reading tests. In contrast to these findings, King[4] found a correlation of −.47 between rate and comprehension. Such variable results appear to be a function of differences in reading materials, reader characteristics, and testing procedures.

READING MATERIAL VARIABLES

The relationship found between rate and comprehension appears to depend, in part, upon whether or not speed and comprehension are tested on the same material. Tinker[5] obtained high correlations between rate and comprehension when comprehension and rate were tested on the same materials. Paterson and Tinker[6] found a correlation of .86 between comprehension and speed on the *Chapman-Cook Speed of Reading Test,* and Gates[7] found correlations ranging from .88 to .96 between speed and comprehension on the *Monroe Silent Reading Test.* When rate has been determined on one test and comprehension on another test, correlations of approximately .30 have been reported.[8] Low correlations between rate and

---

[2] Judd, C. H., "Measuring the Work of the Public Schools," *Cleveland Educational Survey,* 1916, pp. 124–161.

[3] Gates, A. I., "An Experimental and Statistical Study of Reading and Reading Tests," *Journal of Educational Psychology,* 12: 303–314, 378–391, 445–464, Sept., Oct., Nov., 1921.

[4] King, I., "A Comparison of Slow and Rapid Readers," *School and Society,* 4: 830–834, November, 1916.

[5] Tinker, M. A., "Relation of Speed to Comprehension in Reading," *School and Society,* 36: 158–160, July, 1932.

[6] Paterson, D. G., and M. A. Tinker, "Time Limit versus Work Limit Methods," *American Journal of Psychology,* 42: 101–104, January, 1930.

[7] Gates, A. I., "An Experimental and Statistical Study of Reading And Reading Tests," *Journal of Ed. Psych.,* 12: 303–314, 378–391, 445–464, Sept., Oct., Nov., 1921.

[8] Tinker, M. A., "Relation of Speed to Comprehension in Reading." *School and Society,* 36: 158–160, July, 1932.

comprehension scores based on different materials are difficult to interpret in the absence of information concerning correlations between rate scores and correlations between comprehension scores based on these materials. It may be that the different tests are simply not measuring the same thing.

Differences in the subject matter content of materials affect the relationship between reading speed and comprehension. Different correlations between rate and comprehension have been found in various subject matter areas. Thurstone[9] obtained correlations between rate and comprehension of .11 on physical science material, .42 on literary material, and .44 on social science material. Anderson and Dearborn[10] concluded that a negative relationship exists between reading speed and comprehension in the fields of science and mathematics.

Differences in the difficulty and familiarity of materials also affect the relationship between rate and comprehension. Tinker[11] reports progressively lower correlations between speed and comprehension as the difficulty of the material is increased. In addition, Tinker found the relationship to be particularly weak when the material called for an understanding of concepts depending upon a specialized background of experience. Evidence concerning the influence of familiarity of material upon this relationship was obtained by Eurich.[12] Eurich found a stronger relationship between a pre-reading test of information and reading rate than he did between reading rate and a post-reading test of comprehension.

Thus, it appears that the rate-comprehension relationship depends upon (1) whether or not speed and comprehension are tested on the same materials, (2) the subject matter content of the materials, (3) the difficulty of the materials, and (4) the familiarity of the materials.

---

[9] Thurstone, L. L., *A Factorial Study of Perception.* Chicago: University of Chicago Press, 1944.

[10] Anderson, I. H., and W. F. Dearborn, "Reading Ability as Related to College Achievement," *Journal of Psychology,* 11: 387–396, April, 1941.

[11] Tinker, M. A., "Relation of Speed to Comprehension in Reading," *School and Society,* 36: 158–160, July, 1932.

[12] Eurich, A. C., "The Relations of Speed of Reading to Comprehension," *School and Society,* 32: 404–406, September, 1930.

READER CHARACTERISTIC VARIABLES

Variation in the reader's intelligence appears to affect the rate-comprehension relationship. Carlson[13] found some evidence which indicates a tendency for less intelligent readers to read better at slower rates and for more intelligent readers to read better at faster rates. He concluded that this tendency is accentuated when the purpose of reading is more exacting and when the material is more difficult.

It is possible that failure to control the factor of "purpose" is responsible for many of the conflicting results pertaining to this problem. Reported differences in rate-comprehension correlations among various subject matter fields are no doubt partly due to differential reading purposes in these fields. Many of the high correlations between rate and comprehension have been obtained under conditions when reading purposes were not exacting and limited demands were made upon comprehension skills. In studies by Blommers and Lindquist[14] and Shores and Husbands[15] the factor of purpose was controlled by asking questions before reading. These questions made reading purpose more exacting by calling for critical thinking involving interpretations, inferences, and evaluations. These two studies report correlations between rate and comprehension to be either low or non-existent. In Carlson's[16] study, in which purpose was varied as an independent variable, the relationship between rate and comprehension also tended to vary. Thus, it can be seen that the reader characteristics of intelligence and reading purpose clearly affect the relationship between rate and comprehension.

[13] Carlson, T. R., "The Relationship Between Speed and Accuracy of Comprehension," *Journal of Educ. Research*, 42: 500–512, March, 1949.
[14] Blommers, P., and E. F. Lindquist, "Rate of Comprehension in Reading: Its Measurement and Its Relation to Comprehension," *Journal of Educ. Psych.*, 35: 449–473, November, 1944.
[15] Shores, J. H., and K. L. Husbands, "Are Fast Readers the Best Readers?" *Elementary English*, 24: 52–57, Jan., 1950.
[16] Carlson, T. R., "The Relationship Between Speed and Accuracy of Comprehension," *Journal of Educational Research*, 42: 500–512, March, 1949.

TESTING PROCEDURE VARIABLES

Testing procedures play an important role in determining the outcome of studies on the rate-comprehension relationship. Many of the high correlations result from the fact that the "comprehension" tests are, in part, a measure of "rate," so that the reader is working against time. The imposition of time limits which do not permit slow readers to finish answering questions obviously favors the faster reader on the comprehensive score. The inclusion of time to answer questions with the total reading time measurement favors the reader with high comprehension on the rate score. Gates concluded that reading tests, ". . . do not differentiate between rate and comprehension for the correlations of rate tests with the composite of comprehension are about the same as with the composite of rate, and the correlation of comprehension tests are about the same with rate as with comprehension." [17]

When no time limits are imposed upon reading, the correlation between rate and comprehension is considerably reduced. Preston and Botel [18] gave the *Iowa Silent Reading Test* under both timed and untimed conditions. Under timed conditions, the correlations between rate and comprehension were .48, but under untimed conditions the correlation was only .20. Flanagan [19] reported a correlation of only .17 between "rate of work" and his "level of comprehension" score which is an estimate of the comprehension score an individual could be expected to make given unlimited time. Stroud and Henderson [20] found no relationship between rate and comprehension

[17] Gates, A. I., "An Experimental and Statistical Study of Reading and Reading Tests," *J. of Educ. Psych.*, 12: 303–314, 378–391, 445–464, Sept., Oct., Nov., 1921.

[18] Preston, R. C., and M. Botel, "Reading Comprehension Tested Under Timed and Untimed Conditions," *School and Society*, 74: 71, August, 1951.

[19] Flanagan, J. C., "A Study of the Effect on Comprehension of Varying Speeds of Reading." In *Research in the Foundations of American Education*, Washington, D.C.: American Educational Research Association, May, 1939. Pp. 47–50.

[20] Stroud, J. B., and M. Henderson, "Rate of Reading and Learning By Reading." *J. of Educ. Psych.*, 34: 193–205, April, 1943.

when time for answering questions was divorced from the speed score and readers were instructed to read at their own natural rate. Blommers and Lindquist[21] obtained a correlation of only .30 between rate of reading and "power of reading comprehension." Shores and Husbands[22] found little or no relationship between rate and comprehension when no time limits were imposed and the subjects were set to solve problems through reading relatively difficult material. In a correlational study of factors in speed of reading tests, Seashore, Stackford, and Swartz[23] allowed subjects to spend as much time as they needed on a power test. They concluded that individual differences in the speed of reading moderately difficult material are not determined by factors underlying either a reading comprehension test or a vocabulary test.

The relationship between speed and comprehension is influenced by the manner in which comprehension is measured. Letson[24] found high correlations (.46 and .77) between rate and comprehension when comprehension was measured as the number of correct responses. He found a low negative correlation of −.10 when comprehension was measured as the percentage of correct answers in relation to the number attempted. Evidently these findings can be accounted for by the fact that fast readers could read more material during the time limit and therefore could answer more questions. It would seem, then, that the relationship between rate and comprehension is considerably influenced by the testing procedures involved in the measurement of both reading speed and comprehension.

In conclusion, it appears that the confounding of rate and comprehension on measurements is, at least in part, responsible for some of the earlier findings that "fast readers

[21] Blommers, P., and E. F. Lindquist, "Rate of Comprehension in Reading: Its Measurement and Its Relation to Comprehension," *J. of Educ. Psych.*, 35: 449–473, November, 1944.
[22] Shores, J. H., and K. L. Husbands, "Are Fast Readers the Best Readers?" *Elementary English*, 24: 52–57, January, 1950.
[23] Seashore, R. H., L. B. O. Stackford, and B. K. Swartz, "A Correlational Analysis of Factors in Speed of Reading Tests," *School and Society*, 46: 187, August, 1937.
[24] Letson, Charles T., "Speed and Comprehension in Reading," *Journal of Educational Research*, 52: 49–53, October, 1958.

are good readers." Other studies of the relationship between rate and "power of comprehension," find only a slight relationship. When the material is more difficult, when more critical thought processes are involved, and when the reader's purpose is more exacting, the relationship between reading rate and comprehension is minimal.

23

An Investigation of Amount-Limit and Time-Limit Methods of Measuring Rate of Reading

KENNETH H. HUMPHRY

With the increase in high school, college, and industrial reading-rate improvement programs has come a need for better tests of reading rate. Most of the high school and college reading tests currently on the market are subject to criticism. Some are so short as to raise a question about their reliability. Others require a higher level of detailed comprehension than is desirable in a reading rate program. The validity of still other reading-rate tests is open to question in that the tasks required of the examinee are not those performed in a natural reading situation. Not only are efficient measures needed for selecting candidates for the reading course, but suitable measures of rate are necessary for satisfactorily evaluating the extent and performance of gains in reading rate.

Tests of reading rate generally employ either a time-limit or an amount-limit method. In the time-limit method the subject is given a reading selection and is directed to read for a specified period of time. His measure of rate is based upon the amount read and is generally reported in terms of words per minute. In the amount-limit method the subject is given a

REPRINTED with permission of Kenneth H. Humphry, the International Reading Association, and the Department of English of Purdue University. "An Investigation of Amount-Limit and Time-Limit Methods of Measuring Rate of Reading," *Journal of Developmental Reading*, vol. 1 (October 1957), pp. 41–54.

passage which he is told to read in its entirety. His rate is then computed on the basis of the time required to read the entire passage, and is also generally reported in words per minute.

Surprisingly enough, there has been very little research in which these two methods of measuring reading rate have been compared. Furthermore, there is little evidence of the relationship of length, or time requirements, to the reliability of the measures, or of variability in reading rate within individuals throughout a reading test.

PURPOSES

The purposes of this study were to obtain (1) reliability data for three amount-limit reading rate tests of different length, and three time-limit reading rate tests with different time requirements; (2) intercorrelations among the six tests, in order to determine the extent to which they measure the same thing, and to determine the validity of five of the tests when one test is designated as a criterion; (3) evidence on the variability of reading rate within a single long selection for groups of fast, average, and slow readers; and (4) data on the variability of reading rate within an individual for successive periods of time within the same test.

PROCEDURE

The Experimental Reading Tests

Six different rate of reading tests were developed for the purposes of this study, each test consisting of two forms, referred to as A and B. Three of the tests were amount-limit type tests of different lengths, and three were time-limit type tests with different time requirements. Table 1 provides a summary of the fundamental characteristics of the six tests as well as the test procedure. Two forms of each test were prepared and used for purposes of determining reliabilities by the equivalent forms method. During the fall semester 1955 the reading rates of the fastest, average, and slowest reader in each of five classes, after eight 50 minute training sessions, were ascer-

Table 1   Summary Table of the Six Tests of Reading Time

Test and length of selection	Fast Average Slow (times or amounts)[1]	Procedure	Maximum time required
I Amount-limit 7,000 words	11 minutes 17.5 minutes 20 minutes	Timed every minute until finished.	30 minutes
II Amount-limit 2,880 words	4.3 minutes 7.2 minutes 12 minutes	Read until finished. Max. time allowed: 12 minutes.	12 minutes
III Time-limit 2,880 words	2,880 words 1,720 words 1,032 words	Read 4.3 minutes only.	4.3 minutes
IV Time-limit 2,880 words	2,880 words 1,720 words 1,032 words	Time for 4.3 minutes. Then read 7.7 minutes more.	12 minutes
V Time-limit 8,040 words	8,040 words 4,800 words 2,880 words	Read 12 minutes only.	12 minutes
VI Amount-limit 1,720 words	2.6 minutes 4.3 minutes 7.2 minutes	Read until finished.	7.2 minutes

[1] Figured on rates of 670, 401, and 240 words per minute, respectively. The data in this column were used in setting the time limits shown in columns 3 and 4. They do not represent reading times actually employed by fast, average, and slow students used in the experiment.

tained. The average for the five fastest readers was 670 words per minute; for the average reader, 401; and for the slowest, 240. These values were used in setting the lengths and time limits of the various reading selections. In comparing amount-limit and time-limit methods at various lengths it seemed desirable to strive to secure comparable amounts of reading for the two methods.

Thus length and time requirements were chosen to make comparisons possible between different types of tests of the same length and/or time requirements. Three of the tests required twelve minutes total time to administer, i.e., Tests II, IV and V. Three of the tests were alike with respect to length. These were Tests II, III, and IV.

Test I was designated as the criterion against which the other tests were to be compared. This test was 7000 words long and each reader was permitted to read until he finished the test. A minute by minute measure of the number of words each of the subjects had read was obtained. It seemed that this method might provide the most complete picture of each individual's natural rate of reading. Not only could each reader's overall reading rate be determined, but variations in his reading rate at specific time intervals could be ascertained as well.

This method is not thought to be a practical means of measuring reading rate outside of an experimental situation. An involved and lengthy scoring process is required if one wishes to examine the reader's rate within any of the several time segments. It is also not known to what extent periodic interruptions, and subsequent marking of reading times on the test booklet, interfere with the reading process. On an a priori basis, this would seem to be negligible. It is also possible that over an extended period of testing time, reading rates might be slightly lower than otherwise because of the marking time required. In spite of the possible limitations which might have been suggested, this method would still seem to be the best criterion against which to compare other less cumbersome methods of measuring reading rate.

While this study was not primarily concerned with the comprehension aspects of the reading test, it was important that the reader's rate of reading be kept "honest" during the testing period. Therefore, a simple recall test, consisting of ten four-response, multiple-choice items, was developed and used for each of the reading selections to provide a measure of the reader's comprehension. The results served as a check on level of comprehension but were not analyzed in detail.

Selection of the Test Materials

The criteria for the length and time requirements for the tests have been discussed. There were two additional criteria which were considered to be important in the selection of the test materials. First, it was felt that the materials should be comparable in level of difficulty, and should be pitched at approximately the upper senior high school level. A second important characteristic of the materials was that they be high in interest value, and comparable in this respect. Therefore, materials were sought which were likely to be unfamiliar to the readers, and which contained an element of humor or were otherwise likely to be interesting.

TEXTS USED IN EACH READING TEST

I   A   Kenneth Roberts, "It Must Be Your Tonsils," *The Kenneth Roberts Reader,* Doubleday Doran and Company, Inc., Garden City, New York, 1945, pp. 374–394.

I   B   Kenneth Roberts, "An Inquiry into Diets," *op. cit.,* pp. 89–104.

II   A   Mark Twain, "A Scrap of Curious History," *What Is A Man?,* Harper and Brothers, New York, 1917, pp. 182–192.

II   B   Major M. A. Wiener, "100% Below H_2O," *Flying Safety Magazine,* Government Printing Office, Washington, D.C., January, 1955.

III   A   "Thunderbolts in Harness," The General Electric Company.

III   B   Claude D. Kelley, "Game Laws Are No Joke!" Conservation Talks—Leaflet No. 4, The National Wildlife Federation, Washington 12, D.C.

IV   A   Stacy V. Jones, "Life With a Brooklyn Gang," *Harper's Magazine,* November, 1954, pp. 35–43.

IV   B   Bernard De Voto, "Service in Four-Color Gravure," *Harper's Magazine,* February, 1955, pp. 10–15.

V   A   Kenneth Roberts, "An American Looks at Oxford," *op. cit.,* pp. 135–157.

V   B   Kenneth Roberts, "Experiments With a Forked Twig," *op. cit.,* pp. 430–460.

VI   A   Mark Twain, "The Buried City of Pompeii," *The Inno-
cents Abroad,* Leipzig, Bernhard Tauchnitz Edition, 1879,
pp. 311–320.

VI   B   Meeker Oden, "How to Take to the Tropics," *Harper's
Magazine,* January, 1955, pp. 59–65.

Selection of the Subjects

The subjects in the study consisted of 166 students at the State
University of Iowa who had enrolled in the college reading
program during the spring semester of 1955. The majority
were freshmen who were seeking to improve deficiencies in
communication skills through the Communication Skills Program at the University. All of the students from whom the
sample for this study was chosen had voluntarily enrolled in
the reading improvement program and received twenty hours
of reading instruction. The classes met one hour a day, four
days a week, for five weeks. The instruction was typical of
that provided in most college reading programs.

Administration of the Reading Tests

Experience has shown that most of the gain in reading rate,
which a student in these classes may expect to achieve in a
period of twenty hours of instruction, is likely to occur by the
end of the eighth hour of instruction. From that point on,
his reading rate increases much more slowly. Prior to beginning the administration of the reading tests, the students in
this investigation received eight days of intensive practice and
instruction in reading rate. This was done to control somewhat
the effect of practice on subsequent rate scores. The instruction
included lectures on means of improving poor reading habits,
the use of the first seven *Iowa Reading Films,* timed speeded
readings, tachistoscope exercises, and practice on reading ac-
celerators. At the ninth lesson, Test I, Form A, was administered at the beginning of the hour. One reading test was given
at the beginning of each succeeding class meeting until all
twelve tests had been given. The tests were administered in
this order: I A, I B, VI A, VI B, III A, III B, IV A, IV B, V A,
V B, II A, II B. Students were not informed of their performances on these tests until all twelve had been administered.

RESULTS

Comparison of Rate and Comprehension Scores
on Each of the Tests

It is possible to follow several lines of speculation concerning the kinds of results likely to be obtained when employing time-limit and amount-limit tests of reading rate. One might hypothesize that an individual would tend to read faster on a time-limit test than on an amount-limit test because he realized that he could read only for a limited amount of time. Awareness of this element of pressure could, ostensibly, result in his reading the selection at a faster rate than he would employ with an amount-limit test in which such pressure did not exist. Also, one might think that a person would tend to read faster on short tests than on longer tests.

Table 2 sheds some light on the foregoing suppositions. It can be seen that when the means of both Form A and Form

Table 2   Means and Standard Deviations for the Rate
of Reading Tests (In Words per Minute)

	Form M	*A SD*	*Form M*	*B SD*
Test I	372	90	369	107
Test II	371	125	393	122
Test III	375	100	368	104
Test IV	347	93	372	107
Test V	350	101	371	111
Test VI	369	113	337	88

B of each test are considered together, one type of test (amount-limit or time-limit) is not read appreciably faster than the other. It is apparently not true that one tends to read a short selection faster than a long selection, at least within the definition of short and long tests as employed in this study. Again, when both forms of each test are considered, it can be seen that Test VI which was the shortest of all of the reading tests in terms of length, was read most slowly.

Another of the purposes of this study was to examine the extent of variability in reading rate among groups of readers for successive periods of time. One could develop several hypotheses concerning variability in rate of reading. It is possible that a group of readers would read at relatively the same rate from minute to minute, or that their rate might fluctuate markedly from minute to minute. It is possible that rates might vary systematically or fluctuate haphazardly. Other hypotheses are plausible.

The means and standard deviations of the subscores for time segments of Test I are found in Table 3. The evidence of

Table 3   Means and Standard Deviations for Subscores of Rate of Reading Test I (In Words per Minute)

	Form M	IA SD	Form M	IB SD
Total Test	372	90	366	107
1st minute	332	94	366	102
2nd minute	327	87	350	113
4th minute	346	101	364	108
8th minute	374	106	365	123
1st 4 minutes	336	87	363	101
2nd 4 minutes	371	99	362	110

variability in rate revealed in the two forms of the test is inconsistent. The results of Form B refute almost all of the evidence of variability suggested by Form A of Test I.

The comparatively slow reading-rate scores for the first four minutes of Test I A are rather difficult to explain. The material in the reading selection for Test I A likely to be read during the first four-minute period may be somewhat more difficult than that in the second four-minute segment of the reading selection. Another possible explanation is that this was the first of the reading tests to be administered, and it is possible that unfamiliarity with the procedure of marking reading rate at the end of every minute might have adversely affected the rate scores at the beginning of that test.

Reliability of the Reading Tests

The equivalent forms' reliability coefficients of the words per minute scores of the six rate of reading tests are as follows: Test I, .82; Test II, .88; Test III, .84; Test IV, .86; Test V, .86;

Test VI, .85. The differences in the reliabilities of the six tests are small and not statistically significant. There is also little difference between the amount-limit and the time-limit reliability coefficients. The longer test did not yield the greater reliability. The same thing is true of the time-limit tests; Test V (12 minutes) is not appreciably more reliable than Tests III and IV (4.3 minutes).

Reliability coefficients for alternate methods of scoring the amount-limit tests are shown below:

	WPM	*Time*	*T-Scores*
IA vs. IB (Total)	.82	.88	.83
IA vs. IB (First 2880 words)	.77	.84	.76
IIA vs. IIB	.88	.88	.87
VIA vs. VIB	.85	.83	.85

In the first column are reliability coefficients based on rate scores. In the second column, the criterion scores are time scores in 10-second intervals. In the third column, are coefficients based on time scores converted to normalized T-scores. Use of the time scores with this particular sample results in a more reliable Test I, but the advantage does not hold for the other amount-limit tests. The relatively low reliability of the first 2880 words on Test I as compared with Test II, in a way constitutes evidence that the relatively lower reliability of Test I was not due to the fact that the test was longer than the others, but was due to its placement first in the series of tests or to the interruptions at the end of each minute for marking.

The equivalent forms reliability coefficients of the sub-scores (selected time segments) on Test I are shown below:

Time IA vs. IB	*Reliability*
1st minute	.73
2nd minute	.67
4th minute	.72
8th minute	.72
1st 4 minutes	.80
2nd 4 minutes	.76

The first four-minute measure of rate would seem to be slightly more reliable than the second four-minute measure of rate. In fact, the reliability coefficient of the first four minutes is .80 which is almost as high as the reliability coefficient of the total test (.82), and is quite comparable to the reliability of the four minute time-limit test, Test III (.84).

Intercorrelations of the Rate of Reading Tests

Intercorrelations were obtained among all twelve of the tests. Actually, because there were two forms of each of the tests, there are four estimates of the correlation between any two test types. Thus, as estimates of the correlation between Tests I and II, correlations were obtained for I A vs. II A, I B vs. II A, I A vs. II B, and I B vs. II B. These values were averaged by converting the r's to z's (Fisher), obtaining the average of the z's, and then converting back to r. These averages are shown in Table 4.

Table 4   Average Intercorrelations of Scores of the Six Rate of Reading Tests

Test	I	II	III	IV	V	VI
I	—	.77	.77	.78	.76	.81
II	.77	—	.82	.83	.83	.81
III	.77	.82	—	.83	.82	.81
IV	.78	.83	.83	—	.84	.78
V	.76	.83	.82	.84	—	.75
VI	.81	.81	.81	.78	.75	—

It is noteworthy that there is little tendency, if any, for the tests of a given type (amount-limit or time-limit) to show higher correlations with tests of the same type than with tests of the other type. In fact, the intercorrelations are remarkably homogeneous and give little basis for concluding that the tests differ very greatly in what each is measuring.

Test I has been proposed as the logical criterion against which to validate the time-limit tests and the shorter amount-limit tests. If Test I is accepted as the criterion, the intercorrelations of the other tests with Test I may be interpreted as validity coefficients.

The correlations expressing the relationship between both

forms of each test with Tests I A and I B have been corrected for attenuation in both variables and appear below:

	II A	*II B*	*III A*	*III B*	*IV A*	*IV B*	*V A*	*V B*	*VI A*	*VI B*
IA	.77	.80	.84	.81	.82	.78	.76	.80	.84	.82
IB	.93	.87	.87	.89	.91	.92	.88	.89	.95	.93

It will be noted that there is sizable difference in these correlations with Test I Form A as opposed to those with Test I Form B. Because in all cases the correlations are higher with Form B, there appears to be some extraneous variance in Form A scores not present in Form B.

Further Analysis of Test I A

For purposes of analysis of differences in performance for groups reading at different average rates, individual subjects were assigned to groups according to the number of complete four-minute blocks of time required to read the entire test. For example, if a subject read the entire test in thirteen minutes, the average rate can be computed on three four-minute blocks; 1–4, 5–8, and 9–12. This procedure was followed in order to provide a sufficient number of groups for which the variability in reading rate throughout the test could be observed.

Five groups resulted from the procedure described above. The number of subjects in each group varied according to the number of four-minute blocks each individual required to read the entire selection. The number of four-minute blocks required by Groups I through V were three, four, five, six, and seven respectively. From this it follows that Group I would be composed of the fastest readers and Group V the very slowest. Six individuals were excluded from this part of the analysis; two required less than three four-minute periods; three required more than seven four-minute periods; and one subject failed to record some of the time data on his paper.

Average scores, in terms of words per minute, for each four-minute time segment were obtained for each individual. The number of scores for each individual varied according to the number of time segments needed to finish the test.

Table 5 Analysis of Four-Minute Segments of Test I A: Means and Standard Deviations in Words per Minute

		Time segment						
		1–4	*5–8*	*9–12*	*13–16*	*17–20*	*21–24*	*25–28*
Group I (N = 32)	M	433.88	489.38	519.13				
	SD	69.99	49.77	52.67				
Group II (N = 62)	M	354.37	394.81	407.37	398.92			
	SD	38.45	29.60	41.30	32.87			
Group III (N = 39)	M	295.15	324.15	324.54	331.62	325.64		
	SD	25.93	31.32	25.20	23.46	31.03		
Group IV (N = 18)	M	243.44	255.44	274.83	276.06	283.06	298.72	
	SD	25.43	22.31	22.65	26.33	22.10	41.90	
Group V (N = 9)	M	213.44	209.89	227.11	223.89	223.00	241.11	270.33
	SD	33.22	24.45	20.51	17.22	26.44	19.45	41.17

Table 5 presents the means and standard deviations of the five groups for each four-minute segment. This table reveals that the different ability groups did not follow the same pattern in rate of reading. Group I students, the fastest readers, increased their rate of reading systematically from the initial to the final four-minute time segment. The same thing was true of Group IV. Groups II and III increased their rate during the second four-minute period and then tended to become constant. Group V, the slowest group of readers, read at about the same average rate for the first five four-minute periods and then showed a marked increase in rate during the last two periods.

"T" tests for related measures were applied to the differences between the average rate for the first four-minute segment and the average rate for the last four-minute segment for each group. The differences were all significant at the 1 per cent level, indicating a significant increase in rate between the beginning and the end.

Of further interest is within-subject variability in reading rate from one four-minute segment to another. Is variability from one four-minute interval to another the same for fast readers, average readers, and slow readers, or are there differences in within-subject variability associated with reading rate?

To obtain evidence bearing on this question, the mean-square for within-subjects was computed for each of the five groups. These are shown below:

Group	MS
1	3992.83
2	1319.85
3	650.46
4	972.73
5	1088.49

A Bartlett test for homogeneity of variance was applied to these data and resulted in a significant x^2 ($x^2 = 93.71$; $x^2 .01 = 13.28$). This indicates that the within-subject variability differs for the different groups. The data indicate that within-subject variability is greatest for the fast readers and least for the average readers.

SUMMARY

A summary of the most important results of the study is presented below:

Purpose 1: To Obtain Reliability Data

There were no significant differences among the equivalent forms' reliability coefficients for the rate scores of the six tests. The obtained reliability was highest for Test II (.88) and lowest for Test I (.82). In subsequent analysis of Test I A there was evidence of extraneous variance not present in any of the other tests, which might account for the relatively lower reliability of Test I.

There was also little difference between the obtained reliability coefficients of the amount-limit and the time-limit types of tests. Nor were there sizable differences in the reliabilities of tests of different length within the variations in length used in this study.

Purpose 2: To Obtain Intercorrelations Among the Six Rate of Reading Tests

The intercorrelations among the rate measures for the tests were rather homogeneous, indicating that the tests differed very little in what each was measuring. Validity coefficients of Tests II through VI were of about the same magnitude. When Test I A was the criterion, the validity coefficients (corrected for attenuation in both variables) averaged about .80. Similar coefficients with Test I B were considerably more satisfactory, averaging about .90.

Purpose 3: To Obtain Evidence on Variability of Reading Rate for Groups of Fast, Average, and Slow Readers

The evidence from this study suggests that subjects show considerable variability in reading rate during successive time intervals when reading a relatively long selection, and that the rate patterns differ for groups of fast, average, and slow readers. Significant differences between the means of the first four-minute intervals and the last four-minute intervals were found for all rate groups, indicating an over-all increase in rate during the reading of a selection.

Purpose 4: To Obtain Data on Variability of Reading Rate Within an Individual

Within-subject variability in rate of reading differed significantly in the five groups and was greatest for the fast readers and least for the average readers.

On the whole, this study showed that in measuring rate of reading as defined by the tests in this investigation, a fairly short (four-minute) time-limit test appears to be about as valid as other tests which require more time or are more difficult to administer.

24

Appraising Competence in Reading in Content Areas

DOROTHY KENDALL BRACKEN

In order to appraise reading effectively in the content areas, we should consider appraising general reading skills and capacities, appraising reading skills in English, appraising reading skills in social studies, and appraising reading skills in mathematics and science.

APPRAISAL OF GENERAL READING SKILLS AND CAPACITIES

Informal ways of discovering the capacity of boys and girls are as follows:[1] (1) observation of students in classrooms for speed of learning, for use and extent of speaking vocabulary, for organization of ideas and discovery of relationships among them; (2) the use of listening as an indication of capacity. Teachers often use the first method. The second, using listening

---

[1] Ruth Strang, Constance M. McCullough, and Arthur E. Traxler, *Problems in the Improvement of Reading*. New York: McGraw-Hill Book Co., 1955 (2d ed.).

as a measure of reading capacity, has been selected frequently for Grades III to VI since Durrell and Sullivan published their twin tests, Reading Achievement Test and Reading Capacity Test. Betts[2] says that comparison of the student's comprehension of a passage read aloud to him with his comprehension of a comparable passage which he reads silently often shows unrealized reading ability. If he can get ideas from listening, he should be able to get ideas from reading.

It has been suggested that teachers can profitably continue the appraisal of reading ability through a study of interests, informal reading inventories, and detailed case studies. Reading interests may be evaluated[3] by means of questionnaires, responses to essay type questions, check lists, and continuous reading records in order to establish the amount of reading, specific interests of individuals and groups, extent of variety, and quality or maturity of interests.

The informal inventory is described by Stauffer as follows: "The inventory usually consists of a series of graded selections, two at a level, accompanied by ten questions. One selection at a level is read orally at sight; the other is read silently. And, as the words imply, as the pupil proceeds under the careful eye of a trained teacher, an informal inventory of needs is made."[4] A detailed case study is an accumulation of data in the areas of formal and informal tests, observations of classroom activities, results of many interviews, etc. For the average classroom teacher it is perhaps the most impractical method from the point of view of training, time, and effort.

Further suggestions for appraising reading ability are the use of tests of study skills, methods of reading, and flexibility of reading; casual observations of students' reading; and informal teacher-made tests. Various study-skills tests will be mentioned later. Teachers at all levels can profit from ob-

[2] Emmett Albert Betts, "Meeting the Needs of Individual Children," *Reading Teacher*, VI (September, 1952), 4–12.
[3] Henry C. Meckel, "Evaluating Growth in Reading," *Reading in the High School and College*, pp. 251–75. Forty-Seventh Yearbook of the National Society for the Study of Education, Part III. Chicago: University of Chicago Press, 1948.
[4] Russell G. Stauffer, "How the Classroom Teacher Can Locate a Child's Underdeveloped Skills," *Reading in Action*, p. 88. Ed. William S. Gray and Nancy Larrick. New York: Scholastic Magazines, 1957.

servation of students' reading in the classroom. Informal observations[5] can be made of responses in functional reading situations, in instructional reading situations, in work-type activities, and in informal test situations. The use of informal teacher-made tests will be discussed in relation to the various content fields.

APPRAISING READING SKILLS IN ENGLISH

In appraising reading abilities in the English class, "we should use tests which contain the type of material which we expect to use in our English classes." [6] Suggestions for constructing an informal test using this principle follow: (1) make up a test based on materials students will read, (2) arrange in order of difficulty, (3) select passage from book for each level of difficulty identified, and (4) ask questions on each passage, probing kinds of thinking we would expect students to do on that particular piece of material. A test of this type is considered valid because it is made up of materials and questions which are actually used in the classroom.

Besides the responsibility for appraising reading skills in all types of literary selections, the English teacher has responsibilities for determining by both formal and informal means the mechanics his students use in their reading and their reading skills in relation to grammar and composition. Therefore, a few items will illustrate the types of his informal observation: ability to use word-attack skills, syllabication, etc.; ability to use contextual clues and other word-meaning skills; ability to spell; ability to compose and to use writing techniques (for example, paragraph patterns) as reading techniques, etc. Simpson lists others: "Ability to read and understand textbook explanations related to correctness and appropriateness of written and oral expression . . . ability to comprehend and to apply information related to parts of speech and other aspects of grammatical analysis . . . ability

---

[5] Margaret G. McKim, *Guiding Growth in Reading.* New York: Macmillan Co., 1955.
[6] Strang, McCullough, and Traxler, *op. cit.,* p. 145.

to follow directions accompanying exercises to develop grammatical skills and habits . . . ability to use the dictionary to determine the exact and varied meanings of words . . . ability to read punctuation as an aid to comprehension." [7]

APPRAISING READING SKILLS IN SOCIAL STUDIES

Social studies teachers need to appraise their students' ability in many areas. First of all, they need to know how well each student can read the textbook. An oral reading of a paragraph with a few oral questions concerning the main idea and supporting details might be the first approach to an appraisal, followed by a selection read silently with "a free response to a general question such as 'what did the author say?' and objective-type exercises to test the students' comprehension of the main ideas, significant details, key words, inferences, and generalizations. The free response will show better than any other testing device how the student organizes ideas as he reads and whether he can grasp and communicate in writing the author's pattern of thought." [8]

Next, it would be well if social studies teachers checked to find out if their students have good study habits and how they proceed when they study the textbook. One method is to make an assignment and observe the way in which the pupils attack the study problem. Another method is to have students write a short paragraph telling what methods they employ. Still another way is for the teacher to construct a test which shows a pupil's use of the survey, or pre-reading, procedure, his use of self-questions as he surveys, his method of reading in detail, reviewing, and reciting. A good habits-methods test for college students is included in Spache and Berg's *The Art of Efficient Reading* (Macmillan, 1955). An inventory of reading versatility which checks the reader's understanding of purpose and ability to adjust his rate to the purpose has been

[7] Elizabeth A. Simpson, *Helping High-School Students Read Better*, pp. 12–13. Chicago: Science Research Associates, Inc., 1954.
[8] Ruth Strang and Dorothy Kendall Bracken, *Making Better Readers*, p. 222. Boston: D. C. Heath & Co., 1957.

developed by McDonald.[9] Sheldon[10] has also been developing informal tools for assessing the approach each reader makes to reading. Using a different method of estimating flexibility of approach to different types of reading materials, Spache[11] reports the creation of a test of reading flexibility.

Third, in addition to appraising the student's ability to read textbooks, his study method, and his flexibility of reading, the social studies teacher will be interested in checking the specialized abilities particularly useful in social studies reading. These include the ability to locate information, to grasp information from maps, charts, etc., to organize ideas, and to read critically, including efficiency in recognizing propaganda.

Some teachers have used these methods: to appraise locational skills, observe the students in actual situations involving dictionaries, encyclopedias, card catalogues, tables of contents, indexes, headings, and the like. In the upper elementary grades *How To Use an Encyclopedia* and *The Look-It-Up Books* (Field Enterprises, Inc., 1949) are valuable. To appraise ability to grasp information from graphs, charts, and diagrams, allow students to reproduce in a paragraph the information given in the chart and then, vice versa, have them put into a chart information found in a paragraph.

To appraise ability to organize ideas, present a selection orally (either in person or by record or tape recorder) and have students outline or summarize the material. Then have them read a comparable selection silently and organize this material. A comparison of the two will prove interesting. In estimating ability to locate propaganda techniques, a test in two parts has been suggested.[12] Part I deals with generali-

[9] Arthur S. McDonald, "A Reading Versatility Inventory," *Significant Elements in College and Adult Reading Improvement*, Seventh Yearbook of the National Reading Conference, pp. 48–53. Fort Worth: Texas Christian University Press, 1958.

[10] William D. Sheldon, "Diagnostic Techniques and Tools," *Exploring the Goals of College Reading Programs*, Fifth Yearbook of the Southwest Reading Conference, pp. 116–18. Fort Worth: Texas Christian University Press, 1956.

[11] George Spache, "Diagnostic Tools," *Exploring the Goals of College Reading Programs*, pp. 121–23.

[12] Eugene R. Smith *et al.*, *Appraising and Recording Student Progress*, pp. 148–54. New York: Harper & Bros., 1942.

zations based on a selection in the form of conclusions, inferences, or implications. The students evaluate the statements
as to: (1) evidence that the author of the selection wishes
them to agree with or accept the idea in the statement, (2)
evidence that the author wants them to disagree with or reject
the idea in the statement, (3) no evidence as to whether the
author wishes them to agree or disagree. In Part II, students
are asked to identify statements which represent forms of
argument used and to select desirable and undesirable forms
used by the author.

APPRAISING READING ABILITY IN MATHEMATICS

Bond [13] says that the kinds of reading needed in mathematics
are noting and weighing details, following directions, organizing contents, drawing inferences, and discriminating between relevant and irrelevant information. In reading mathematics, therefore, the rate is slow, with careful attention to
detail. In order to appraise the speed and care with which
mathematics students read mathematical materials, try some
suggestions to combat skimming made by Schubert:[14] spot
irrelevant sentences and phrases which have been inserted in
problems from supplementary texts, read want-ad sections of
the newspaper for specific facts, approximate answers before
working out in detail, and read orally to determine difficulty.

An informal test to determine the way students read
mathematics materials might be set up in which no computations were asked for. The pupil would simply read the problems and answer questions such as, What is asked for? What
is given? What computations would you use?

In mathematics the vocabulary is a specialized one and
is often the stumbling block in students' progress. Strang[15]
suggests informal teacher-made tests. The teacher makes a
list of difficult words found in the text, and from this list she

[13] Guy L. Bond and Eva Bond, *Developmental Reading in High School.*
New York: Macmillan Co., 1941.
[14] Delwyn G. Schubert, "Formulas for Better Reading in Mathematics,"
School Science and Mathematics, LV (November 1955), 650–52.
[15] Strang, McCullough, and Traxler, *op. cit.*

devises a test, a list of words for which she asks the definition. This is the easiest for the teacher but the most difficult kind of response for the student. A better procedure would be the construction of a test of the multiple-choice type. After giving this kind of test, the teacher can list the names of students in the class down the left side of the page and the numbers of the items on the test across the top. Then he can see at a glance which items are unknown to the whole class, which to groups, and which to individuals only.

APPRAISING READING ABILITY IN SCIENCE

The problems of reading in science and mathematics are related. Both require a slower rate, both have distinct and unique vocabularies, both use ideas compressed into little space, with many ideas and a multiplicity of details.

One of the best informal tests which has been suggested is one by Strang.[16] She suggests that the teacher assign a passage from the textbook, time the reading, and administer a test built upon these lines: *Part I:* What did the author say? *Part II:* Check the best, most complete, most accurate main idea (multiple-choice) ; *Part III:* True-false test on details; *Part IV:* Answering questions; *Part V:* Drawing conclusions; *Part VI:* Vocabulary (words in a phrase or clause with four choices given) ; *Part VII:* Processes used in reading this article. Then ask the following questions: How did you get the main idea? How did you find and remember the details? What did you do when you read that made it possible for you to answer questions? What did you do when you read that made it possible for you to draw conclusions? How did you find out the meanings of unfamiliar words?

It has been suggested that a "readiness" test be given by the science teacher to determine the vocabulary level of the class and to indicate which terms are known and which are unknown. Furthermore, Leary[17] indicates that in a science vocabulary test some mathematical terms should be included

[16] *Ibid.*
[17] Bernice E. Leary, "Meeting Specific Reading Problems in the Content Fields," *Reading in the High School and College,* pp. 136–79.

which are frequently employed in science reading—symbolic language, expressions of relationship (formulas, equations, and graphs).

Spache and Berg, in *The Art of Efficient Reading,* suggest a method for checking the plan the college student has for reading in science. Present the class with a science selection; then ask the students both to read the introductory paragraphs and preview the selection, raising questions that come to mind, and to indicate their plan for reading the selection. The second step should include approach (intensive reading, critical reading, rapid reading), style (formal or textbook, informal or literary, mixed), difficulty (very difficult, average difficulty, fairly easy, very easy), and rate (slowly and carefully, at average rate, quickly, very rapidly).

With the many standardized tests now available, and from our knowledge of the use and importance of planned observation and informal testing, it is possible, as a result of accumulating a wealth of data, for teachers to appraise effectively the reading abilities of both classes and individuals in the content areas.

For Further Reading

Bormuth, John R. "Comparable Cloze and Multiple-Choice Comprehension Test Scores," *Journal of Reading* 10 (February, 1967) : 291–99.

Bryan, Fred E. "How Large Are Children's Vocabularies?" *Elementary School Journal* 54 (December, 1953) : 210–16.

Carlson, Thorsten R. "Effect of Certain Test Factors in Measurement of Speed of Reading," *Journal of Educational Research* 44 (March, 1951) : 543–49.

Davis, Frederick B. "Research in Comprehension in Reading," *Reading Research Quarterly* 3 (Summer, 1968) : 499–545.

Feifel, Herman, and Lorge, Irving. "Qualitative Differences in the Vocabulary Responses of Children," *Journal of Educational Psychology* 41 (January, 1950) : 1–18.

Hunt, Lyman C. "Can We Measure Specific Factors Associated

with Reading Comprehension?" *Journal of Educational Research* 51 (November, 1957) : 161–72.

Preston, Ralph C., and Botel, Morton. "Reading Comprehension Tested Under Timed and Untimed Conditions," *School and Society* 74 (August, 1951) : 71.

Ruddell, Robert B. "The Effect of Oral and Written Patterns of Language Structure on Reading Comprehension," *Reading Teacher* 18 (January, 1965) : 270–75.

Russell, David, and Saadeh, Ibrahim Q. "Qualitative Levels in Children's Vocabularies," *Journal of Educational Psychology* 53 (August, 1962) : 170–74.

Weber, Rose Marie. "The Study of Oral Reading Errors: A Survey of the Literature," *Reading Research Quarterly* 4 (Fall, 1968) : 96–119.

Section Five

ESTIMATING CHANGE
IN READING ABILITY

Ways to evaluate reading growth are needed by the teacher and administrator to plan further instruction and to judge the effectiveness of teaching procedures, instructional materials, and curriculum organization. Tests have been used more frequently for estimating growth in reading ability than for any other purpose. However, nowhere are tests more often misused than when change is being evaluated. The articles in this section contain practical suggestions for overcoming some of the problems inherent in any measurement of change in behavior.

Stroud's article points out the shortcomings of standardized tests for estimating growth and provides a useful background for understanding the articles that follow. In Article 26, Davis discusses four major steps that should be followed in assessing change. He then outlines specific steps to be followed in evaluating reading growth of an individual or of an entire class; his use of specific examples should aid in the utilization of the procedures. In Article 27, Davis describes the types of measurements that should be utilized in evaluating improvement in Reading Skill courses.

Reading and measurement specialists quite often hold that the use of alternate forms of standardized reading tests is preferable to using the same test over again when measuring reading growth. However, in Article 28, Karlin and Jolly examine the assumptions underlying this contention and present evidence that indicates that it may be just as valid to readminister a pre-test rather than use an alternate form.

Problems of evaluating "new methods" of teaching reading are examined by McDonald in Article 29. The rash claims for new methods of teaching reading are usually based on erroneous measurements of students' reading abilities.

In Article 30, Tracy and Rankin describe a procedure of great use to classroom teachers in estimating reading improvement and in evaluating these gains. Article 31, by Bliesmer, describes some of the special problems in evaluating the progress of remedial readers. Both articles include valuable suggestions for reading teachers and supervisors facing the problems of evaluating students' reading improvement.

The articles in this section seek answers to these questions:

1. How should standardized reading tests be used to estimate reading growth?
2. Is the best procedure for estimating reading growth the subtraction of a post-test score from a pre-test score?
3. Should grade-level norms be used for estimating growth?
4. What procedures will increase the accuracy of reading improvement estimates?
5. Should a ten-point gain be evaluated equally for all students even if they begin a program with different reading achievement levels?

25

Background of Measurement in Reading Improvement

J. B. STROUD

All research presupposes measurement. In a sense all improvement in instruction in reading depends upon measurement. To be sure a given teacher may reflect that he feels more comfortable and self-assured teaching reading by procedure A than by procedure B. This is scarcely measurement. But if a hundred teachers or eight in a hundred make such a report, we have something approaching measurement. One could write a descriptive history of methods of reading instruction without reference to measurement. However, when one attempts to investigate the relative effectiveness of the respective methods, seen in historical perspective, he must sooner or later come to terms with measurement.

If for the moment we consider the sum total of our knowledge of reading, such as might be encompassed in a course of instruction bearing the title Psychology of Reading, knowledge which certainly has had a profound effect upon reading instruction, we are impressed with the cruciality of measurement. Javal must have made his original observations upon the saccadic nature of eye movement in reading without

REPRINTED with permission of J. B. Stroud and the National Reading Conference, Inc. "Background of Measurement in Reading Improvement," in *Starting and Improving College Reading Programs:* Eighth Yearbook of the National Reading Conference, Oscar S. Causey and William Eller, eds. (Fort Worth, Texas: Texas Christian University Press, 1958), pp. 77–88.

the aid of measurement. Indeed it seems unlikely that one would have ever attempted to investigate the behavior of the eyes in reading had he not observed that they move in unusual ways. However, all subsequent knowledge of eye movements has been derived through measurement. The period from 1878, the date of Javal's original observations, to 1917, the date of Schmidt's monograph, was marked by attempts to measure eye movements in reading.[1]

A similar history characterizes the work on the relationship between reading rate and comprehension. In his book, *Mental Evolution in Animals,* published in 1883, Romanes described some work upon this problem.[2] Here he measured reading rate much as we do today. Tests of reading comprehension as we know them had not appeared upon the scene. He resorted to the method of written reproduction. In passing, it may be noted he observed "astonishing differences in reading rate," amounting to as much as 4 to 1. He also observed a lack of relationship between slowness of reading and power of assimilation. Investigations to the same effect, using more or less similar methods were reported by Abell (1894) and Quantz (1897).[3] As you well know, the problem of the relationship between reading rate and reading comprehension is still with us. I think it may be said that the advent of the reading test as you and I know it has contributed more to confusion than to the solution of the problem. To this issue we shall return later.

If we look at almost any of the practical problems of reading instruction we again see the significant role of measurement. Without measurement, without measurement of some kind, we do not know what the instructional needs are and do not know the effectiveness of instruction once it has been undertaken. Any consideration of such practical problems as reading readiness, reading level, individual differences, homogeneous grouping, establishing special classes for the retarded or gifted, referring pupils for remedial instruction,

[1] W. A. Schmidt, *An Experimental Study in the Psychology of Reading.* Supplementary Educational Monographs, No. 2, Chicago: University of Chicago Press, 1917.
[2] New York: D. Appleton and Co., 1833.
[3] A. M. Abell, Rapid Reading, *Educational Review,* 1894, Vol. 8, pp. 283 ff. J. O. Quantz, Problems in the Psychology of Reading, *Psychological Review, Monograph Supplements,* 1897, Vol. 2, No. 1.

investigating factors associated with reading deficiencies, calls for measurement appropriate to the problem.

In thus recognizing that measurement occupies a crucial place in the improvement of reading instruction we should not lose sight of the role of subjective judgment upon the part of the teacher. The judgment of the shrewd, experienced teacher may approach an unstandardized form of measurement and should always be given weight in pupil appraisal procedures. Moreover, in thinking of measurement we envisage more than measurement of reading proper. It is really the child and his development that concerns us, not merely his reading. Thus the professional worker in reading must be conversant with measurement of intelligence, of personality, especially as it may affect or be affected by reading performance, and with the measurement of scholastic achievement generally as this reflects the use of reading.

We are all familiar with the fact that writers recognize two kinds of reading tests, the so-called survey test and the diagnostic or analytical test. The survey test whose purpose seems to be that of ranking pupils in over-all proficiency in reading or perhaps determining the general developmental level of reading of a class or school system appears to be most appropriate to a general educational achievement battery. The professional worker in reading will probably insist upon the use of the best tests he can get—tests that yield the maximum amount of information about the reading performance of the pupils being tested. Having made this point it still may be questioned whether or not analytical testing has lived up to its earlier promise, in the field of reading, in the field of intelligence, or elsewhere. What I mean to suggest is that diagnostic testing is something to be critical about.

Analytical testing seems to imply that reading performance may be analyzed into a number of separate and at least somewhat independent abilities, that these abilities develop in a given pupil at rates that are somewhat independent, and that we have separate and independent instructional procedures for their development. In the light of these three conditions we seem to do pretty well at the beginning and early levels, and less well at later levels.

There are certain abilities which we associate with reading readiness, which are correlated with one another and with intelligence, but which vary somewhat independently. Moreover specific training designed to foster the development of these abilities or skills is at hand. I have in mind such abilities as auditory discrimination, visual discrimination, matching objects whose names begin with the same sounds, choosing pictures of objects whose names begin like the names of certain objects or persons named in stories, and discerning the meaning of stories heard orally. Of course the meaning of the obtained scores on such tests will depend upon the measured intelligence and perhaps the social background of the individual child. Thus the intelligence becomes a factor, perhaps the most important single factor, in assessing readines for reading.

At the first and second grade levels diagnosis may also feature an intelligence score or some kind of reading capacity score. Especially at these stages of reading development the teacher or reading specialist will wish to make sure that adequate auditory and visual discrimination abilities have been acquired. In addition it would seem to be profitable to test for word analysis, sight vocabulary, use of contextual clues in attacking new words, and of course, reading comprehension. In the latter the test designer may make use of sentences, paragraphs, or somewhat longer connected stories, or of all three. I think some caution should be observed in attributing diagnostic significance to the separate scores. At least, when the three types are used there appears to be no reason why the scores cannot be combined to form a total reading comprehension score. It is not sufficient, in order to enlarge the count of diagnostic features of a test, to call one of these sentence comprehension; another, paragraph comprehension; and the other, story comprehension; and to provide subtest scores and norms, as if the three separate scores had some diagnostic significance. At least, the test author should be expected to demonstrate that the part scores have some analytical value or present plausible argument that they do so. It seems probable that the pupils who can read and successfully respond to such sentences as (1) Can some animals live under water all their lives? or (2) Do birds like to have you touch them? or (3) Would you be surprised if you saw a monkey drying the dishes? could successfully read stories of comparable levels of difficulty and vocabulary. This in no sense is offered as a criticism of test authors for using a variety of devices for testing reading comprehension. They always work under rigid limitations of space. They face the problem of the most efficient use of space. They also face the problem of holding the interest of the pupils. Obviously they are justified in employing any stratagem available. Upon our part, as professional workers in the field of reading, we do not have to attribute diagnostic significance to these separate tests simply because they exist.

The reading test author always faces the problem of how to combine the subtest scores to form composite scores. As a kind of rule of thumb I think it might be suggested that scores which have separate diagnostic or teaching significance should not be combined into composites. For example, work-study skills such as the use of indexes, the use of the library, or the ability to read maps, hardly belong with reading comprehension, not in a diagnostic test. They might be grouped together to form a total work-study skill score. Measures of reading capacity, if they form a constituent part of a reading test, should be kept separate from work-study skills and reading comprehension. As much may be said of word attack skills or sight vocabulary. A composite score comprised of all the part scores on a reading test is not very meaningful and tends to obscure its diagnostic features. The practice of providing such scores may not be objectionable at all in a survey type of test.

Once we are past the primary grades, appraisal of reading performance in the ordinary course of school work resolves itself pretty largely into measures of capacity, measures of rate, and measures of comprehension. One of the most engaging tests to this purpose, one which unfortunately for some time has been out of print, is the *Van Waganen–Dvorak Diagnostic Examination of Silent Reading Abilities*. As measures of capacity this battery features subtests of Vocabulary, Analogies, and General Information. As a measure of reading rate these authors make use of a test of the Chapman-Cook type, consisting of a number of short paragraphs in each of which is imbedded an incongruent word or phrase. The reader is asked to mark out these words or phrases.

Upon the face of it this would look like a good procedure, since it provides evidence that the reader did or did not read with understanding the passages upon which his rate of reading was established. However, this method has some inherent disadvantages. Such tests are ordinarily administered by the time-limit method. If the number of items attempted is taken as the rate score nothing is gained by requiring the reader to show evidence that he understood what he read. If the number right, or worse still the number right minus a fraction of the number wrong, is taken as the score, we confound the rate score with the comprehension score. One who attempts 15 items and gets 10 right reads faster than one who attempts 10 items and gets 10 right. He would not receive a higher rate score by this method. Indeed if a correction formula is applied he would receive a lower score.

There is the further fact that the reading rate score is contaminated by the pupils' habits of work and thought. A meticulous worker may earn a lower score than another student who reads no faster but is less careful about his work. Both of these criticisms of the Chapman-Cook type of test apply to any work-type reading rate tests.

The Van Waganen–Dvorak examination provides for five comprehension scores, as follows: (1) generalizing, (2) drawing inferences, (3) noting and remembering clearly stated detail, (4) drawing conclusions, and (5) combining ideas that belong together in thought but are not presented together. These subtests of comprehension are of high quality. They sample most of the important aspects of good reading comprehension. At least these are aspects of intelligent reading. I think the merit of these subtests lies chiefly in their quality and in the ampleness of their coverage of comprehension abilities. I feel less assured about the diagnostic significance of the part scores. I doubt that these abilities vary independently to any great extent, or that we can or should provide instruction designed to foster their development independently. Certainly this is a case in which a total comprehension score is most meaningful.

There are some traits which we simply associate with intellect. A hundred years ago in Europe, as railroads and highways were being built and gravel pits dug, men were finding stone implements, eoliths dating back to the Tertiary period, and later, shaped tools of the second inter-glacial. No fossil men were found to go with these implements in those far-off periods. Yet, scholars recognized them as the work of man. These are among the things we expect of intellect, and only creatures capable of higher intelligence can do these things. Of course intelligent pupils can generalize, draw inferences and conclusions, can summarize, and combine ideas that go together in thought but are not presented together in time and space. Indeed they can combine and synthesize information acquired at different periods in their lives.

A test author can make more efficient use of his reading text by getting at comprehension in different ways. One good inference item may be all he can get out of a paragraph. But he may also be able to get an information item or two, a generalization item, or a conclusion item. This fact alone would justify the use of a variety of types of comprehension items.

At this point the question arises as to the rightful relationship between tests of reading comprehension and tests of intelligence. Suppose one of you, or for all I know, a bright sixth grade pupil read the following statements: The Caspian Sea, situated between Europe and Asia, is 92 feet below sea level. It is fed by two large rivers, the Volga and the Ural, which drain vast areas of Russia. You or he would be able to infer that this is quite a large sea; that it is a body of salt water; that it has no outlet to any of the oceans, among other things. Such statements and such inferences might well go into an intelligence test at age levels to which they are appropriate. I would not think them appropriate to a reading comprehension test. The inferences must be drawn from too much information not contained in the two-sentence story. Conversely, in a reading comprehension test we might think that the stories to be read should contain all or most of the information the pupil would require in order to draw the inferences, to make the generalizations or draw the conclusions called for. Obviously different levels of reading comprehension will require different levels of intelligence.

I have suggested that there are three major facets to pupil appraisal in the field of reading and that the question of improvement of reading be considered in the light of these three facets. As indicated, these are reading rate or fluency, reading comprehension, and reading capacity, perhaps chiefly intelligence. It is of the greatest consequence that measures of these three aspects of pupil growth be kept separate one from another in so far as possible.

It seems fairly easy to secure independent measures of reading rate. As Professor Eller and his students have demonstrated, fair reliability can be achieved in reading rate scores, either by the time-limit or amount-limit method, based upon three or four minutes' reading time.[4] At least rate scores based upon reading times of such lengths appear to be about as reliable as those based upon reading time of much longer length. Now, the test author, being under press to make the most efficient use possible of his allotted space, commonly prepares a comprehension test over passages thus read to establish reading rate. In so far as I can see this does no harm to the rate score. But it does in some cases, for some reasons unknown to me, introduce a correlation between rate and comprehension, as for example on the Pressey and Traxler tests. In the case of these two tests, as you will recall, the pupil proceeds to read a somewhat long selection and after a length of time marks the line he is reading when a pre-arranged signal is given. The pupil then completes the reading of the entire selection and straightway takes an untimed comprehension test. With these two tests I have repeatedly obtained correlations in the range of from .30 to .40 between the rate and comprehension scores. We would of course expect positive, and somewhat higher, correlations between rate and comprehension on those tests in which the comprehension section is timed. I have also repeatedly obtained zero correlations between rate and comprehension in other situations in which pupils read entire selections each at his own rate and proceeded to take untimed comprehension tests over the passages. Another of our students, Mr. Thalberg, has obtained correlations of zero, more or less, between rate of reading established on one set of selections and comprehension scores

---

[4] K. Humphry, Amount-Limit and Time-Limit Methods of Measuring Reading Rate, Doctor's Dissertation, State University of Iowa, 1955.

established on entirely different sets of selections.[5] The latter were, of course, read.

It is suggested that there might be some merit in using different reading selections for the establishment of rate from those used to establish comprehension scores. At least this procedure would permit us to conclude that any relationship found to exist between rate and comprehension were real, and not a consequence of some kind of dependence of one of the measures upon the other. This would look like a legitimate thing to do. If reading rate has any generality, if there are persons who are rapid, average, and slow readers, this fact can be ascertained, and such persons identified, by one reading passage as well as another. If reading comprehension scores have any generality, good, average, and poor comprehension can be ascertained on reading selections quite independent of those used to establish rate. Moreover, the rate and comprehension tests could be thus administered weeks or months apart.

It is true that the rank and file of reading comprehension tests are confounded by a rate factor. It has seemed expedient in the marketing of tests to be able to inform school officials precisely how long it takes to administer a test. For this reason, and also perhaps to enhance the reliability of the tests, reading tests commonly are strictly timed. Thus the comprehension score reflects not only power of comprehension but also reading rate and rate of work. An excellent substitute for a comprehension test of unlimited time is the "level of comprehension" feature of the Cooperative tests. Here, even though there is a specified time for administration, the level of comprehension score is reasonably uninfluenced by rate of reading. Suffice it to say that it is possible for a slow reader to make as high a comprehension score as a rapid reader. It is rather surprising that this procedure has not been used more extensively than has been the case.

In my insistence that reading rate and comprehension be measured by methods that yield scores that are independent

[5] S. P. Thalberg, Reading Rate and Comprehension in a College Reading Program, Master's Thesis (in preparation), State University of Iowa.

of each other I am not assuming that rate and comprehension never bear any genuine relationship to each other. I think in the ordinary course of events, and in the case of most reading tests, rate and comprehension vary independently, more or less. Either this is true or I, and some of you, have had no business teaching that slow reading is the consequence of bad habits. On the other hand I feel sure there are conditions under which rate and comprehension vary concomitantly. I think the question that should be asked is, What are the conditions that influence the relationship between rate and comprehension? not, Is there a relationship? My interest in the relation between rate and comprehension at the moment centers not so much in the phenomenon itself as in its bearing upon problems of measurement.

I shall use an illustration or two. On some of the items in intelligence tests, such as "block design" and "object assembly" on the *Wechsler Intelligence Scale for Children,* or the problems in Raven's *Progressive Matrices,* it may mean one thing to solve or fail to solve the problems at all. It may mean another thing to be able to solve them quickly. In such cases speed signifies power. Power makes speed possible. In power situations speed may signify intelligence. In mine-run situations it may not do this. Speed in mine-run situations may not correlate positively at all with speed in power situations. In certain test situations power of intelligence may make for rapid reading and for high comprehension. Another kind of power may come from training. We would expect an instructor in chemistry to read a chapter in a chemistry text more quickly than an instructor in psychology and to show better comprehension.

Thus in reading situations in which there is a premium upon power we would expect both reading rate and comprehension to vary with the power of the readers. Even here, prior habits of work and thought may operate to upset the relationship. In order to demonstrate a positive relationship between rate of reading and comprehension even in a power situation it probably would be necessary to arrange for some kind of work-type reading, in which all readers could be held to some kind of uniform reading requirements.

As already said, pupil appraisal in our work requires the

use of measures of capacity. Here also we are concerned about the independence of the measures, especially when certain group intelligence tests are used for purposes of assessing capacity. Since the inception of group testing, users of tests have been concerned about the effects of reading proficiency upon the scores, since these tests are administered under rigid time limits. Apparently we face here a somewhat complex set of relationships. As before, we are not so much concerned with knowing what the relationships are as what they mean in our work.

If reading rate is determined in power situations, as mentioned above, and if the group intelligence tests are power tests there is not much doubt that the reading rate scores thus derived would correlate positively with the intelligence scores. And under such circumstances probably no one would think it unfortunate that the fastest readers tended to make the highest scores. Twenty-five or thirty years ago psychologists were concerning themselves with the speed-power issue in group intelligence tests. One of the procedures used in investigations of the problem was to administer a test under standard time limits, then, after changing to pencils of different colored lead, to allow additional time equal to the standard limits or in some cases more. The workers did not quite agree upon what the results signified regarding the speed-power issue, but they were agreed in showing that pupils who made the lowest scores in standard time improved their scores least when allowed additional time. At least we may conclude that their low scores were not a consequence of slow reading.

We have reason to believe that the typical reading rate test is not a power test, at least not so to any considerable extent, even when it employs the work-type procedure. We know, I think, that slow, poor readers, slow readers with poor comprehension, do not improve their scores very much when allowed practically unlimited time on group intelligence tests. They do not seem to be penalized by their slowness. Their low scores are not attributable to slowness of reading. Typically such pupils do not do well on intelligence tests that do not require reading at all. Nor does a rapid, poor reader, as determined by the typical reading test, a rapid reader with poor comprehension, fare appreciably better upon a group intelligence test than a slow, poor one. On the other hand, there is some evidence that pupils who read rapidly and well, read fast with good comprehension, do somewhat better on group intelligence tests than slow readers who enjoy good comprehension. The differences are not great. We should not expect them to be great. The number of words to be read in a typical group intelligence test is not great. One who reads at a rate of 100 words per minute could cover an equal number of words of ordinary prose within the time allotted to the intelligence test.

Perhaps one would be inclined to the conclusion that group intelligence tests, which we use to measure capacity, are not seriously contaminated with the thing we are trying to predict, reading itself. Naturally, there is a relationship, rather a high one, between intelligence and reading. That, of course, is the reason for our administering intelligence tests in reading work in the first place. But so that we may work with true relationships we want our methods of determining intelligence to be relatively free, operationally, of reading proficiency itself.

Obviously in clinical work we would insist upon individual psychological examinations. The reasons for this are numerous and obvious. In the ordinary course of school work this is, to say the least, impractical.

I should like to close with the general observation that the best intelligence tests to use for purposes of pupil appraisal in reading are the best tests of intelligence available. This would seem pretty obvious, but I think the statement deserves a little further development. The best intelligence test to use for the prediction of reading achievement is also the best test to use for the prediction of achievement in arithmetic, spelling, language, or in other subject matter fields. In our work over the years we have studied the relationships among various achievement tests and subtests and the following intelligence tests: *Primary Mental Abilities*, the *Stanford-Binet*, *Wechsler Intelligence Scale for Children,* verbal and nonverbal, *Davis-Eells Games*, *Progressive Matrices*, and *Lorge-Thorndike Intelligence Tests* (verbal and nonverbal). We have found little evidence of differential predictive power among these tests or among any of their subtests. In general those tests and subtests which yield the highest correlations with reading also yield the highest correlations with arithmetic, language, spelling, and so on. For example, in our work, the two subtests out of the eleven subtests on the WISC which yielded the highest correlation with reading were "block design" and "object assembly." It is significant that these same two subtests yielded the highest correlations, of any of the eleven, with the other achievement measures used.

26
The Assessment of Change

FREDERICK B. DAVIS

To assess a pupil's current level of proficiency in any skill, ability, or subject-matter field, it is first necessary to define carefully and explicitly the variable being measured. Second, a test of the variable, or as close an approximation to it as can be secured, must be administered under conditions that assure a high degree of cooperation on the part of the pupil. Third, a pupil's obtained score must be compared with suitable norms, such as percentile ranks in his own age or grade group. Fourth, the possibility that the pupil's obtained score represents a sizable deviation from his true score must be considered. To do so, the standard error of measurement of the pupil's obtained score must be used to construct an appropriate confidence interval.[1] For practical purposes, the 15-per-cent

---

[1] In practice, the standard error of measurement precisely applicable to a given pupil's obtained score is rarely obtainable. If standard errors of measurement for several levels of score value are available, the one for the value closest to that of the pupil's score should be used. If not, the over-all standard error of measurement for the pupil's age or grade group may be employed.

REPRINTED with permission of Frederick B. Davis and the National Reading Conference, Inc. "The Assessment of Change," in *Phases of College and Other Adult Reading Programs:* Tenth Yearbook of the National Reading Conference, Emery P. Bliesmer and Albert J. Kingston, eds. (Milwaukee, Wisconsin: The National Reading Conference, 1961), pp. 86–95.

confidence interval is often satisfactory and forms a basis for asserting that the chances are 85 out of 100 that the range of scores so designated includes the pupil's true score.

These four steps may seem unduly elaborate to many teachers and supervisors, but the task of assessing the pupil's improvement in any skill, ability, or subject-matter field may be even more complicated. This assessment is, however, of great practical importance to pupils and their parents as well as to teachers, school administrators, and supervisors. After all, the primary purpose of teaching is to produce improvement in the learner. Procedures that may be used in assessing improvement in learning will be discussed under the four main headings indicated.

OBTAINING APPROPRIATE MEASURING INSTRUMENTS

Test Validity

The first consideration in selecting an instrument for estimating improvement is the validity of the instrument for measuring what the examiner wants to measure. Teachers and administrators should give careful thought to the appropriateness of their measuring instruments prior to the beginning of the instructional period and select for detailed study tests that appear to measure the most relevant combination of skills, abilities, and knowledges. Ordinarily, a teacher interested in measuring the improvement of a pupil during all or part of a school year wants to know how well the pupil has learned certain specific skills that he has been practicing and how much effect his specific practice and his general maturation have had on his over-all proficiency. For example, to measure reading ability it is usually fairly easy to select tests of specific skills (such as oral reading, word recognition, or use of an index), but it is more difficult to decide which test of over-all reading ability measures the most appropriately weighted combination of skills. The total scores of tests of comprehension in reading commonly used in American secondary schools constitute measures of rather different combinations of skills and abilities. The *Iowa Silent Reading Tests* (4) include measures of study skills and rate of reading in the total scores; the *Nelson-Denny Reading Test* (9) consists of rather highly speeded tests of word knowledge and paragraph comprehension; and the *Cooperative Reading Comprehension Test* (2) includes in its total score an essentially unspeeded test of word knowledge and both speeded and unspeeded measures of paragraph comprehension. It tends to have a more literary flavor than the two tests mentioned previously. *The Davis Reading Test* (3) yields two scores, the first an unspeeded measure of comprehension and the second a speed-of-comprehension score.

A source of unwanted and invalid variance in scores on aptitude and achievement tests that is often unrecognized even by sophisticated examiners is the practice of guessing on the part of many examinees. The effect of this practice is particularly troublesome when tests are used to measure *improvement* because, over a period of time, pupils are apt to change their rates of work or methods of approach to the task set by the test. If tests are scored with an appropriate correction for chance success, the directions for administration can legitimately discourage guessing and can reduce the effect of such guessing as nonetheless takes place. For these reasons, among others, the writer strongly recommends that only tests scored with correction for chance success be employed to estimate improvement resulting from learning. This is especially important in measuring growth in comprehension in reading because many courses designed to improve reading stress speed of reading as well as depth of comprehension. Improvement in both objectives of instruction should, therefore, be measured separately. Unless the test of comprehension is scored with correction for chance success, it is, in practice, likely to become partly a measure of the examinee's tendency to mark answers to items even when he does not understand the material on which they are based. Since many teachers, psychologists, and school administrators are not familiar with the way guessing on the part of the examinee can impair the validity of test scores, illustrations will be provided here to show how it can spuriously increase or decrease the observed change in a pupil's score.

In 1949, Murphy and Davis administered Form B of the

Nelson-Denny Reading Test to 393 eleventh- and twelfth-grade
pupils in Nashville, Tennessee (8). The 47 pupils who obtained
the lowest scores were called in for retesting. They were encouraged to do better and to mark an answer to every item
even if they did not know the answer. These instructions
changed their mental sets toward the task and their methods
of work. Their average score rose from 25.53 on Form B to
46.32 on Form A. Part of this increase was the result of regression to the group mean, but most of it resulted from the
fact that pupils marked answers to a greater number of test
items than they had at first. Since the scores on the test are
not corrected for chance success, a pupil is likely to increase
his score simply by marking answers to more items. After
correction for chance success, the average score of the same
pupils rose only from 13.62 to 15.62, a difference largely accounted for by regression to the group mean. Correction for
chance success removed the spurious *inflation* of the observed
gain in the average reading-test scores of the 47 pupils.

Another example will illustrate how correction for chance
success can remove a spurious *reduction* of the observed
change between testings. A ninth-grade pupil, markedly retarded in recognition vocabulary, was given the vocabulary
section of Form B of the *Nelson-Denny Reading Test* at the
beginning of the school year in September. Finding that he
had great difficulty in reading the words, he moved rapidly
along, marking every item and hoping to get a few of them
correct on the basis of what he could read. Since he actually
did know the answers to some of the items, his score was better than could most reasonably have been expected on the
basis of chance alone; he got a score of 23. The published
norms indicated that this corresponded to a grade score of
11.0. After 9 months of school, including special tutorial work
in reading with emphasis on word-recognition skills, he was
given Form A of the same test. This time he approached the
test differently because he could read the words more readily.
He tried each item seriously and was able to read 34 of them
in the time limit. Of the 34 he tried, he marked 14 correctly.
The published norms indicated that this corresponded to a
grade score below the beginning of grade 9. These scores might

lead one to conclude that the boy had retrogressed markedly in recognition of words during the course of the school year. But we can easily show that this conclusion is unjustified. After correction for chance, the boy's score on Form B in September was 4; on Form A in June it was 9. Thus correction for chance success removed the spurious *reduction* of the amount of improvement that the boy had actually made and showed that, in fact, he had increased his score.

Availabilty of Parallel Forms

Since the estimation of *improvement* demands testing at two different times, the availability of parallel forms is important. Thus, a teacher might prefer to use the *Neal Analysis of Reading Test,* of which several parallel forms are available, rather than the *Gray Oral Paragraphs Test,* of which only one form is available. It is undesirable to use the same form of a test more than once because a pupil may remember part of it or even look up some of the material in it during the interim between testings.

Accuracy of Measurement

Because the amount of improvement that can be shown to be statistically significant at any given level of confidence varies with the accuracy of the measuring instruments employed, it is desirable to use, among tests of equal validity and availability, those with the smallest standard errors of measurement at the score levels obtained by the pupils for whom improvement is to be established. In practice, it is often impossible to make comparisons among tests on this basis because few test publishers provide standard errors of measurement at several score levels. If reliability coefficients are compared, it is important that they shall have been obtained by similar methods on reasonably similar groups, such as pupils in a given age or grade group. Whenever a test is appreciably speeded, reliability coefficients computed by split-half or Knuder-Richardson techniques are spuriously high in comparison with those computed by parallel-forms techniques.

SECURING CONSISTENT RAPPORT
WITH THE EXAMINER

It is important that the degree of cooperation and motivation shown by the examinee be as nearly the same as possible during all testing sessions. Otherwise, differences between the resulting scores cannot properly be ascribed to changes in the pupil's level of skill or ability. For the same reason, the approach of the examinee to the mechanics of testing should be consistent at all testing sessions. This does not mean that the mental set of the pupils should not change; after successful training in reading, for example, it is to be expected that pupils will anticipate and work on a reading test with greater confidence than they did before. Changes of this kind in mental set are a natural concomitant of the successful teaching of reading. What is meant is that mere familiarity with the format of items and answer sheet should not serve to increase a pupil's score. To minimize these irrelevant influences and, at the same time, to minimize the effect of regression to the group mean on the difference between test scores, two equivalent forms of a test may be administered to a class or grade group. Scores for the first of the two forms may be used to identify pupils for remedial instruction before the second set of test papers has been scored. Scores from the latter may be obtained from a third parallel form given at the end of the period of remedial work.

Teachers and others may be surprised to find that considerable improvement in test scores ordinarily takes place between the first and second testings—improvement that would erroneously be ascribed to the effects of the remedial teaching if the second test had not been given prior to the training period.

One of the most important factors in keeping constant the pupil's approach to the mechanics of testing is the type of directions used. These should be clear-cut, understandable, unambiguous, and honest. If standardized tests are used, the directions given by the publisher must be followed precisely;

otherwise, the norms may not be applicable. Therefore, when tests are selected, consideration should be given to the adequacy of the directions. These should provide at least a brief explanation of how the scoring is to be done. Directions for tests corrected for chance success can, and ordinarily do, state this. The following phraseology has been found satisfactory for secondary-school pupils: "You should mark answers to items even when you are not sure that your answers are correct, but it is better to omit an item than to guess *wildly* because each one of your incorrect answers results in a small subtraction from the number of your correct answers."

SELECTING TESTS THAT HAVE APPROPRIATE STANDARDS OR NORMS

Tests used to measure a pupil's improvement should have norms appropriate for representative groups at the pupil's grade level even though the pupil's score may be equivalent to the norm scores of pupils in grades considerably higher or lower. Say, for example, that a pupil entering the ninth grade is scheduled to take the *Stanford Reading Test* in September along with his class. Even though his reading ability is known to be low, it is best to administer the Advanced reading test, which has norms appropriate to Grade 9 and is intended for pupils having the backgrounds and experiences of ninth graders. The change in this pupil's reading ability can then be estimated by one of the methods described in the next section of this paper. If the pupil answers no items correctly in September, the Advanced test will have been shown to be unusable and one of the lower-level tests in the same series should be administered to him. In fact, if the pupil's September grade score were below 40 (the lowest grade score on the Profile Chart of the *Stanford Reading Test,* Advanced) the inaccuracy of measurement would be sufficiently great to warrant the use of a lower-level test—say, the Intermediate test if his grade score were 30–39; the Elementary test if it were 20–29; or the Primary test if it were below 20. To measure progress the June test should be an equivalent form of the level of test given in September.

ESTIMATING THE AMOUNT OF CHANGE

There are many ways of estimating the true amount of improvement (or retrogression) of an individual or of a group. In Table I, five methods for estimating the change in an individual and three methods for estimating the change in the average of a group are provided.[2] These range from crude to sophisticated estimates. Choice among them is determined by the data available and by the use to be made of the data. A classroom teacher might have available only the data and time required for using Method 1 for individuals or Method 6 for groups. An experimenter, conducting a study to determine the gains made by certain individuals or groups, should make plans to obtain and use the data required by Method 5 for individuals or Method 8 for groups.

To illustrate the application of several of the methods presented in Table I to practical data, information about the scores of the 200 pupils in a public high school has been used. These data are shown in Table III. The pupils were tested in September with Form A of the *Davis Reading Test* and in June with Form B of the same test. Only the Speed-of-Comprehension scores of the pupils are considered for illustrative purposes. From the group of 200 pupils, one named Hazel Brown was selected at random prior to the first testing and was also given Form C in September and Form D in June. Her scores are denoted in Table III as A, B, C, and D. Averages of the scores on Forms A and B in the entire group are indicated by placement of a bar over the form letter.

Various estimates of Hazel's true gain in Speed of Comprehension are shown in Table IV. As noted in Table I, Methods 1, 2, and 3 should be used only if an individual pupil has been selected for retesting at random from an age or grade group. Even then, they provide no more than crude estimates

---

[2] Tables I, II, III, and IV are presented at the end of this paper.

unless the number of equivalent forms used in Method 3 is fairly large. In practice, a sufficient number of equivalent forms is not likely to be available for published tests. Hence, it is ordinarily best to plan to use either Method 4 or Method 5 if the requisite data and computing time can be obtained. Method 1 is the simplest and by far the most commonly used estimate of a pupil's gain. It consists simply of getting the difference between his initial and final scores. For Hazel, the difference (d_1) is shown in Table IV to be 5 scaled-score points. When the appropriate expression for D_1 in Table II is employed to find the smallest difference obtained by Method 1 that is significantly different from zero at the 15-per-cent level, Hazel's gain of 5 points is not established as significant. Hence, we cannot conclude that she has made any real gain in speed of comprehension in reading. It should be noted that the 15-per-cent level is not a stringent requirement for significance.

Let us see what our conclusion would be if we were to use the data from both Form A and C (given in September) and Form B and D (given in June). If we employ Method 2, as indicated in Table I, and find the difference between the average of these two pairs of scores, we obtain an estimated gain of 5 points, as before. Use of the appropriate equation from Table II to compute the smallest difference obtained by Method 2 that is significantly different from zero at the 15-percent level yields 4.3, as shown in Table IV. Hazel's gain of 5 points is larger; hence we may conclude that this gain is significant. Increased accuracy of measurement provided by the use of averages of pairs of scores permits the 5-point gain to be regarded as significant.

Method 3 is presented in Table I to show how the average of any number of equivalent forms at either the initial or final testings may be employed. The corresponding test of significance for the 15-per-cent level is shown in Table II.

Methods 4 and 5 for estimating change may be employed even in the case of an individual pupil who was selected for retesting because he had an unusually high or unusually low score in the initial test. In practice, pupils are often assigned to remedial work in reading if their scores on a suitable test, administered at the beginning of the school year, are low.

Then they are retested in June to find the extent of their gains, if any. Such gains should be estimated by Method 4 or 5. Let us say that Hazel's September score of 59 was one of the lowest in her grade and that she was one of the lowest-scoring 20 pupils assigned to remedial work. For her, Method 4, as specified in Table I, yields an estimated gain of 4.6 scaled-score points. Since a gain of less than 4.9 points, computed by Method 4, cannot be considered significant at the 15-per-cent level, as shown in Table IV, we cannot conclude that she has made a real gain.

It should be noted that use of Method 4 requires that the initial and final tests be administered to the entire group of 200 pupils in Hazel's grade group. Their scores provide the means, $\bar{A}$ and $\bar{B}$, and are used to estimate reliability coefficients, r_{aA} and r_{bB}, as follows:

$$r_{aA} = 1 - \frac{S^2_{\text{meas}_p}}{S_A{}^2}, \qquad \text{and} \qquad r_{bB} = 1 - \frac{S^2_{\text{meas}_p}}{S_B{}^2},$$

where S_{meas_p} is the standard error of measurement given by the publisher for a sample of twelfth-grade pupils reasonably similar to the 200 in Hazel's grade group.

In addition to the data required for Method 4, Method 5 demands that the correlation of scores of the 200 pupils on the initial and final tests, r_{AB}, be computed. If Method 5 is used to estimate Hazel's change, a gain of 4.2 points is found. However, the increased accuracy of estimation provided by taking into account the correlation of September and June scores among the 200 pupils in Hazel's grade group permits establishment of the significance of this gain at better than the 15-per-cent level. The clear implication of this illustration for psychologists, teachers, and remedial workers is to make provision in advance for obtaining the data required for use of Method 5 whenever the effects of remedial or other special treatment are to be evaluated.

Estimates of change for a group of pupils chosen at random from an age or grade group can be made by Methods 6, 7, and 8 presented in Table I. If the members of the group have been chosen on the basis of their initial test scores, Method

6 should not be used for this purpose. As shown by the data in Table IV, an average gain of 1.3 points would be significant at the 15-per-cent level for a group of 20 pupils chosen at *random* from the 200 in Hazel's grade group. The amount of change in the group of 20 pupils selected from the group because of low initial test scores should be estimated by either Method 7 or 8. The former yields an estimate of 5.5 points and the latter 4.9 points. Both estimated gains are highly significant statistically since they both greatly exceed the smallest differences of 1.1 and .8, respectively, required to establish significance at the 15-per-cent level.

A word of caution may be in order with respect to the tests of significance of the estimates of mean gain obtained by Methods 6, 7, and 8. These should be used as a basis for drawing inferences about the gain (or loss) estimated for any given group. They should *not* be used as a basis for drawing inferences about the gains (or losses) that could be expected in other comparable samples drawn at random from the same population and exposed to the same influences between tests. The bases for inference of the latter kind are the conventional appropriate standard errors of differences between means.

Table I   Methods of Estimating True Change

Estimate of change (d) for an individual pupil

A. *Chosen at random from an age or grade group*

The difference between equivalent scores:

1. $d_1 = B - A$

2. $d_2 = \dfrac{B + D}{2} - \dfrac{A + C}{2}$

3. $d_3 = \dfrac{\sum\limits^{m} Y}{m} - \dfrac{\sum\limits^{n} X}{n}$

B. *Chosen on the basis of initial test scores*

The difference between regressed equivalent scores:

4. $d_4 = r_{bB}B - r_{aA}A + (\overline{B} - \overline{A} + r_{aA}\overline{A} - r_{bB}\overline{B})$

An estimate of the true difference between equivalent scores:

5. $d_5 = W_B B + W_A A + (\overline{B} - \overline{A} - W_B\overline{B} - W_A\overline{A})$

Estimate of change (d) for a group of pupils

A. *Chosen at random from an age or grade group*

    The difference between averages of equivalent scores:

    6. $d_6 = \overline{B}_g - \overline{A}_g$

B. *Chosen on the basis of initial test scores*

    The difference between averages of regressed equivalent scores:

    7. $d_7 = r_{bB}\overline{B}_g - r_{aA}\overline{A} + (\overline{B} - \overline{A} + r_{aA}\overline{A} - r_{bB}\overline{B})$

    An estimate of the true difference between averages of equivalent scores:

    8. $d_8 = W_B\overline{B}_g + W_A\overline{A}_g + (\overline{B} - \overline{A} - W_B\overline{B} - W_A\overline{A})$

Explanation of symbols used (tables I–IV)

A, B, C, D	represent individual obtained scores on equivalent forms of the same test (1:164)
X, Y	represent individual obtained scores on any equivalent form of the same test
m, n	represent the numbers of equivalent forms of the same test administered to one individual
N	represents the number of pupils in an age or grade group
N_g	represents the number of pupils in a subgroup of the N pupils
$\overline{A}, \overline{B}$	represent arithmetic averages of individual obtained scores of N pupils on equivalent forms of the same test
$\overline{A}_g, \overline{B}_g$	represent arithmetic averages of individual obtained scores in a subgroup of N_g pupils on equivalent forms of the same test
s_{meas}	represents the standard error of measurement of individual scores on equivalent forms of the same test in the group of N pupils
r_{aA}, r_{bB}	represent the reliability coefficients of individual scores on equivalent Forms A and B of the same test in the group of N pupils

$$W_A = \frac{s_B r_{AB}(1 - r_{bB}) - s_A(r_{aA} - r_{AB}{}^2)}{s_A(1 - r_{AB}{}^2)}$$

$$W_B = \frac{s_B(r_{bB} - r_{AB}{}^2) - s_A r_{AB}(1 - r_{aA})}{s_B(1 - r_{AB}{}^2)}$$

Table II   Smallest Change (D) Significant at
the 15-Per-Cent Level*

1. $D_1 = 2s_{\text{meas}_A}$

2. $D_2 = 1.44s_{\text{meas}_A}$

3. $D_3 = 1.44 \sqrt{\dfrac{s_{\text{meas}_A}^2}{m} + \dfrac{s_{\text{meas}_B}^2}{n}}$

4. $D_4 = 1.44s_{\text{meas}_A} \sqrt{r_{aA}^2 + r_{bB}^2}$

5. $D_5 = 1.44s_{\text{meas}_A} \sqrt{W_A^2 + W_B^2}$

6. $D_6 = \dfrac{D_1}{\sqrt{N_g}}$

7. $D_7 = \dfrac{D_4}{\sqrt{N_g}}$

8. $D_8 = \dfrac{D_5}{\sqrt{N_g}}$

* Changes significant at any other level can be identified by appropriate changes in the equations. For example, if the expression on the right-hand side in each of equations 1 through 8 is multipled by 1.36, the 5-per-cent level is provided. If each is multiplied by 1.79, the 1-per-cent level is provided.

Table III   Data Pertaining to Davis Reading Test Scores in
a Twelfth-Grade Class

	Scaled score		*Scaled score*		*Number*
A_i	59.0	r_{aA}	.84	N	200
B_i	64.0	r_{bB}	.87	N_g	20
C_i	61.0	r_{AB}	.65		
D_i	66.0	W_A	−.57		
$\overline{A}$	70.3	W_B	.61		
$\overline{B}$	74.5				
$\overline{A}_g$	60.1				
$\overline{B}_g$	66.1				
s_A	7.3				
s_B	8.0				
s_{meas}	2.9				

Table IV   Estimated Changes (d) and Smallest Changes Significant at the 15-Per-Cent Level (D) for Pupil i and Group g

Estimated change (in scaled scores)		Smallest change significant at the 15-per-cent level	
d_1	5.0	D_1	5.8
d_2	5.0	D_2	4.2
$d_3{}^*$	6.0	$D_3{}^*$	5.1
d_4	4.6	D_4	4.9
d_5	4.2	D_5	3.4
d_6	6.0	D_6	1.3
d_7	5.5	D_7	1.1
d_8	4.9	D_8	0.8

$^* d_3 = \left(\dfrac{B + D}{2} \right) - A$ (average of two tests *vs* score on one test)

References

1. Davis, F. B., "Interpretation of Differences Among Averages and Individual Test Scores," *Journal of Educational Psychology*, 50:162–170, 1959.
2. Davis, F. B., et al., *Cooperative Reading Comprehension Test*, Forms Q–Z, Educational Testing Service, Princeton, New Jersey, 1940–53.
3. Davis, F. B., and C. C. Davis, *Davis Reading Test*, Psychological Corporation, New York, 1958.
4. Greene, H. A., A. N. Jorgensen, and V. H. Kelley, *Iowa Silent Reading Tests* (New Edition, Revised), Advanced Test, World Book Company, Yonkers, New York, 1943.
5. Kelley, T. L., *Fundamentals of Statistics*, Harvard University Press, Cambridge, Massachusetts, 1947.
6. Lord, F. M., "Measurement of Growth," *Educational and Psychological Measurement*, 16:421–437, 1956.
7. McNemar, Q., "On Growth Measurement," *Educational and Psychological Measurement*, 18:47–55, 1958.
8. Murphy, H. D., and F. B. Davis, "A Note on the Measurement of Progress in Remedial Reading," *Peabory Journal of Education*, 27:108–111, 1949.
9. Nelson, M. J., and E. C. Denny, *Nelson-Denny Reading Test*, Houghton Mifflin Company, Boston, 1938.

27

Measurement of Improvement in Reading Skill Courses

FREDERICK B. DAVIS

To the layman the measurement of rate of reading seems at first thought to be a simple undertaking. Just ask a person to read for five minutes, count the number of words read, and divide the number by five to get his average rate in words per minute. Unfortunately, thoughtful consideration of the problem quickly reveals that the measurement of rate of reading is a complicated and troublesome matter.

It is apparent that any reader's rate is greatly affected by his purpose in reading. How greatly is illustrated by some data obtained by Laycock (8). The rate of reading in words per minute of 391 applicants for admission to college is shown in Table 1. The average scholastic aptitude score of these examinees was slightly above that of the median applicant for admission to college. When asked to read a passage at their normal rate, they averaged 220.4 words per minute. Asked to read a similar passage as fast as possible without missing important points on which test questions would be based, they

REPRINTED with permission of Frederick B. Davis and the National Reading Conference, Inc. "Measurement of Improvement in Reading Skill Courses," in *Problems, Programs and Projects in College-Adult Reading:* Eleventh Yearbook of the National Reading Conference, Emery P. Bliesmer and Ralph C. Staiger, eds. (Milwaukee, Wisconsin: The National Reading Conference, Inc., 1962), pp. 30–40.

averaged 308.1 words per minute. In other words, a simple request for them to increase their speed of reading without sacrificing comprehension resulted in an immediate 40 per cent average gain in rate.

After eliminating from consideration students whose comprehension scores were below 75 per cent, the gain made

Table 1   Rate of Reading of 391 Applicants
for College Admission*

		Rate in words/min.			
Group	N	Normal rate	After request to read rapidly	Gain in rate	Training
All applicants	391	220.4	308.1	88.7	None
Among applicants with comprehension scores of 75%, or more:					
Highest	37	231.1	420.0	188.9	None
Lowest	35	219.3	255.0	35.7	None
Second testing among applicants with comprehension scores of 75%, or more:					
Highest	37	355.8	533.1	177.3	
Lowest	35	321.6	428.0	106.4	

* After (7).

by the 37 fastest readers is even more suprising. Their normal average rate was 231.1 words per minute, which increased to 420 words per minute for an average gain of 82 per cent. Lest it be thought that gain would largely disappear on another testing because of regression toward the average gain for all 391 students, the results of a second testing should be noted. These 37 applicants read an average of 355.8 words per minute on the first selection in the second testing and an average of 533.1 words per minute on the second selection. The gain made by the 35 slowest readers who obtained comprehension scores of 75 per cent or more is also shown in Table 1 and indicates that changes in the purpose of slow readers cause marked increases in rate of reading even though the average per cent of increase is smaller than that of the initially rapid readers.

Three important implications follow from data of this type:

a. The measurement of rate of reading must be made under conditions that unambiguously define the purpose for which the reading is being carried on and that provide assurance that this purpose is being fulfilled by the reader.
b. Quite different instruments are needed for measuring the rate at which material is covered for the several important but very different purposes for which reading is done.
c. Since a mere request to a typical reader to step up his rate without sacrificing comprehension may result in a marked increase in his speed of reading many kinds of material without serious loss of comprehension, the results of training programs for increasing speed of reading should always be judged on the basis of procedures that exclude any increase in speed that a reader can make before the training is begun simply by stepping up his speed of reading without appreciable loss of comprehension.

The purposes of readers vary so widely that some of them hardly result in what is commonly defined as reading. For example, a student may wish to determine what topics are taken up in a book or an essay and how they are organized. He therefore skims through the material rapidly without making any effort to understand the content. This accomplishes his purpose, but his activity can scarcely be described as reading, in any ordinary sense of the term. He has used techniques that are well suited to his purpose, but he has not *read* the material.

A second purpose characteristic of many readers is that of following the main thread of a story. This purpose is uppermost in the minds of many readers of novels. A third purpose that commonly motivates reading is that of grasping an author's ideas, of understanding them, and of weaving them together in order to draw conclusions or to apply them in practical situations. A fourth purpose in reading is to learn certain facts or statements so that they can be reproduced from memory. Students must read many assignments with this purpose in mind.

Tests are needed to measure the rate at which reading can be carried on to fulfill each of these four purposes. Thus, at least four separate rate-of-reading tests should be made available, as follows:

a. A test of rate of covering words during skimming;
b. A test of rate of covering words while following the main thread of thought;
c. A test of rate of covering words while understanding the content;
d. A test of rate of covering words while learning the principal ideas in the content.

The level of complexity of material greatly affects the speed at which it can be read by an individual seeking to maintain a high level of comprehension. This fact can be illustrated by data published by Flanagan in 1939 (6). He administered 20 items in each of 3 equivalent reading scales in Form O of the *Cooperative Literary Comprehension Test* to 317 twelfth-grade pupils in such a way that they worked at different pre-determined rates on the 3 scales. The resulting data are shown in Table 2. The average score of the group of 317 pupils was

Table II Comprehension at Varying Rates of Speed in Reading Cooperative Literary Comprehensive Test, Form O*

	Mean scores on 20 items		
Group	*Time: 18 mins.*	*Time: 12 mins.*	*Time: 6 mins.*
317 pupils in grade 12	10.5	9.7	7.0
Highest third in 18 mins.		11.74	8.38
Middle third at 18 mins.		9.65	7.02
Lowest third at 18 mins.		7.59	5.26

* After (6).

10.5 in 18 minutes of working time, 9.7 in 12 minutes of working time, and 7.0 in 6 minutes of working time. Thus, with a clear purpose (that of responding correctly to test items illustrated in advance by practice exercises), these twelfth-grade pupils sustained an average loss of comprehension in reading materials of equivalent difficulty and type when their working time was cut by one-third and by two-thirds.

An analysis of the data was made to determine whether different percentages of loss of comprehension occurred between the 12-minute and 6-minute working periods for the groups of pupils comprising the *highest* third of the 317, the *middle* third, and the *lowest* third with respect to comprehension scores in the 18-minute working time. As shown in Table II, the precentages of loss of comprehension between 12-minute and 6-minute working times were nearly the same for all three thirds of the original group. This result suggests that, with the purpose of the reader and the complexity of the content held constant, there is a fairly direct *inverse* relationship throughout the range of ability to comprehend between rate of reading and extent of comprehension. It may be noted that the pupils could refer back to the reading material as they responded to the comprehension questions, so memory played no appreciable part in determining the results of this experiment.

These results are so fundamental to understanding the process of reading that they warrant discussion. The inverse relationship between rate of reading and extent of comprehension under the conditions set by Flanagan's experiment makes such good common sense that one wonders why anyone ever doubts it. The reason is probably that other types of relationships between rate of reading and extent of comprehension have been obtained and confused with it. For example, Flanagan also found that in the group of 317 twelfth-grade pupils the product-moment coefficient of correlation between rate of reading (indicated by the score on a test when every pupil has a chance to try every item) was .17. The fact that this relationship is *positive* (though low) does not contradict the finding that there is a *negative* relationship between rate of reading and extent of comprehension if other factors are held constant. The coefficient of .17 represents a relationship in a group of pupils who differ among themselves with respect to verbal aptitude (as well as with respect to other variables). Verbal aptitude is positively correlated in the group with both rate of reading and extent of comprehension. It serves as a common linkage, therefore, and largely accounts for the correlation of .17 between them. The point of practical importance is that pupils at any given initial level of comprehension tend to sustain a loss in comprehension as they are given less time to read the material and answer questions about it.

Two other studies of the relationship between rate of reading and extent of comprehension that should be mentioned are those of Blommers and Lindquist (1) and Carlson (2). In a sample of 672 pupils in grades 11 and 12, the former found a correlation of .30 between rate of reading and extent of comprehension. Working with elementary school pupils, Carlson found in a group of 330 fifth-grade pupils that the correlation between rate of reading (expressed as the average number of words per minute for reading passages and test questions based on them) and extent of comprehension (expressed as the per cent of questions answered that were correctly answered) varied somewhat with the purpose of the reader, the level of difficulty of the content, and the type of material read. Most of the coefficients that he obtained were insignificantly different from zero and about as many were positive as negative. The data have been summarized in Table III.

Table III   Correlations Between Rate and Extent of Comprehension in Reading*

Reading skills	N (*grade 5*)	r_{RC}
Central thought	330	.09
Making inferences	330	.29
Following directions	330	.09
Noting details	330	.00
Reading and then answering questions		
Grade 3 level	330	−.03
Grade 5 level	330	−.04
Reading and answering questions interspersed		
Grade 3 level	330	.04
Grade 5 level	330	−.10
Grade 7 level	330	−.29
Reading short passages with questions at the end of each		
Grade 3 level	330	−.02
Grade 5 level	330	−.06
Grade 7 level	330	−.02

* After (2). Rate expressed as words per minute required to read the material and answer questions about it. Comprehension score expressed as percent of questions marked correctly.

The technique commonly used for measuring changes in rate of reading brought about by reading skill courses and by various mechanical devices have been inadequate for the purpose. First, tests needed to measure the rate at which reading takes place to fulfill each of the four major purposes listed previously in this paper have not been available. Second, tests used to check comprehension have often been administered with time limits so have often included items that could be answered by many examinees before they read the material. Third, tests used to check comprehension have often been administered with time limits so short that every examinee did not have time to try each item and scored without a correction for chance success. In these circumstances, when an examinee is tested at the beginning and at the end of a reading skill course he may read so rapidly on the second testing that his comprehension is markedly reduced and yet obtain a higher comprehension score than at the beginning of the course simply by marking answers (at random, if necessary) to a greater number of items. Thus, his test scores give the false impression that he has greatly increased his rate of reading while maintaining or even improving upon his original extent of comprehension. Fourth, estimates of individual and group gains during reading skill courses have often been based on a comparison of scores on comparable forms of a test properly administered according to directions before and after the course without considering the fact that the training received during the course may have so altered the purpose of the examinee or examinees that, despite careful adherence to published directions for test administration, the initial and final scores are not truly comparable. In many instances, they could be made more nearly comparable if the examinees were instructed prior to the initial testing that they should read as rapidly as possible while still getting the information needed to answer questions about the material. Fifth, estimates of individual and group gains during reading skill courses have rarely taken into account possible regression to the population means. Still more rarely have estimates of individual or group gains been compared with the appropriate standard error or standard error of measurement of the gains to determine their statistical significance. Procedures for estimating individual and group gains and for testing their statistical significance were presented by Davis in the *Tenth Yearbook of the National Reading Conference* (3).

COMPREHENSION

Evaluation of the effect of training in reading skills on comprehension poses fewer practical problems than does evaluation of the effect of such training on rate of work in various reading skills. Analyses of the components of comprehension, using tests especially designed to measure the skills believed by most authorities in the field to be part of the process of comprehension, have been reported by Davis (4), Hunt (7), and others. Leaving aside minor differences in the interpretation of these studies, we are safe in concluding that knowledge of word meanings and ability to weave together ideas and to draw inferences and conclusions from them are the two most important mental skills involved in comprehension. Since the ability to weave verbal ideas together cannot be measured directly without the use of word meanings, these two fundamental elements in comprehension are inextricably interwined. Of the tests now available for measuring comprehension in reading at the secondary-school and college levels, the *Cooperative Reading Comprehension Test,* the *Davis Reading Test,* Series 1, and the *Diagnostic Reading Test,* Survey Section, yield scores obtained under essentially unspeeded conditions. Of these only the *Davis Reading Test* yields a rate-of-comprehension score that is scored with correction for chance success. The rate-of-comprehension score is quite different from the conventional rate-of-reading score, expressed in terms of the number of words covered per minute. It is intended to measure the degree of understanding attained in reading the amount of material that an individual can cover in a specified time limit. Since random marking of responses to items that an individual has not had time to read during the time limit can increase his score when correction for chance is not employed in scoring a test of this type, in which the time limits are set to permit few examinees to finish, it is best to use rate-of-comprehension tests only if they are scored with the correction for chance success.

The correlation of scores on rate-of-comprehension tests and essentially unspeeded tests of comprehension are ordinarily rather high. For scores derived from Series 1 of the *Davis Reading Test*, for example, the correlation coefficient is about .77 among twelfth-grade pupils when entirely different items are included in the two comparable forms of the test from which the scores are derived (5).

To make possible checks on the extent of comprehension during the measurement of rate of reading, at least two forms of four separate comprehension tests, based on the same material used for measuring rate of work for different purposes, should be constructed, equated, and provided with norms in the same samples of examinees. Long passages should be used to provide a basis for measuring rate of work in reading of various kinds. Care must be taken to use passages about which it is possible to prepare questions that can be answered correctly (more often than chance will permit) only if the examinee has read the passage.

CONCLUSIONS

The measurement of rate of work in reading for various purposes poses many difficult problems. Number of words read per minute is, in itself, a meaningless score. To be meaningful, it must be associated with a score indicating the extent of comprehension that has been attained. If the comprehension score is based on a test that permits the examinee to look back to the material he read while his rate of work was being measured, we cannot be sure how much he comprehended on the first reading. If it is based on a test that does *not* permit the examinee to look back, we cannot be sure to what extent we are measuring memory as well as comprehension. It is probable that speed-of-comprehension tests should be adopted as the standard form of measuring instruments for rate of work in skimming, in following the main thread of thought, and in understanding the main ideas and weaving them together. Rate-of-work scores expressed as words read per minute should probably find use only for research purposes in these three fields.

For measuring rate of work in learning the principal

ideas in the material read, a weighted combined score based on words read per minute and number of questions answered correctly in unlimited time may be found most useful. For this type of measurement, the amount of time and the kind of activities permitted between the reading and the testing would have to be carefully controlled.

Tests of the types described in this paper for use with secondary-school and college students and with adults are urgently needed to permit realistic evaluation of improvement produced by reading skill courses.

References

1. Blommers, P., and E. F. Lindquist, "Rate of Comprehension of Reading: Its Measurement and Its Relation to Comprehension," *Journal of Educational Psychology*, 35:449–73, 1944.
2. Carlson, T. R., "The Relationship Between Speed and Accuracy of Comprehension," *Journal of Educational Research*, 42:500–12, 1949.
3. Davis, F. B., "The Assessment of Change." In E. P. Bliesmer and A. J. Kingston, Jr. (Eds.), *Tenth Yearbook of the National Reading Conference*, Milwaukee, Wisconsin: The Conference, 1961, pp. 86–89.
4. Davis, F. B., "Fundamental Factors of Comprehension in Reading," *Psychometrika*, 9:185–97, 1944.
5. Davis, F. B., and C. C. Davis, *Manual for the Davis Reading Test, Series 1*. New York: Psychological Corporation, 1953, p. 13.
6. Flanagan, J. C., "A Study of the Effect on Comprehension of Varying Speeds of Reading." In *Research on the Foundations of American Education*, Official Report of the American Educational Research Association, 1939. Washington: The Association, 1939, pp. 47–50.
7. Hunt, L. G., "Can We Measure Specific Factors Associated with Reading Comprehension?" *Journal of Educational Research*, 51:161–172, November, 1957.
8. Laycock, F., "Significant Characteristics of College Students with Varying Flexibility in Reading Rate," *Journal of Experimental Education*, 23:311–30, 1955.

28

The Use of Alternate Forms
of Standardized Reading Tests

ROBERT KARLIN AND HAYDEN JOLLY

Before reporting the results of a study which attempted to
clarify some aspects of the use of alternate forms of standardized reading tests to measure growth in reading over a period
of time, let us look briefly at two related questions:

1. How parallel may we expect alternate forms of reading tests
   to be?
2. Why shouldn't the *same* form of a standardized reading test be
   used to measure growth?

Is it possible to devise standardized reading tests whose
alternate forms are exactly parallel? Perhaps a tentative
answer to this question will be found if we consider the factors
which contribute to the difficulty of reading materials. Such
factors as sentence and word length, sentence and paragraph
structure, number and difficulty of concepts, load of specialized
vocabulary, use of figurative language, timeliness of the content, and others can and do influence the responses of individuals to printed material. Although it may be possible, for example, to prepare paragraphs containing "identical" elements

REPRINTED with permission of Robert Karlin and Hayden Jolly and the
International Reading Association. "The Use of Alternate Forms of
Standardized Reading Tests," in *The Reading Teacher*, vol. 19 (Decem-
ber 1965), pp. 187–91, 196.

such as those mentioned, an examination of alternate forms of reading tests reveals a lack of consistency among these and related elements. Statistical treatments cannot explain away real differences among items of standardized reading tests that are supposed to be identical or nearly so. Perhaps we may go so far as to suggest that our present inability to identify and deal with all the factors that affect the difficulty of reading materials vitiates any effort to equalize alternate forms of reading tests.

Why do we need alternate forms of standardized reading tests? Possibly the most common answer to this question is related to the influence of practice. Familiarity with test items, we are told, may affect the results. How much of any given standardized reading test will any single individual remember? Or the group, for that matter? Will a second or sixth grader remember 5 items or 12 items, or perhaps 22? Will he recall these items after 3 days, 6 weeks, or 9 months? Perhaps we have assumed that he will. Even if he were to recall that a given number of items appeared on an earlier test, would such recollection automatically alter the results? How many youngsters, after completing a standardized reading test, will attempt to verify their responses? It is unlikely that many will. Is it reasonable to suggest that the influence of practice as it relates to standardized reading test performance has been given weight far beyond its real significance? This concern and the need to verify it might well be the subject of another study.

Let us now turn our attention to an investigation which attempted to deal with some of the questions that we have raised. Specifically, the study attempted to determine the need for using alternate forms of selected standardized reading tests to measure growth in reading over a period of nine months.

SUBJECTS AND PROCEDURE

The subjects of this study were 161 pupils enrolled in grades 4–8 at the University School of Southern Illinois University, Carbondale, Illinois, during the 1962–63 school year. The entire student population of Grades 4, 5, and 6 served as an elementary level group, and all the students in Grades 7 and 8 served as a junior-high group. Only students present for all of the tests administered in both the fall and spring were included in the study.

In September 1962, Form A of the Science Research Associates Reading Tests, Grades 4–6, and Form W of the California Reading Test, Elementary Level, were administered to the subjects in Grades 4–6. Form A of the SRA Reading Test, Grades 6–9, and Form W of the California Test, Junior-High Level, were administered to the subjects in Grades 7 and 8. The tests were given by the experimenters on alternate days at the same time period. The presentation of the test was alternated, Grades 4 receiving the SRA Test first, Grade 5, the California, etc.

In May 1963 these same tests were readministered to the subjects along with their alternate forms. Forms A and B of the SRA Test, Grades 4–6, and Forms W and X of the California Test, Elementary Level, were given to the subjects in Grades 4–6. Forms A and B of the SRA Test, Grades 6–9, and Forms W and X of the California Test, Junior-High Level, were given to the subjects in Grades 7 and 8. Each subject received four tests, the original and alternate forms of both

Table 1   Order of Final Testing, May 1963

Level I, California and SRA Tests, Grades 4–6

Grade	1st Test period	2nd Test period	3rd Test period	4th Test period
4	Cal., Form W	SRA, B	Cal., X	SRA, A
5	SRA, Form A	Cal., X	SRA, B	Cal., W
6	Cal., Form X	SRA, A	Cal., W	SRA, B

Level II, California and SRA Tests, Grades 7 and 8

Grade	1st Test period	2nd Test period	3rd Test period	4th Test period
7a	Cal., W	SRA, B	Cal., X	SRA, A
7b	SRA, A	Cal., X	SRA, B	Cal., W
8a	Cal., X	SRA, A	Cal., W	SRA, B
8b	SRA, B	Cal., W	SRA, A	Cal., X

tests. In an effort to control the effects of practice and test fatigue, the tests were presented as indicated in Table 1.

Every attempt was made to make administration of the tests identical for each group. All tests were given by the experimenters, and the instructions in the accompanying test manuals were followed precisely, particularly the specified time allotments. Raw scores for each test were determined, and corresponding grade equivalent scores were used in the statistical treatment.

To determine whether significant variance existed in the difference scores among the test treatments of fall and spring, between the two tests used, or among the levels tested, the grade scores from the fall and spring tests were analyzed by an IBM 1620 computer using a FORTRAN program which submitted the data to a "treatment × treatment × subject × levels" analysis of variance.

RESULTS

The summary tables of the variance analysis together with the treatment, level, and related interaction means for the elementary and junior-high groups are presented in Tables 2, 3, 4, and 5.

Table 2   Analysis of Variance, Grades 4–6 (I, Test Treatments, J, Time Treatments, L, Levels)

Source	Sum of squares	Deg. of freedom	Est. of variance	F test
Total	1080.81	353		
Among subjects	781.54	58		
Among levels	247.81	2	123.906	13.0004*
Error among	533.72	56	9.530	
Within subjects	299.27	295		
Among I treatments	76.90	1	76.906	144.2198*
Among J treatments	53.39	2	26.697	50.0641*
IJ interaction	2.82	2	1.414	2.6516
IL interaction	6.69	2	3.346	6.2756*
JL interaction	2.95	4	.737	1.3834
IJL interaction	6.12	4	1.531	2.8724
Error within	150.37	282	.533	

* Significant at the .01 level.

The results of these analyses relevant to the purpose of this study are:

1. The F-ratio of 144.2198 (Grades 4–6) and 19.7867 (Grades 7–8) for among test treatments (I) indicates sig-

Table 3   IJL Interaction*

I (test and form)	J (time)	L (grade level)	Mean
SRA A	Fall	4	5.142
SRA A	Fall	5	6.338
SRA A	Fall	6	7.270
SRA B	Spring	4	5.719
SRA B	Spring	5	7.714
SRA B	Spring	6	8.011
SRA A	Spring	4	5.314
SRA A	Spring	5	7.252
SRA A	Spring	6	7.782

* Difference needed for significance at the .01 level: Level 1, .5814; Level 2, .5814; Level 3, .6462.

nificant differences (beyond the .01 level of confidence) between the mean scores on the SRA and California tests of both the elementary and junior-high levels.

2. The F-ratios of 50.0641 (Grades 4–6) and 133.8378 (Grades 7–8) for among time treatments (J) indicate significant differences (beyond the .01 level) between the mean scores of the fall and spring test results. This is an expected difference, attributable to reading growth over the nine-month period.

3. The F-ratios of 1.6516 (Grades 4–6) and 1.3822 (Grades 7–8) for the IJ interaction indicate no significant differences at the .01 level between the mean scores on Forms W and X of the California Test or Forms A and B of the SRA test administered in the spring.

4. With the exception of the IL interaction F-ratio for Grades 4–6 and Grades 7–8 (this is an expected difference between the mean scores obtained for each level), the remaining interaction F-ratios are not significant at the 0.1 level of confidence.

On the basis of the mean scores on these two tests the

Table 4   Analysis of Variance, Grades 7–8 (I, Test Treatments, J, Time Treatments, L, Levels)

Source	Sum of squares	Deg. of freedom	Est. of variance	F test
Total	1806.55	611		
Among subjects	1407.53	101		
Among levels	111.90	1	111.907	8.6373*
Error among	1295.62	100	12.956	
Within subjects	399.02	510		
Among I treatments	9.86	1	9.863	19.7867*
Among J treatments	133.42	2	66.713	133.8378*
IJ interaction	1.37	2	.689	1.3822
IL interaction	1.74	1	1.745	3.5007*
JL interaction	.36	2	.184	.3701
IJL interaction	2.50	2	1.254	2.5167

* Significant at the .01 level.

sample used in this study appears to consist of superior readers. Although the investigators do not have data from a group of "normal' or "average" readers, they have reason to believe that similar results would be obtained with the latter group.

Table 5   IJL Interaction*

I (test and form)	J (time)	L (grade level)	Mean
SRA A	Fall	7	9.233
SRA A	Fall	8	10.362
SRA B	Spring	7	10.323
SRA B	Spring	8	11.096
SRA A	Spring	7	10.178
SRA A	Spring	8	11.162
Cal. W	Fall	7	9.568
Cal. W	Fall	8	10.278
Cal. X	Spring	7	10.601
Cal. X	Spring	8	11.521
Cal. W	Spring	7	10.647
Cal. W	Spring	8	11.262

* Difference needed for significance at the .01 level: Level 1, .3607; Level 2, .3607.

CONCLUSIONS AND IMPLICATIONS

The results of this study indicated no significant difference in measures of reading growth over a nine-month period obtained from the original and alternate forms of the SRA or the California Reading Tests at the elementary and junior-high levels.

May we conclude from this result that the use of alternate forms of reading tests should be discontinued? Certainly not. That these statistical findings are limited to the particular subjects, levels, time interval, and test is clear. Nevertheless, it seems certain that many of the arguments upholding the need for alternate forms (such as the effect of practice or the possibility of the students remembering items) have questionable value.

At the beginning of this paper we raised several questions regarding the parallelism of alternate forms of reading tests and the need for using alternate forms. It appears that while the data obtained in this study do not answer these questions fully, they do offer a tentative solution to the practical problem of measuring reading growth over extended periods of time. The data suggest that, within the limits of the investigation, there is no real justification for using alternate forms. And it is entirely possible that similar results may be obtained with other samples, other tests, other levels, and for other intervals of time. This possibility is certainly worth additional investigation.

Incidental to the major purpose of this study is the finding that there *is* a significant difference between the results of the two tests. Any close examination of various reading tests may lead one to the conclusion that they are quite dissimilar. The levels of difficulty of items, the nature of the subtests, the population used for the establishment of norms—in general, the total make-up—may differ significantly. In light of the tendency to accept different reading grade scores as having essentially the same meaning, we may profit from this objective verification that they do not necessarily have the same meaning.

The implications of this finding are potentially crucial for all teachers and researchers faced with the need to measure reading growth resulting from regular classroom instruction or a particular experimental program. How valid can the evaluation be unless the instruments employed actually measure the facets of the reading process given emphasis in the instructional program? Too often, perhaps, we (or our principal) "order" rather than "select" a test to do the important job of measuring reading growth and, indirectly, our teaching skill.

29

Some Pitfalls in Evaluating Progress in Reading Instruction

ARTHUR S. McDONALD

In the past few years, dramatic results have been claimed for one after another "new method" of teaching reading. In the January, 1963, *Phi Delta Kappan,* the editor warned that most of these results had not been evaluated for possible contamination by the "Hawthorne effect." In point of fact, a number of pitfalls have been overlooked by many researchers in assessing reading instruction.

From the beginning of formalized reading instruction, various kinds of appraisal have been carried on to ascertain progress of an individual and/or a group. Research studies aimed at assessing the effectiveness of different kinds of reading instructional programs have also been conducted.

My own review of published studies in the past ten years shows that the three most commonly used methods for evaluating progress in reading programs are:

1. Determining reading gains by comparison of pre- and post-test scores on alternate test forms of both standardized and informal tests, and finding difference in test performance from that ex-

REPRINTED from *Phi Delta Kappan* (April 1964), pp. 336–38, "Some Pitfalls in Evaluating Progress in Reading Instruction" by Arthur S. McDonald by permission of Phi Delta Kappa.

pected (e.g., "Johnny gained six months in reading test performance during a six-week reading program").

2. Comparing test gains with the national average yearly gains made with those made in the local reading program.

3. Comparing test-retest results of the remedial group with test-retest performance of a control group.

Of these three methods, the first one is most commonly used in classroom and reading clinic descriptive reports. The third is most usual in published reports of research studies.

SOURCES OF ERROR

In recent years, several writers have pointed out the dangers inherent in these methods. Among pitfalls are these:

1. Failure to correct for regression to the mean. (Most remedial students are selected on the basis of low initial reading test scores. On a second testing, persons so selected are likely to make higher test scores whether or not they have *actually* improved in reading ability.)

2. Treating reading grade scores as empirically obtained indications of month-by-month progress. In reality, reading grade scores are extrapolated from one grade level to another. (Spache has pointed out that experiments using repeated testing indicate that reading growth is not evenly distributed throughout the year but occurs in an initial spurt during the first few weeks or months of the year.[1])

3. Interpretation of test scores on the assumption that the tests used provide reliable and valid measures of the most important aspects of reading.

4. Spurious scores obtained from the use of a single test over wide educational (or performance) levels. (For instance, on one commonly used type of reading test a non-reader can miss all the questions and earn a reading grade score of 1.6. If another level of this test were used with the same child, his score would be approximately third reading grade level.)

5. Use, for checking reading comprehension of test ques-

---

[1] George D. Spache, *Toward Better Reading*. Champaign: Gerrard Press, 1963.

tions which can be answered by most children from their background knowledge (i.e., without even reading the selection).

6. Errors in interpretation because of use of inappropriate norms, failure to allow for interform differences in equivalence, etc.

7. Failure to select a really comparable control group.

OTHER SOURCES OF ERROR

Even a carefully designed study, however, one carried out with comparable experimental and control groups under conditions providing for control of many important variables (including student and teacher motivation), may still be vitiated by errors. These errors may arise, in part, because too little attention is paid to reading as a *form of behavior* and, in part, because of errors *inherent in the experimental model itself*.

Thus, in the absence of special precautions, the results obtained by use of comparable-groups methods are likely to be confounded by "Hawthorne" and "placebo" effects.

Cook has defined the Hawthorne effect as ". . . a phenomenon characterized by an awareness on the part of the subjects of special treatment created by artificial experimental conditions." [2]

As partial explanation of this consequence, Orne has shown that "as far as the subject is able, he will behave in an experimental context in a manner designed to play the role of a "good subject." [3] In other words, the student in either an experimental or control group will try to validate the experiment as he understands it.

A special form of the Hawthorne effect accompanies the use of apparatus, equipment, drugs, special instructional ma-

[2] Desmond L. Cook, "The Hawthorne Effect in Educational Research," *Phi Delta Kappan*, 44, 1962, p. 118.
[3] Martin T. Orne, "On the Social Psychology of the Psychological Experiment: With Particular Reference to Demand Characteristics and Their Implications," *American Psychologist*, 17, 1962, p. 778.

terial, ritual, "secret methods," etc. This is called "placebo response."

Following Fischer and Dlin,[4] a "placebo" may be defined as a chemical, mechanical, electronic, or psychological agent or treatment employed, with or without ritual, but always with the suggestion or implication of its powerful and helpful properties. The "placebo response" is that effect of the agent or treatment which cannot be due to the agent or treatment itself but which must be due to some other aspect of the situation.

Thus the placebo effect may be related to the attitude (enthusiasm, belief, optimism, etc.) of the administrator, to the administrator, to the atmosphere (security, insecurity, competitiveness, challenge, etc.), to the treatment situation itself, to the expectancy of *both* the subjects and the experimenter.

Often overlooked in assessment studies, in fact, is the considerable research evidence available that the subject's expectations, the cues provided by the environment and the attitudes and expectations of the instructor or experimenter, may significantly alter the effectiveness of the treatment used and the consequences of the study.

As an example, college students who believed they were getting dexedrine (and who *were* receiving dexedrine) had typical energizer-like reactions in both mood and psycho-motor performance, while students who received dexedrine (but believed they were getting a barbiturate) showed a tendency toward barbiturate-like reactions. It should be noted that the percentage of such typical *student* responses, however, dropped markedly when the *experimenters* knew what drug was being administered.[5]

In another experiment college students were *not* aware that decaffeinated and regular coffee were administered (to the entire group) at different times, but were told that tests

[4] J. K. Fischer and B. M. Dlin, "The Dynamics of Placebo Therapy: A Clinical Study," *American Journal of Medical Science*, 232, 504–512, 1956.

[5] Jonathan O. Cole, "The Influence of Drugs on the Individual," in Seymour M. Farber and Roger H. L. Wilson (eds.), *Control of the Mind*, New York: McGraw-Hill, 1961, 110–120.

were being made to check certain effects of caffeine. The same effects were reported in a similar way for *both* kinds of beverage. When the subjects were told, however, that decaffeinated coffee was being used "just to prove that it was the caffeine that produced the changes" (but *both* regular and decaffeinated coffee were administered as before to all students), *all* effects being measured returned to pre-test conditions.[6] (It is interesting to note that an earlier variation of this experiment, using milk, has often been cited in popular articles as proving that caffeine does not keep one awake.)

Considerable research has shown that the *mere act* of using special treatment or instructional devices, material, drugs, etc., strongly increases their effect. Furthermore, the *intra*individual variation in response to Hawthorne and placebo effects has been shown to be as great as the *inter*individual variation of such responses. The Hawthorne and placebo effects produced depend not only on the particular agent or ritual used and the method of administration but also on the circumstances under which these are used and how the effects are measured. Thus the expectations of the subject, the experimenter, and the nature of the situation in which an agent is administered, a device used, or a course of remediation carried out are important determiners of the effects. Vague means of measuring outcomes, tests with low reliability, and heavy reliance on subjective evaluation strongly favor contamination of results with placebo and Hawthorne responses.

Thus unwanted Hawthorne and placebo contamination is particularly likely in reading programs where the instructors rely heavily on special instrumentation (and themselves believe in the unique beneficial effects of the instruments), or believe strongly in the "powerful" effects of a novel method of instruction, or have found a completely new means of instruction which they believe cannot be measured by existing assessment instruments.

The greater the stress, anxiety, or hope surrounding the circumstances of the treatment of experiment, the greater the desire of the subject to improve, the higher the enthusiastic

---

[6] L. D. Goodfellow, "Significant Incidental Factors in the Measurement of Auditory Sensitivity," *Journal of General Psychology*, 35, 33–41, 1946.

belief of the experimenter or instructor in the agent and technique used, the greater the tendency for Hawthorne and placebo responses to appear.

Investigations have shown that completely inert substances, useless agents, or exhortations (such as "read faster, comprehend more"), when used with the understanding that they would produce certain effects, did indeed cause such effects to appear in 20 to 60 per cent of the subjects. Lehmann reported that "giving a placebo capsule in a well-controlled, double-blind experimental procedure produced test-retest differences which were larger and of greater significance than the administration of effective doses of psychoactive drugs." [7]

EXPERIMENTER MUST BE "BLIND"

Nash has pointed out the importance of measures taken by the experimenter to increase his "blindness" concerning the subjects in the experiment and the absolute necessity of his paying close attention to his own desires regarding the outcome of the experiment so that he can erect safeguards against the operation of bias or placebo effects arising from experimenter or subject expectancy. He concludes that systematic errors due to suggestion can be reduced if the conditions affecting suggestion and expectancy are kept approximately the same for control and experimental subjects. [8]

Thus in any study of the effects of initial instruction or corrective or remedial treatment, it is absolutely necessary to assess the Hawthorne and placebo reactions. To show that a certain kind of program or type of reading instruction produces more than a nonspecific Hawthorne or placebo response, it must be shown that its effects are stronger, last longer, and are qualitatively different from those produced by placebo

[7] Heinze E. Lehmann, "The Place and Purpose of Objective Methods in Psychopharmacology," in Leonard Uhr and James G. Miller (eds.), *Drugs and Behavior*, New York: John Wiley and Sons, 1960, pp. 107–127.

[8] Harvey Nash, "The Design and Conduct of Experiments on the Psychological Effects of Drugs," in Leonard Uhr and James G. Miller (eds.), *Drugs and Behavior*, New York: John Wiley and Sons, 1960, pp. 128–156.

agents (as defined in this article) or by the Hawthorne effect, or that the program affects different kinds of subjects than do placebo and Hawthorne reactions.

In this connection, Spache has warned that by dramatic use of novel methods or impressive equipment "it is possible to produce for a brief space of time what appears to be more than normal progress by remedial techniques or methods that are completely contradictory or even irrelevant to the causes of the reading retardation." [9]

My review of relevant research published in the last ten years shows that more than 80 per cent of the studies dealing with evaluation of progress in reading programs of various types at all levels of instruction from elementary to college suffer from serious (but apparently unsuspected or unassessed) contamination due to the Hawthorne and placebo effects.

IMPLICATIONS

Improved evaluation of reading progress requires:

1. Careful delineation of objectives in *operational* terms. (What kinds of reading problems can we help with testable techniques and materials? What kinds of reading problems remain unaffected by our current procedures or show only Hawthorne and placebo reactions?)

2. Appropriate generalization from the experimental or clinical situation to the daily teaching situation *elsewhere.*

3. Controlling for Hawthorne and placebo contamination. (Cook cites suggestions that the placebo treatment be used to control the Hawthorne effect. For example, avoid singling out experimental and control groups. Use some form of special instrumentation, specially scheduled time and instructional material, stamped "Experimental Edition," with all students. This approach must contain safeguards against teacher expectancy.[10])

[9] Spache, op. cit.
[10] Cook, op. cit.

4. What conditions and procedures in commonly used remedial programs are especially favorable for the occurrence of Hawthorne and placebo responses? What are the most common responses of the nature encountered?

30

Methods of Computing and Evaluating Residual Gain Scores in the Reading Program

ROBERT J. TRACY AND
EARL F. RANKIN, JR.

The "RESIDUAL GAIN" statistic has been developed by Manning and DuBois[1] as a powerful tool for the measurement of individual differences in improvement resulting from training. This technique permits the measurement of differences in improvement with subjects who have been equated statistically on the basis of the pre-training measurement. Unlike other common measures of improvement, residual gain does not require that pre- and post-training measures be expressed in equal interval scales, and it removes the influence of regression effects upon the measurement of improvement.

Rankin and Tracy[2] and Rankin[3] have utilized residual gain measures in evaluating reading progress and have pointed

[1] Manning, W. H., and P. H. DuBois. "Correlational Methods in Research on Human Learning," *Perceptual and Motor Skills*, 15 (1962), 287–321, Monograph Supplement 3–V15.
[2] Rankin, E. F., Jr., and R. J. Tracy. "Residual Gain as a Measure of Individual Differences in Reading Improvement," *Journal of Reading*, 8 (March, 1965), 224–233.
[3] Rankin, E. F., Jr. "A New Method of Measuring Reading Improvement," *International Reading Association Conference Proceedings*, 10 (1965), 207–210.

REPRINTED with permission of Robert J. Tracy and Earl F. Rankin, Jr., and the International Reading Association. "Methods of Computing and Evaluating Residual Gain Scores in the Reading Program," in *Journal of Reading*, vol. 10, no. 6 (March 1967), pp. 363–71.

out its potentialities as a research tool in studying correlates of reading improvement. In comparing residual gains with "crude gain" (i.e., the simple difference between pre- and post-training measures) they found a discrepancy in grades assigned for improvement in almost half the cases. They noted that crude grades tend to underestimate the progress of superior "improvers" (as measured by residual gain) and to overestimate the progress of inferior "improvers."

The purpose of this paper is to present computational and graphical methods for arriving at residual gain scores and for evaluating such scores. The computational methods will illustrate the meaning of residual gain for both the reading teacher and researcher. Since the computation of residual gain is somewhat arduous, the use of the two computational formulae will be of primary interest to the research scientist. Fortunately, the graphical procedures for estimating residual gains and for assigning grades to such gains are relatively simple and are recommended for classroom use.

COMPUTATIONAL METHODS

There are two methods for computing residual gains. One is the "z-score method" and the other is the "raw score method." Both have certain advantages and disadvantages which will be described.

The z-score formula is:

$$Z_{y \cdot x} = Z_y - r_{xy}Z_x$$

where Z_y represents the post-test score in z-score form, r_{xy} is the correlation between pre- and post-tests, and Z_x represents the pre-test score in z-score form. The formula reveals that residual gain is the difference between a predicted and an observed measure. The predicted score for a particular individual (i.e., $r_{xy}Z_x$) is subtracted from his obtained score after training (i.e., Z_y). Technically, residual gain represents the deviation of final scores from the regression line of final on initial scores.

The following steps are involved in computing a set of residual gain scores in z-score form:

1. Convert both pre- and post-reading test scores to z-scores for each student.
2. Compute the r between pre- and post-test raw scores.
3. Obtain predicted post-test z-scores by multiplying the correlation coefficient by the pre-test z-score for each student.
4. Subtract the predicted post-test z-score from the obtained post-test z-score for each student.

Table I (Column D will be discussed later) shows a convenient format and the essential data for computing z-score residual gains for a small sample of 10 students.

By expressing pre- and post-test scores in comparable units, the z-score method makes it easy to interpret the mean-

Table I   The Z-score Method for Obtaining Residual Gains

Student	X Pre raw score	z_x pre z	Y Post raw score	z_y post z	$z_x r$ predicted post z	$zy \cdot x$ residual gain	D derived score
1	69	−.500	79	+1.149	−.338	+1.487	95
2	75	+.750	75	+.343	+.506	−.163	73
3	70	−.292	70	−.665	−.197	−.468	69
4	70	−.292	77	+.746	−.197	+.943	88
5	84	+2.625	81	+1.552	+1.772	−.220	72
6	67	−.917	67	−1.270	−.619	−.651	66
7	70	−.292	68	−1.068	−.197	−.871	63
8	73	+.333	78	+.947	+.225	+.722	85
9	67	−.917	69	−.867	−.619	−.248	72
10	69	−.500	69	−.867	−.338	−.529	68

Summary statistics

1. $\bar{X} = \dfrac{\Sigma X}{N} = 71.4$

2. $s_x = \dfrac{1}{N} \sqrt{N\Sigma X^2 - (\Sigma X)^2} = 4.8$

3. $\bar{Y} = \dfrac{\Sigma X}{N} = 73.3$

4. $s_y = \dfrac{1}{N} \sqrt{N\Sigma Y^2 - (\Sigma Y)^2} = 4.96$

5. $r = \dfrac{N\Sigma XY - (\Sigma X)(\Sigma Y)}{\sqrt{N\Sigma X^2 - (\Sigma X)^2} \sqrt{N\Sigma Y^2 - (\Sigma Y)^2}} = .675$

ing of residual gain and to compare residual gain with the crude gain for a particular individual. For example, Student #2 (see Table I) made the same score of 75 on both pre- and post-tests. However, his z-scores reveal that he has dropped from .750 to .343 (a crude z-score gain of −.407). A glance at the predicted post-test z-score reveals that it was predicted that he would drop down from his initial high z-score of .750 to .506, and therefore his residual gain was only −.163.

Unfortunately, this method is rather tedious. It takes some time to convert all scores to z-scores; and in subtracting predicted scores from obtained scores, the plus and minus numbers are conducive to error. Therefore, some may prefer the raw score method to the z-score method.

The raw score formula is:

$$Y \cdot S = Y - [bX + C]$$

where

$$Y = \text{post-test score}$$
$$X = \text{pre-test score}$$
$$b = \frac{N\Sigma XY - (\Sigma X)(\Sigma Y)}{N\Sigma X^2 - (\Sigma X)^2}$$
$$C = \overline{Y} - b\overline{X}$$
$$\overline{Y} = \text{post-test mean}$$
$$\overline{X} = \text{pre-test mean}$$

Table II shows a format for computing residual gain in raw score form. Although the formula may look somewhat complex, the raw score method is easier and quicker to use than the z-score method.

The raw score method does not yield as much information for interpreting gains on the z-score method. For example, although Students #2 and #3 (see Table II) show no change in raw scores from before to after training, Student #3 shows a greater negative residual gain than Student #2. This would be difficult to interpret without the z-scores.

However, the raw score formula is easier to compute and may also avoid some rounding errors. Scores do not have to be converted to z-scores, and the numbers involved in subtraction are always positive. Since b and C in the formula are constants, computation is rapid on a calculator. (A faster formula

Table II   The Raw Score Method for Obtaining Residual Gains

Student	X pre raw score	Y post raw score	$bX + C$ predicted post raw score	$Y \cdot X$ residual gain	Derived score
1	69	79	71.625	+7.375	95
2	75	75	75.813	−.813	73
3	70	70	72.323	−2.323	69
4	70	77	72.323	+4.677	88
5	84	81	82.095	−1.095	72
6	67	67	70.229	−3.229	66
7	70	68	72.323	−4.323	63
8	73	78	74.417	+3.583	85
9	67	69	70.229	−1.229	72
10	69	69	71.625	−2.625	68

Summary statistics

1. $C = \overline{Y} - b\overline{X} = 23.463$

2. $b = \dfrac{N\Sigma XY - (\Sigma X)(\Sigma Y)}{N\Sigma X^2 - (\Sigma X)^2} = .698$

for computing raw score residual gain is $Y \cdot S = Y - bX - C$. This would not yield the interpretative information provided by the Table II format but would be much faster to compute.)

Another advantage of the raw score method is that residual gain can be easily expressed in normative units. For example, a raw score residual gain could be interpreted in terms of increase in age units or percentiles. This would provide an accurate evaluation of change for each individual which would not be possible with simple crude gain measurements.

GRAPHICAL METHOD FOR ESTIMATING RESIDUAL GAIN

For classroom use, where less accuracy is necessary than that demanded by research, raw score residual gains can be estimated easily and very quickly by a graphical procedure. Essentially, this involves plotting a regression line on a graph and then subtracting scores on the regression line from obtained post-test scores. Figure 1 represents the regression line based on the data in Table II.

Figure 1   Regression Line

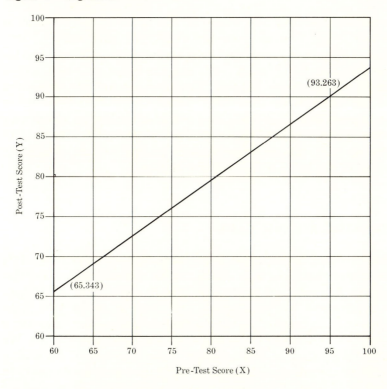

To make a graph, plot the Y scores (i.e., post-test scores) on the ordinate and the X scores (i.e., pre-test scores) on the abscissa. (See Figure 1.) Next, draw the line of the best fit which defines a residual gain of 0 for each X and Y combination. The formula for the predicted post-test score (Y') for a given value of X is:

$$Y' = bX + C$$

where

$$b = \frac{N\Sigma XY - (\Sigma X)(\Sigma Y)}{N\Sigma X^2 - (\Sigma X)^2}$$

$X =$ any arbitrary pre-test score value, and $C = \overline{Y} - b\overline{X}$. The above formula should be repeated twice using two arbitrary extreme values of X to facilitate the drawing of the line connecting these two points. (A large piece of finely ruled graph paper will allow greater accuracy in plotting points and interpreting results.) For example, in Figure 1, the Y' value is 65.343 for an X value of 60 and 93.263 for an X value of 100. These two points are joined by a straight line. This is the regression line for Y on X (i.e., the predicted post-test scores for all pre-test score values). Now one can quickly determine the approximate residual gain for any individual by locating the intersecting lines for X and Y and counting up (or down) to the regression line. These residual gains can then be used to compare the relative improvement of various individuals or to assign grades in a classroom situation.

EVALUATING RESIDUAL GAINS

Once residual gains have been computed or estimated, it is sometimes desirable to evaluate an individual's progress relative to the class and to express this in some form which can be interpreted to the student. One way of doing this is to represent the residual gain as a derived score—for example, a T-score with a mean of 50 and a standard deviation of 10. We have found that a derived score with a mean of 75 and a standard deviation of 10 is more easily accepted by students in reading classes. This permits the assignment of grades or evaluation categories for improvement in terms of the normal distribution curve with A = 90–100, B = 80–89, C = 70–79, etc. Students will more readily accept a derived score of 75 as representing average improvement than a derived score of 50.

The formula for converting residual gains to derived scores (d) is:

$$D = \frac{S_d}{\sqrt{1 - r^2}} (Z_{y \cdot x}) + \overline{D} \text{ (z-score method)}$$

$$D = \frac{S_d}{S_y \sqrt{1 - r^2}} (Y \cdot X) + \overline{D} \text{ (raw score method)}$$

where

D = derived score
S_d = standard deviation of the derived score (i.e., 10)
S_y = standard deviation of post-test scores
r^2 = squared correlation between pre- and post-test scores
$Z_{x \cdot y}$ = residual gain for an individual z-score form
$Y \cdot X$ = residual gain for an individual in raw score form
$\overline{D}$ = mean of derived scores (i.e., 75)

Column D in Tables I and II presents derived scores based on residual gains for each of 10 students. Note that derived scores are the same with z-score and raw score methods.

GRAPHICAL METHOD FOR ESTIMATING DERIVED SCORES

A much quicker method is available for assigning an individual student to a relative evaluation category or a grade classification on the basis of residual gain. A graphical method can be used very easily to achieve this purpose. If a graphical method is used, a student may be assigned to a given evaluation category without computing either a residual gain score or a derived score. All that is needed is to determine the residual gain scores defining the boundaries of 50, 60, 70, 80, and 90 and to plot these boundaries on a graph. The formula for obtaining residual gains corresponding to boundaries between evaluation categories is:

$$Y \cdot X_b = \frac{(D_b - \overline{D})S_y\sqrt{1 - r^2}}{S_d}$$

where

$Y \cdot X_b$ = residual gain score defining a given boundary (Due to the difficulties involved in plotting z-scores on a graph, only the raw score residual gains are considered here.)
D_b = the desired boundary (i.e., 90, 80, etc.)
$\overline{D}$ = mean of derived score (i.e., 75)
S_y = standard deviation of post-test scores
S_d = standard deviation of derived scores (i.e., 10)
r^2 = squared correlation between pre- and post-test scores

This formula is repeated for each boundary.

To set up the graph, first draw the regression line on a piece of graph paper as previously described. Next, to draw the boundary line for a derived score of 70, plot $Y \cdot X_b$ for two arbitrary extreme values of X by counting down from the regression line the amount indicated by the magnitude of $Y \cdot X_b$ for a boundary of 70. For example, in Figure 2, $Y \cdot X_b$ for a boundary of 70 is -1.83. Therefore, the extremes of the boundary line are determined by counting down 1.83 points below the regression line at an arbitrary X values of 60 and of 100. These two points are then connected by a straight line. The above operations are repeated for each boundary line (as in Figure 2).

Now all one needs to assign any student to an evaluation or grade category on the basis of residual gain is his pre- and post-test score. The point where lines for X and Y intersect will fall in the proper evaluation category. For example, Student #1 in Table II has an X score of 69 and a Y score of 79. The coordinate for these two lines in Figure 2 places this student in the "A" category, which is in accordance with his computed derived score of 95 in Table II.

Of course, it should not be necessary to draw a different graph each semester for the reading class. If one has a fairly large representative group, the same graph can be used to evaluate gains for subsequent semesters.

A glance at Figure 2 reveals some interesting characteristics of residual gain evaluations. An increase of two points, for example, would yield a letter grade of C for a person with pre-test score of 65, a letter grade of B for a person with a pre-test score of 85, and a letter grade of A for a person with pre-test score of 95. If crude gains had been used, these three persons would each have received the same grade. If percent gain had been used, grades would have been assigned in reverse order with the student making an initial score of 65 making the highest grade for improvement and the student with an initial score of 95 making the lowest grade. Both crude gain and per cent gain measures fail to reflect the influence of re-gression effects upon gain. Due to regression effects, a person with a low initial test score would tend to score higher on retesting even without training and a person with a high initial score would tend to go down on retesting. Hence an increase

Figure 2   Evaluation Categories

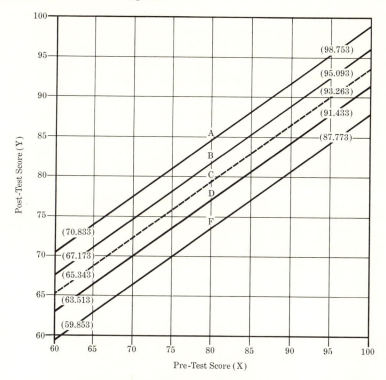

of 2 points yields a lower residual gain grade for a low pre-test score than for a high pre-test score.

Similarly, as revealed in Figure 2, an increase of 10 points is necessary to achieve a residual gain grade of A with an initial score of 65, an increase of only 4 points would yield a grade of A for a pre-test score of 85, and a person with an initial score of 95 could get an A grade even if he increased only 1 point on the post-test. If either crude gains or residual gains had been used to evaluate improvement, the student with the 10-point increase would have received a much higher grade than the student with a 1-point increase.

In summary, this paper has presented two computational methods for measuring residual gains and a short graphical method for estimating such gains for classroom use. In addition, a computational method for evaluating residual gains in terms of derived scores based on the normal distribution curve has been described. A short graphical method for assigning evaluation categories to residual gains in the classroom has been presented. The short-cut methods for estimating and evaluating residual gains without laborious calculation represent a technical breakthrough which should make this valuable technique readily available to any classroom reading teacher with an elementary knowledge of statistics.

31

Evaluating Progress in Remedial Reading Programs

EMERY P. BLIESMER

A typical and apparently widely accepted procedure for determining progress of participants in remedial reading programs is to administer alternate forms of some standardized reading test at the beginning and at the end of a given instructional period. The differences between beginning and ending test scores are then viewed as evidences of gains. However, some question might be raised concerning this evaluation procedure. Children in remedial programs are usually participating because they have not been making at least "normal" progress in the attainment of reading skills; but use of the evaluation method described above appears to ignore the fact that what has been "normal" progress for the average child usually has not been "normal" progress for the remedial case. A point relative to the reading potential or reading capacity levels of children might also be raised. Children in a remedial program are usually selected because there is evidence that they stand some chance of profiting from a program; that is, children are considered to be "retarded" in reading and likely prospects for a remedial program if their reading achievement levels are below their reading potential levels. If, then, the difference (or gap) between the potential and the actual read-

REPRINTED with permission of Emery P. Bliesmer and the International Reading Association. "Evaluating Progress in Remedial Reading Programs," in *The Reading Teacher*, vol. 15 (March 1962), pp. 344–50.

ing achievement levels of an individual is considered as the amount of actual retardation in reading, it would seem reasonable to consider a decrease in this gap after a period of instruction as a valid indication of progress also. However, various reports of programs indicate that, while the reading potential level may be involved as an acceptance criterion in a remedial program, it is usually not given any really definite or active recognition in evaluating the progress made in a program. (For exceptions to this trend, see the last three studies listed in the References.)

Several years ago this writer had the opportunity to plan and direct an exploratory study relating to the points just raised. Three specific methods for evaluating progress in remedial programs were analyzed: (1) determining gains by the typical method of finding differences between before and after reading test scores, (2) comparing remedial program gains with average yearly gains made before the remedial program, and (3) finding differences between reading potential and reading achievement levels (potential-achievement gaps) at the beginning and at the end of a remedial program.

The various data involved were gathered on two groups of children who were participating in the remedial reading programs of the two reading clinics of a city public school system during the school year 1955–56. Group A was made up of forty children from Grades 4 through 8; Group B consisted of forty-one children from Grades 4 through 7. Among the tests used with the children in Group A during the latter part of September and early October were the Revised Stanford-Binet Scale (Form L), The Gates Reading Tests (Primary, Advanced Primary, and Survey), and alternate forms of the reading subtests of various batteries of the Metropolitan Achievement Tests (which had been used annually in the school system for a number of years). Alternate forms of the Metropolitan and Gates tests were administered in early May of 1956.

Similar testing procedures were used for Group B, except that scores obtained with the Gates tests were not used in analyses involving Group B; and the intelligence test used was a group, rather than an individual, intelligence test. It was originally planned to use the Wechsler Intelligence Scale for

Children to obtain reading potential levels for children in Group B. However, unforeseen schedule changes for psychometric personnel made it impossible to obtain the Wechsler data; so a group intelligence test, the California Short-Form Test of Mental Maturity (Elementary, 1951 S-form) was used with Group B. All three types of I.Q. scores (Language, Non-Language, and Total) yielded by the California test were used in the analyses of Group B data.

The cumulative records of all subjects were used for determining yearly gains in reading before the remedial program year. Reading subtest scores on the Metropolitan tests, obtained at nearly the same time each fall, were available for each child for each year beyond the first he had been in school before the remedial year. The difference between "total" or "average" reading achievement scores obtained from two successive fall administrations was viewed as the gain during the year. The average of each child's yearly gains before the remedial year, hereafter referred to simply as "average yearly gains," was then determined.

The first, or typical, method for evaluating progress involved simply determining differences between reading test scores obtained at the beginning and those obtained at the end of the period of remedial instruction. These differences then represented "remedial gains." Scores obtained with both Gates and Metropolitan reading tests were used with Group A; but only Metropolitan results were used with Group B. The average remedial gains of the grade placement level sub-groups of both Groups A and B and of the intelligence level sub-groups (grouped in terms of intervals of ten I.Q. points) of Group B were determined; and these remedial gains are presented in the table.

The second evaluating method involved a comparison of remedial year gains with average yearly gains during the years in school before the remedial year. The ratio of the average remedial gain to the average yearly gain was determined for each total group and for each grade level sub-group on Metropolitan scores. Similar comparisons for the Gates scores were made only for Group A. These ratios may also be seen in the table.

The third method of determining progress was the one

Table 1 Average Remedial Gains, Average Yearly Gains Before Remedial Year, Ratios of Average Remedial to Average Yearly Gains, and Average Potential-Achievement Gap Decreases*

Groups	N	Av. remedial gain Met.	Av. remedial gain Gates	Av. yearly gain	Ratio: av. remedial gain to av. yearly gain Met.	Ratio Gates	Av. potential-achievement gap Met. Oct.	Met. May	Gates Oct.	Gates May	Av. gap decrease Met.	Av. gap decrease Gates
Group A (Stanford-Binet)												
Grade Groups												
4	12	.81	1.28	.57	1.4	2.2	2.70	2.49	2.88	2.20	.21	.68
5	14	.72	1.42	.50	1.4	2.8	3.01	2.84	3.41	2.54	.17	.87
6	4	.90	1.25	.50	1.8	2.5	2.73	2.38	3.30	2.60	.35	.70
7	3	1.60	1.23	.74	2.2	1.7	2.07	.84	2.77	1.91	1.23	.86
8	7	.69	1.02	.58	1.2	1.8	3.12	2.71	3.77	3.03	.41	.74
Total	40	.83	1.28	.55	1.5	2.3	2.84	2.52	3.26	2.40	.32	.77
I.Q. Group												
120–139	2	1.05	1.35				4.50	4.15	5.05	4.40	.35	.65
110–119	5	1.16	1.96				3.62	3.04	3.72	2.50	.58	1.22
100–109	21	.80	1.16				2.71	2.45	3.19	2.47	.26	.72
90– 99	11	.64	1.05				2.41	2.22	2.76	2.06	.19	.70
70– 89	1	.90	1.00				3.00	2.40	3.10	2.40	.60	.70
Group B (California Test of Mental Maturity)												
Language I.Q.												
Grade Groups												
4	7	1.14		.39	2.9		.14	.14			.00	
6	25	1.70		.55	3.1		1.07	.17			.90	
7	9	2.27		.56	4.1		1.73	.14			1.59	
Total	41	1.73		.51	3.4							
I.Q. Group												
100–109	7	2.03					2.04	.61			1.33	
90– 99	13	2.07					1.45	.05			1.40	
– 89	21	1.41					.49	-.39			.78	
Non-Language I.Q.												
Grade Groups												
4	.7	1.14		.39	2.9		2.47	1.76			.71	
6	25	1.70		.55	3.1		1.56	.36			1.20	
7	9	2.27		.56	4.1		3.54	1.75			1.79	
I.Q. Group												
110–	9	2.19					3.91	2.36			1.55	
100–109	9	1.52					2.32	1.44			.88	
90– 99	11	1.47					2.14	1.08			1.06	
– 89	12	1.77					.63	-.75			1.38	
Total I.Q.												
Grade Groups												
4	7	1.14		.39	2.9		1.30	.53			.77	
6	25	1.70		.55	3.1		1.43	.60			.83	
7	9	2.27		.56	4.1		1.30	.74			1.57	
I.Q. Group												
110–	2	2.30					2.90	1.20			1.70	
100–109	9	2.13					2.21	.62			1.59	
90– 99	12	1.66					1.60	.28			1.32	
– 89	18	1.50					.74	.03			.71	

* All differences, gaps, and gains (or decreases) are expressed in terms of school years.

which involved consideration of the amount of decrease in the potential-achievement gap after a period of remedial instruction. For the purposes of this study, the California I.Q.'s, as well as the Stanford-Binet I.Q.'s, were viewed as ratios of mental age to chronological age. The MA's of the children as of October 5, 1955 (the approximate starting date of remedial instruction) were then determined by using the CA's of the children as of that date. Tables presented in manuals accompanying the California tests were then used to determine the grade placement level corresponding to each obtained mental age. The resulting grade placement levels were then considered as indications of potential reading achievement levels. Next, for each child, the difference between his potential reading level and his reading achievement level (his potential-achievement gap) was found; and this difference, or gap, was viewed as the amount of reading retardation at the beginning of remedial instruction. Similar procedures were used for determining potential reading levels and potential-achievement gaps as of May 6, 1956 (the approximate ending date of remedial instruction) ; and the decrease in potential-achievement gap was then determined for each subject. Average potential-achievement gap decreases for each of the total groups (A and B) and for each of the various sub-groups (grade placement level and intelligence level) have been presented in the table.

Obviously, the methods and data of the study had some limitations. These limitations included using a group, rather than an individual, intelligence test with Group B (even though such practice may obtain in a number of school reading clinics) ; converting Stanford-Binet mental age scores to grade equivalent scores on the basis of tabular data obtained with another intelligence test; having a very small number of cases in some of the sub-groups; and failing to equate adequately the length of time of remedial instruction (two hours a week for seven months) and that of yearly instruction during the years in school before the remedial reading year. However, despite these and other possible limitations, a number of observations and trends conclusions might even be drawn.*

* A more detailed report (1) of the procedures and the results of this study is available.

Examination and analysis of the various data presented in the table will show that, in the case of average remedial gains for Group A, those indicated by Metropolitan scores were at least equivalent to what might be considered a "normal" amount of gain for the average child in the typical classroom (seven months of gain) and were definitely above this amount in a number of instances. The finding that, in general, remedial gains indicated by Gates test scores were noticeably greater than those indicated by Metropolitan test scores is also of interest. (The obtained October and May Gates scores tended to be lower and higher, respectively, than the corresponding Metropolitan scores.) Comparison of remedial gains and average yearly gains reveals Metropolitan remedial gains to be about one and one-half to over two times as great as average yearly gains in the case of Group A and from about three to over four times as great in the case of Group B. Remedial gains for total groups, A and B, were approximately one and one-half to three and one-half times as great, respectively, as the corresponding average yearly gains. If length of time for remedial instruction had been equated with that of yearly instruction before the remedial year, the ratios would have been even greater; and if consideration had been given to equating actual hours of instruction, results might have been rather dramatic in some instances.

With one exception, definite potential-achievement gap decreases were indicated by all the various types of analyses. In the case of Group A, gain indications involving Gates scores were again greater than those involving Metropolitan scores. No definite or consistent gap decrease trend was indicated for Group A; but there did appear to be somewhat of a trend for greater gap decreases to occur in the case of Group B at the higher grade placement and intelligence levels. (Even though a number of subjects in Group B did not fall into the same intelligence level sub-groups for all types of I.Q.'s, this tendency tended to be consistent.) Examination of May potential-achievement gaps (listed along with October gaps in the table) reveal that, despite positive gain indications (that is, gap decreases), there were still a number of appreciable gaps existing in May in a number of instances. Perhaps it should be pointed out here that no decrease in gap for a given individual would not indicate that he had made no progress; but, rather, it would indicate that the individual had progressed the amount which might have been expected of him had he not been retarded in reading at the beginning of the instruction period. It may also be noted that the negative May gaps in two instances in the case of Group B (obtained for subjects on whom some of the lowest intelligence scores were obtained), indicating that achievement levels exceeded potential levels, gives cause for question about the validity of the obtained potential estimates in these cases.

Effectiveness of remedial instruction was shown favorably by all methods of evaluating progress which were used in the study. While differences in reading test scores obtained at the beginning and at the end of a given period of remedial instruction might be most familiar and meaningful to a large number of teachers and parents, the amount of gain thus shown will often need to be considerably greater than that expected of the average child before such gain is commonly viewed as an impressive one. Comparing remedial gains with average yearly gains tends to reveal effectiveness of remedial instruction more immediately, definitely, and impressively. In view of the comparison of data based on the two reading tests used, a question might also be raised relative to the extent to which the degree of gain indicated is a function of the particular tests used. Evaluation of progress in terms of potential or capacity levels (or potential-achievement gap decreases) might seem to have the most desirable and valid rationale; but it does not tend to give results which appear as immediately definite and impressive as do the results obtained with other methods. More extended and refined study of this approach or method (and of the others also) would certainly seem to be merited, however, especially if the objective of "helping each child achieve commensurate with his capacity" is to be given more than lip service.

References

1. Bliesmer, Emery P. "Methods of Evaluating Progress of Retarded Readers in Remedial Reading Programs," in Edith M. Huddleston (Ed.), *The Fifteenth Yearbook*

73

of the National Council on Measurements Used in Education. New York: The Council, 1958. Pp. 128–134.

2. Bond, Guy L., and Fay, Leo C. "A Report of the University of Minnesota Reading Clinic," *Journal of Educational Research,* XLIII (January, 1950), 385–390.

3. Mouly, G. J., and Grant, V. F. "A Study of the Growth to Be Expected by Retarded Readers," *Journal of Educational Research,* XLIX (February, 1956), 461–466.

4. Scott, Frances Deane. "Evolution of a College Reading Program," *Journal of Developmental Reading,* II (Autumn, 1958), 33–42.

For Further Reading

Harris, Chester W. *Problems in Measuring Change.* Milwaukee, Wis.: Univ. of Wisconsin Press, 1967.

Lennon, Roger T. "The Stability of Achievement Test Results from Grade to Grade," *Educational and Psychological Measurement* 2 (Spring, 1951) : 121–27.

Libaw, Frieda, Berres, Frances, and Coleman, James, "A New Method for Evaluating the Effectiveness of Treatment of Learning Difficulties," *Journal of Educational Research* 55 (August, 1962) : 582–84.

Smith, Donald, and Wood, Roger. "Reading Improvement and College Grades: a Follow-up," *Journal of Educational Psychology* 46 (March, 1955) : 155–59.

C
D
E
F   4
G   5
H   6
I   7
J   8

P   24